International Political .

Series Editor: **Timothy M** ... 'assachusetts
Boston, USA and Emeriti

CW01656599

The global political ecor ... of cumulative crises impacts its organization and governance. The IPE series has tracked its development in both analysis and structure over the last three decades. It has always had a concentration on the global South. Now the South increasingly challenges the North as the centre of development, also reflected in a growing number of submissions and publications on indebted Eurozone economies in Southern Europe.

An indispensable resource for scholars and researchers, the series examines a variety of capitalisms and connections by focusing on emerging economies, companies and sectors, debates and policies. It informs diverse policy communities as the established trans-Atlantic North declines and 'the rest', especially the BRICS, rise.

Titles include:

Kobena T. Hanson, Cristina D'Alessandro and Francis Owusu (*editors*)
MANAGING AFRICA'S NATURAL RESOURCES
Capacities for Development

Daniel Daianu, Carlo D'Adda, Giorgio Basevi and Rajeesh Kumar (*editors*)
THE EUROZONE CRISIS AND THE FUTURE OF EUROPE
The Political Economy of Further Integration and Governance

Karen E. Young
THE POLITICAL ECONOMY OF ENERGY, FINANCE AND SECURITY IN THE UNITED ARAB EMIRATES
Between the Majilis and the Market

Monique Taylor
THE CHINESE STATE, OIL AND ENERGY SECURITY

Benedicte Bull, Fulvio Castellacci and Yuri Kasahara
BUSINESS GROUPS AND TRANSNATIONAL CAPITALISM IN CENTRAL AMERICA
Economic and Political Strategies

Leila Simona Talani
THE ARAB SPRING IN THE GLOBAL POLITICAL ECONOMY

Andreas Nölke (*editor*)
MULTINATIONAL CORPORATIONS FROM EMERGING MARKETS
State Capitalism 3.0

Roshen Hendrickson
PROMOTING U.S. INVESTMENT IN SUB-SAHARAN AFRICA

Bhumitra Chakma
SOUTH ASIA IN TRANSITION
Democracy, Political Economy and Security

Greig Charnock, Thomas Purcell and Ramon Ribera-Fumaz
THE LIMITS TO CAPITAL IN SPAIN
Crisis and Revolt in the European South

Felipe Amin Filomeno
MONSANTO AND INTELLECTUAL PROPERTY IN SOUTH AMERICA

Eirikur Bergmann
ICELAND AND THE INTERNATIONAL FINANCIAL CRISIS
Boom, Bust and Recovery

Yildiz Atasoy (*editor*)
GLOBAL ECONOMIC CRISIS AND THE POLITICS OF DIVERSITY

Gabriel Siles-Brügge
CONSTRUCTING EUROPEAN UNION TRADE POLICY
A Global Idea of Europe

Jewellord Singh and France Bourgouin (*editors*)
RESOURCE GOVERNANCE AND DEVELOPMENTAL STATES IN THE GLOBAL SOUTH
Critical International Political Economy Perspectives

Tan Tai Yong and Md Mizanur Rahman (*editors*)
DIASPORA ENGAGEMENT AND DEVELOPMENT IN SOUTH ASIA

Leila Simona Talani, Alexander Clarkson and Ramon Pachedo Pardo (*editors*)
DIRTY CITIES
Towards a Political Economy of the Underground in Global Cities

Matthew Louis Bishop
THE POLITICAL ECONOMY OF CARIBBEAN DEVELOPMENT

Xiaoming Huang (*editor*)
MODERN ECONOMIC DEVELOPMENT IN JAPAN AND CHINA
Developmentalism, Capitalism and the World Economic System

Bonnie K. Campbell (*editor*)
MODES OF GOVERNANCE AND REVENUE FLOWS IN AFRICAN MINING

Gopinath Pillai (*editor*)
THE POLITICAL ECONOMY OF SOUTH ASIAN DIASPORA
Patterns of Socio-Economic Influence

Rachel K. Brickner (*editor*)
MIGRATION, GLOBALIZATION AND THE STATE

International Political Economy Series
Series Standing Order ISBN 978–0–333–71708–0 Hardcover
978–0–333–71110–1 Paperback

You can receive future titles in this series as they are published by placing a standing order. Please contact your bookseller or, in case of difficulty, write to us at the address below with your name and address, the title of the series and one of the ISBNs quoted above.

Customer Services Department, Macmillan Distribution Ltd, Houndmills, Basingstoke, Hampshire RG21 6XS, England

---

Al bambino Gabriellino

Contents

List of Figures

List of Tables

Introduction

Starting in December 2010, the Arab world was swept away by a wave of demonstrations that soon became known as 'The Arab Spring'.[1]

It is still early to talk about an established academic account of the motivations behind the dramatic events in the region during 2010/11, but it seems to the author that it is about time to try and insert this issue into the broader picture of the latest changes in the global political economy. It seems indeed inappropriate to emphasise the sudden nature of the 'Arab Spring' when so many of the latest vicissitudes of the region were already pointing towards a soon-to-come crisis.[2] These vicissitudes, in turn, cannot be disentangled from the wider context of the global political economy and of globalisation, where the political economy origins of the Arab Spring need to be found.

There seems to be a certain degree of consensus in the literature on the fact that the process of globalisation has indeed modified the political equilibrium not only at the global level but also at the regional and local ones.[3] However, scholars are still divided on the assessment of the 'hows' and 'whys' of the impact of globalisation on regional and local dynamics.

This is partly due to the fact that the definition itself of globalisation seems surrounded by a certain degree of mystery, invoked often in different contexts or debates without a proper systematic attempt to define it.[4]

The main objective of this book is to study the impact of globalisation on regionalisation and the crisis of the Nation State from a distinct International Political Economy perspective, with particular attention on the dynamics of the MENA area, especially Egypt, Libya and Tunisia.

The theoretical aim of the book is, firstly, to understand the problem of regionalisation, both political and economic, in the context of globalisation; and, secondly, to assess the relation between globalisation, marginalisation and the local more or less violent responses to the loss of power by the state to address economic vulnerabilities and threats of exclusion from the Global Political Economy.

The book therefore focuses on the following theoretical questions:

> How is the process of globalisation related to the increase of social unrest and revolution in marginalised countries of the world? What is marginalisation and how is it related to a lack of regionalisation? What political economy factors create the tensions which could lead civil society to make pressure for regime change?

From an empirical point of view, the book will present the cases of Egypt, Libya and Tunisia.

> What are the dynamics of the revolutionary waves in Egypt, Tunisia and Libya? In which political economy context did the crises spark? What was the relation between the economic and political grievances in these cases? Is there a relation between globalisation and the Arab Spring? Are a lack of regionalisation and the marginalisation of Egypt, Libya and Tunisia an intervening factor?

The empirical analysis is based on the experience of the author as Junior Professional Officer for the United Nations in the MENA region, based in Cairo, and includes direct contact with people involved in the Midan Tahrir protests.

The book argues that the lack of regionalisation and the progressive marginalisation of the region, and in particular the countries under analysis, represent the political economy context in which the increase in political discontent and the outbursts of rage of a more or less violent character took place. This is in turn inserted in the broader debate concerning the loss of power by the nation state to guarantee jobs and social protection as a consequence of globalisation thus potentially leading to social unrest and revolt.

The book is divided into two parts. The first deals with the political economy context within which to analyse the Arab Spring. It assesses the relevance of different definitions of globalisation to explain global imbalances. It then introduces the definition of the new global division of labour and identifies three basic theoretical paradoxes through which to analyse the issue of the Arab Revolutions. These paradoxes are:

1. The paradox of regionalisation within globalisation.
2. The paradox of marginalisation within globalisation.
3. The paradox of the empowerment of civil society in the midst of the crisis of the Nation State.

The second part presents the cases of the Egyptian, Tunisian and Libyan revolutions, identifying their dynamics, the motivations behind the crises and the differences between the countries considered. Reference is made to the contacts made by the author on the sites.

In the conclusions, the cases of Egypt, Tunisia and Libya will be inserted into the broader theoretical context to verify whether the previously identified theoretical paradoxes are capable of framing a more informed analysis of the political economy of the Arab Spring.

The events of the Arab Spring

When, on the 17th of December 2010, the young Mohamed Bouazizi set himself on fire to protest against the Tunisian police confiscating the poor fruits and vegetables he was selling in the streets, few thought that this would be the beginning of a wave of violent protests, not only across the country but over the entire MENA region. These would eventually lead to the ousting of political establishments believed to be immovable until a few days earlier. Hundreds of youths gathered in the streets of Tunisian provincial towns. The protests started in Sidi Bou Zid, some 200 km away from the capital Tunis, but spread unexpectedly all over the country until Zine al-Abidine Ben Ali fled the country on 14 January, after 23 years in power. On the same day, Muhammar Ghadhafi, the leader of Libya since 1969, condemned the events of Tunisia amid reports of riots all over the Libyan territory (The Guardian, various issues).

Also, in Egypt people started to make comparisons between the political regime in Tunisia and the regime of Hosni Mubarak, long-time Egyptian President (The Guardian various issues). Indeed, on 17 January an Egyptian man too set himself on fire to denounce his incredibly low standards of life. The man was reported to be the owner of a small restaurant who could no longer endure his poverty.

On 25 January Egyptian protesters blocked Midan Tahrir in Cairo and mass demonstrations erupted all over the country in a fashion unseen in the country for decades. From this moment onwards events unfolded at a rapid pace. On 27 January the Egyptian opposition leader El Baradei returned to Egypt to join the anti-government protests. On the 28th, 25 people were reported killed and Mubarak appeared on television, dismissing his government but without leaving power. On 31 January the army explicitly backed the protesters by refusing to attack them in the streets. A few days later a horde of pro-Mubarak youths clashed with protesters in Tahrir square but was unable to deter them, confirmed by a mass demonstration on 4 February which saw hundreds of thousands take to the streets. On 11 February Mubarak was compelled to stand down and hand power to the military following 18 days of mass revolts (The Guardian various issues).

On 16 February it was the turn of Libya. Violent demonstrations erupted in the second biggest town of the country, Benghazi, to protest against the imprisonment of a human rights activist by the government. As pro-government forces mobilised, violence spread, especially in eastern towns such as Benghazi where dozens were reported dead. Cities were set on fire and disputed between loyalists and opposition parties. On 8 March, the fights moved to the oil site of Ras Lanuf, whilst the UK and the US announced that they were prepared to deploy a full range of military responses, including the imposition of a no-fly zone (The Guardian various issues). A few days later, on 18 March, the UN Security Council voted in favour of a resolution authorising all necessary measures to protect civilians under threat of attack, in particular in Benghazi. Ten members voted in favour with five abstaining, including China, Russia and Germany. The resolution ruled out putting troops on the ground. Operation Odyssey Dawn started the day after, with air and missile strikes against the military forces of Ghadhafi in order to stop them from taking back Benghazi. However the fights between the rebels and the Ghadhafi loyalists went on for months until the new Libyan government, the National Transitional Council, was able to move into the capital, Tripoli, on 26 August. Nevertheless, the search for Ghadhafi was not over until he met his death at the hands of the forces loyal to the new government on 20 October, whilst escaping from NATO airstrikes in Sirte (The Guardian various issues).

'Sic Transit Gloria Mundi', commented Berlusconi, the then Italian Prime Minister, at the news of the death of his long-term friend, the Libyan dictator (La Repubblica). However the roots of these extraordinary events should not be traced back only through the unpredictability of political fortunes, but need to be sought in the more structural consequences of the redefinition of political and economic equilibriums brought about by globalisation. Indeed, more than political factors, economic ones seem to link together the fate of the three countries. It was poverty in Tunisia and Egypt that brought about the extreme protest of self-immolation at the onset of both revolutions, and it was oil that stimulated Western interest in the Libyan civil war. What this book hypothesises is that the progressive impoverishment of marginalised countries of the globe, as well as the quest for energy, are some of the most important consequences of the process of globalisation. This, coupled with the incapacity of the Nation State to control economic dynamics in the age of globalisation, and with the lack of any regional layer of governance in the MENA area, created a power vacuum which is still to be filled.

There is already a part of the literature stressing that what really motivated the impoverished popular and middle classes of these countries to go to the streets was a structural lack of economic opportunities.[5] This book brings this argument a step forward by claiming, and hopefully demonstrating, that such a structural lack of opportunities was a consequence of the marginalisation of the area and of the countries considered from the process of globalisation and of the contextual lack of power of the nation state to address similar problems.

This perspective de-emphasises somewhat the role of social networks in the Arab uprisings and the idea that the Arab Spring was mainly sparked by middle class youths with access to social networks. With respect to the role played by the social network in sparking the revolutions, there is evidence that in the case of Tunisia, for example, the protests initially spread amongst the unemployed youth of Sidi Bou Zid after the death of Bouazizi mainly by word of mouth, and it was only afterwards that Facebook played a role in communicating what was happening.[6] According to West (2011), after the uprising in Sidi Bou Zid had gone on for some days the rest of Tunisia was mainly mobilised through the television (state TV Channel 7 and Al –Jezeera especially).[7] Of course, social networks also played a role but as a means of communication rather than as the spark of the uprisings. Moreover, the role played by the muted acquiescence of Muslim organisations to the popular uprising, especially in Egypt, should also not be underestimated, especially in the light of later events.[8]

Referring to the role played by the middle class, it is important to stress that also the progressive impoverishment of the middle classes in the MENA area is one of the main consequences of its marginalisation and lack of integration in the global political economy. There is indeed plenty of evidence that impoverishment of the middle classes in the area was a fact since the beginning of the globalisation era. Farah (2009) demonstrates that already at the beginning of the 1990s the worsening economic conditions in Egypt and the subsequent implementation of the Economic Reform and Structural Adjustment Programme (ERSAP) had resulted in the withdrawal of the privileges granted by Nasser to 'the middle class, the workers and the peasants'.[9] This was exacerbated by inflationary pressures which lowered real incomes in rural and urban areas, deepening poverty also amongst the middle class.[10] The dichotomy between the popular classes and the middle classes is therefore a false one: both have experienced a marked worsening of their standards of life in the areas concerned by the analysis. Furthermore, although it might be true that the first demonstrations in the streets might have been sparked by the middle classes, subsequent events demonstrate that the majority of the population was firmly behind them.[11] In theoretical terms this confirms the hypotheses proposed by some scholars (Mittelman 2000) that globalisation leads to two interrelated phenomena: on the one hand the subordination of politics to economics and the loss of power by the state to control economics and, on the other hand, the empowerment of civil society and its consequent increased tendency to protest in favour of more equal and democratic regimes. In the MENA area this is accompanied by a structural lack of economic and political integration at the regional level which makes the crisis of the nation state ever more dramatic and therefore dangerous (Overbeek 2000; Van der Pijl 2011).

The academic rationale: a qualitative definition of globalisation and its impact on the MENA region

The notion of globalisation is by no means an uncontroversial one in academic debates, as well as in wider public discourse.[12] Yet it seems possible to classify the positions adopted by scholars on the subject into three broad groups:[13] those who deny the existence of the phenomenon of globalisation;[14] those who accept it but tend to give only a quantitative definition of globalisation,[15] and those who adopt a qualitative definition.[16]

The theoretical background of the book is represented by the traditional qualitative[17] definition of globalisation. This identifies the process of globalisation as a qualitatively new phenomenon, characterised by the dramatic increase of foreign direct investment (FDI), the transnationalisation of social groups, including labour and business, and by an unprecedented interdependence of financial markets.[18]

For the purposes of this book, technological transformation is considered an exogenous component of the qualitative definition of globalisation, and it is the factor which brings about transformation in the realms of financial transactions and production. This, in turn, triggers related changes in the economic, social and political spheres.

Technological transformation is also the driving force behind the process of transformation of global production and the related global reallocation of production alongside the dramatic increase of foreign direct investment and mergers and acquisitions, and the creation of export processing zones.

As a consequence of the restructuring of production, the labour structure also changes with a substantial reallocation of labour intensive production to Third World countries. However, this outcome is compounded by the opposite effects of technological development in terms of the increase of distant work and of labour mobility, including mass migration.

Indeed, on the one hand, production tends to move to some specialised regions of the globe[19] where it is possible to exploit the advantages of lower production costs both in the form of lower labour costs and/or in the form of lower costs of primary resources. This phenomenon gives rise to the paradox of regionalisation within globalisation, characterised by the creation of economically integrated regions. On the other hand, however, the populations of those marginalised zones of the globe whose economic conditions are deemed to worsen as a consequence of the process of globalisation, experience increased strains and difficulties.

Moreover, globalisation reduces the capacity of the nation state to guarantee social protection and jobs to its citizens and to control its territory and economy (Strange 1998; Sassen 1996; 2006). The crisis of the state in the age of globalisation is compounded in some regions of the globe by a new multi-layered system of governance which diffuses the tensions created by this phenomenon of erosion of national authority. However in the MENA area both subnational and supranational levels of organisation are pretty underdeveloped exacerbating a power vacuum which is potentially very destabilising (Van der Pijl 2011). Here lie the roots of economically motivated social unrest leading civil society to multiply its calls for regime change and democratisation even in a violent way (Mittelman 2000).

In conclusion, from a theoretical point of view the following issues appear particularly relevant:

1. The paradox of regionalisation within globalisation, or lack of it.
2. The paradox of marginalisation within globalisation and its consequences in terms of decreased economic opportunities.
3. The crisis of the nation state within globalisation and its potentially destabilising consequences.
4. The empowerment of civil society within globalisation and its renewed propensity to require change.

Egypt, Tunisia and Libya, although with major differences, are considered here as clear cases of marginalisation within globalisation, whilst the MENA area represents a case in which the process of regionalisation within globalisation failed to materialise. However, the MENA area is also the locus of the struggle for the control of energy resources, which the globalisation process makes scarcer and more contested.

This is considered as the political economy context into which the events of the Arab Spring should be inserted.

The structure of the book

The book is divided into two parts. The first part investigates the political economy context of the 2010/11 upheavals, starting from the different definitions of globalisation and its consequences. As such, it contributes directly to the current debate among scholars of political science and international relations concerning the nature of the process of globalisation, its origins, its characteristics and its impact on other socio-economic and cultural phenomena. The second part provides an in-depth analysis of the three case studies and of the marginalisation of the MENA area, and the implications in terms of increased political discontent and reactions of a more or less violent nature.

In **Part I** of this volume the author analyses the competing definitions of globalisation and identifies the theoretical paradoxes arising from a qualitative interpretation of the phenomenon.

From the quantitative point of view, globalisation is defined as:

> ...The intensification of economic, political, social and cultural relations across borders.[20]

This definition leaves a number of issues unsolved. On the one hand, these regard the means by which the degree of economic, social and cultural relations across the border, as well as their intensification, can be measured. On the other hand, it also leaves the kind of relationships between the economic, social and political aspects of globalisation unclear and indeed, it does not even specify whether there is any relationship at all. Moreover, by accounting for the phenomenon of globalisation only in quantitative terms, one can hardly manage to grasp its causes and consequences. This makes it extremely difficult to relate it to other phenomena such as regime change of a more or less violent nature in marginalised countries of the world. It is therefore necessary to deepen the perspective by adopting a qualitative definition of globalisation.

From the qualitative point of view, globalisation is defined as a process comprising a number of qualitative transformations, which in turn characterise the current phase of capitalist development. The analysis of this debate and all its implications for the Arab Spring is contained in Chapter 1 of the book.

Chapter 2 deals with the paradox of regionalisation within globalisation. Technological change is recognised by transnationalist scholars of globalisation as the motor of a set of transformations affecting both the productive and the financial structures. The restructuring of production through the geographical reallocation of production is characterised by the creation of Export Processing Zones in developing countries, a policy of Mergers and Acquisitions and straightforward Foreign Direct Investment.[21] However, not all areas of the globe are equally involved in the reallocation of production.

Some regions of the world experience high levels of integration in the global economy and a high degree of regional economic and political integration, giving rise to the paradox of regionalisation within globalisation. On the contrary, some other areas of the globe are increasingly marginalised from the global political economy, producing negative economic dynamics and exacerbating internal discontent. The chapter will identify the main approaches to regionalisation and provide evidence in support of this thesis.

In Chapter 3 the analysis moves to the socio-economic consequences of this particular definition of globalisation. The process of globalisation in social and wealth terms, as defined in the book, is not neutral but entails new social cleavages and challenges, as well as new winners and new losers. In fact, given the innovative nature of the technological tools necessary to grasp the opportunities of globalisation, the necessity arises for a continuous updating and requalification of skills. This poses the problem of the polarisation of skills and access to technological devices both in social and geographical terms adding to the paradox of marginalisation within globalisation. The chapter will address the issue by making reference to the debate amongst scholars and to appropriate figures. It will then investigate the consequences of social exclusion for civil society and social capital in the three countries considered.

In **Part 2**, the author applies the theoretical context defined in the first part to the case of the marginalisation of the MENA area and of Tunisia, Libya and Egypt in particular.

Chapter 4 reconstructs the historical developments of regionalisation in the MENA area and assesses the consequences of the lack of regionalisation. The paradox of regionalisation within globalisation is one of the pillars of the qualitative, transnationalist approach to the impact of globalisation on local dynamics. As underlined above, it entails that those regions experiencing a high degree of integration into the global economy tend to increase their level of economic and, to a certain extent, also political and institutional integration. The Middle East and Northern Africa region is instead a clear example of the opposite.[22] Leaving aside a more detailed analysis of the theoretical aspects of the concept of integration[23] and of the political and institutional dimension of Arab integration (or rather 'disintegration')[24] what mainly concerns this contribution is the degree of economic integration, or lack of it.[25]

In Chapter 5 Tunisia is singled out as the country where the turmoil first began and ended. In December 2010 violent protests arose, and already by 14 January 2011 the government had been overthrown with the ousting of President Ben Ali and Prime Minister Mohammed Ghannouchi, the dissolution of the political police, the demise of the RCD (the former ruling party of Tunisia) and liquidation of its assets, the release of political prisoners, and the election of a Constituent Assembly with a clear majority for the Muslim party on 23 October 2011. Was this impossible to foresee, or was it somehow the likely outcome of a more generalised process of marginalisation which produced its consequences within a relatively long period of time? This and similar questions will be considered in the analysis undertaken in this chapter.

Chapter 6 investigates the case of Egypt, a country that, despite managing to change the political regime led by Mubarak, seems still far from having identified a stable political equilibrium.How did the global political economy affect the Egyptian crisis? To what extent is Egypt marginalised and how does this relate to the continuing turmoil in the country after the Arab Spring?

Finally, in Chapter 7 the attention moves to the case of Libya, where the death of its historical leader Ghadhafi in October 2011 seemed to have put an end to the civil war starting in February of the same year. What was the role played by the West in the unfolding of the crisis and, most importantly, in the development of the political economy of isolation? How is the political economy of oil related to the marginalisation of the country from the global political economy?

The conclusion proposes a discussion of the political economy of the Arab Spring in the context of globalisation. In particular, the attention focuses on the precarisation of nation state authority in developed and in less developed countries, the increase of the role of economic factors and actors, and the reaction of civil society through increased social unrest and requests for economic growth, jobs and regime change.

Notes

1. In Yemen, the fourth country where the protests produced a change in government, the outcome was bound up in pre-existing fights between north and south, between Houthi Shi'ah and Sunnis, and between various pro- and anti-Saleh tribes. Yemen underwent a period of political transition following the signature in November 2011 of a Gulf Cooperation Council-brokered Initiative and UN transition plan by former President Saleh and the leaders of the main political parties in Yemen. It brought to an end months of political turmoil and committed Yemen to a two-year period of political transition. Under the Initiative, former President Saleh resigned from office and was succeeded by Abd Rabbo Manscur Hadi following interim Presidential elections in February 2012. See Pollack (2011: 5). Although many of the Middle East and North Africa region countries have since witnessed more or less violent riots, the only three countries which actually underwent true regime changes, often referred to as 'revolutions', are Tunisia, Egypt and Libya, hence the focus of the book on these three North African countries.
2. See Bradley (2008, 2012); Alterman (2000).
3. See for example, Gardezi (1995); Ghosh (1998, 2000); Sassen (1996, 1998); Weiner (1995).
4. See the Conclusions of this book for a more detailed account of this debate.
5. See Bradley (2012); West (2011).
6. See West (2011: 338–367), Kindle edition.
7. See West (2011: 338–367), Kindle edition.
8. See Wickham (2002); Bradley (2012).
9. See Farah (2009: 42).
10. See Farah (2009: 47).
11. See Bradley (2012).
12. See conclusions in Talani (2004).
13. A similar distinction is contained in Dicken (1998: 5).
14. See, for example, Hirst and Thompson (1999).

15. See, for example, Garret (1998).
16. See, for example, Mittelman (2000). For the relations between globalisation and migration see, for example, Sassen (1998); Weiner (1995).
17. For the debate on the definition of globalisation see, for example: Hirst and Thompson (1999); Mittleman (2000). For the relations between globalisation and migration see, for example, Sassen (1998); Weiner (1995).
18. See Overbeek (2000).
19. Scholars refer to the 'triad' to indicate the three main zones of production of the globe, that is the Asian–Pacific region, America and Europe.
20. See Holm and Sørensen (1995: 12).
21. Dicken (2003).
22. For an analysis of the reasons underlying the lack of integration of the ME area see Kubursi (1999).
23. For useful reference on this issue see Hudson (1999).
24. See Hudson (1999: 1).
25. For the historical account of the development of intraregional economic relations in the Middle East North Africa see Owen (1999).

References

Alterman, J.B. (2000). Egypt: Stable But for How Long? *The Washington Quarterly*, Autumn 2000, 107–118.

Bradley, J.R. (2008). *Inside Egypt: The Land of the Pharaohs on the Brink of a Revolution*. Palgrave.

Bradley, J.R. (2012). *After the Arab Spring*. Palgrave.

Dicken, P. (1998). *Global Shift*. Paul Chapman Publishing.

Dicken, P. (2003). *Global shift: Reshaping the Global Economic Map in the 21st century*. Sage.

Farah, N.R. (2009). *Egypt's Political Economy*. American University in Cairo Press.

Gardezi, H. (1995). *The Political Economy of International Labor Migration*. Black Rose Books, Montreal.

Garret, G. (1998). *Partisan Politics in the Global Economy*. Cambridge University Press.

Ghosh, B. (1998). *Huddled Masses and Uncertain Shores: Insights into Irregular Migration*. Martinus Nijhoff Publishers, London.

Ghosh, B. (ed.) (2000). *Managing Migration: Time for a New International Regime*. Oxford University Press, Oxford.

Hirst, P., and Thompson G. (1999). *Globalization in Question*. Polity Press.

Holm, H.H., and Sørensen, G. (1995). *Whose World Order? Uneven Globalization and the End of the Cold War*. Westview Press, Boulder.

Hudson, M.C. (ed.) (1999). *Middle East Dilemma: The Politics and Economics of Arab Integration*. Columbia University Press, New York.

Kubursi, A. (1999). 'Prospects for Arab Economic Integration After Oslo', in Hudson, M.C. (ed.) *Middle East Dilemma: The Politics and Economics of Arab Integration*. Columbia University Press, New York, ch. 14.

Mittelman, J.H. (2000). *The Globalization Syndrome: Transformation and Resistance*. Princeton University Press, Princeton.

Overbeek, H. (2000). 'Globalization, Sovereignty and Transnational Regulation: Reshaping the Governance of International Migration', in Gosh, B. (ed.) *Managing Migration: Time for a New International Regime.* Oxford University Press, Oxford.

Owen, R. (1999). 'Inter-Arab Economic Relations During the 20th century: World Market vs Regional Market?', in Hudson, M.C. (ed.) *Middle East Dilemma: The Politics and Economics of Arab Integration.* Columbia University Press, New York, ch. 10.

Pollack, K.M. (2011). *The Arab Awakening: America and the Transformation of the Middle East,* e-book, http://kcl.eblib.com/patron/FullRecord.aspx?p=795889, accessed 9 May 2013.

Sassen, S. (1996). *Losing control.* Columbia University Press, New York.

Sassen, S. (1998). *Globalization and Its Discontents.* The New Press, New York.

Sassen, S. (2006). *Territory, Authority, Rights: From Medieval to Global Assemblages.* Princeton University Press, Princeton NJ.

Strange, S. (1996). *The Retreat of the State.* Cambridge University Press, Cambridge.

Talani, L.S. (2004). *European Political Economy: Political Science Perspectives.* Ashgate, London.

Weiner, M. (1995). *The Global Migration Crisis: Challenge to States and Human Rights.* HarperCollins College Publishers.

West, J. (2011). *Karama! Journeys through the Arab Spring.* Heron Books, Kindle edition.

Wickham, C.R. (2002). Mobilizing Islam: Religion, Activism, and Political Change in Egypt. Columbia University Press, New York.Van der Pijl, K. (2011). 'Arab revolts and nation-state crisis', *New Left Review* 70, July–August 2011, pp. 27–49.

1
The Chinese Butterfly and the Arab Spring: Bread and Globalisation

Bread and the Arab Spring

There is no denying the role that the economy played in the revolts going under the name of the Arab Spring. The two people who set fire to themselves in Tunisia and Egypt, sparking the uprisings, did so for economic motivations.[1] The protesters who took to the streets in Cairo, did so screaming 'Bread' (*Aish*) as one of their main slogans. Even in the academic literature on the Arab Spring there seems to be now some agreement on the relevance of economic factors (Noueihed and Warren 2012: 5–6; Maloney 2011: 66).[2]

Furthermore, it is impossible to deny that the global economic crisis which started in 2008 as a consequence of the global financial crisis played a fundamental role in the outburst and spreading of protests across the region (Lagi 2012). The price of oil increased significantly, reaching a peak of $147 per barrel on 11 July 2008, as a consequence of investors' crave for secure assets, and speculative investment followed in other commodities. This characterised the 4th phase of the development of the global financial crisis and certainly contributed to the unsustainable rise in the cost of basic foodstuffs which produced a wave of protest in many Middle Eastern and North African (MENA) countries in the Spring of 2008 (Orlowski 2008: 11; Talani 2013).[3]

In Egyptian the word for 'bread', *Aish,* is also the word used for 'life'. Bread is life for Egyptians in many ways; Egypt is the world's larger importer of wheat and Egyptians are the world's larger consumers of it (FAO 2011). It is no surprise, then, that increases in the price of bread have often meant mass demonstrations in the country. Previously, in 1977 'Bread Riots' had broken out in Egypt, though the reason was not so much scarcity of bread itself, but the decision of President Sadat, within his Infitah policy,[4] to end subsidies for basic food staples (Roccu 2012). In this case, a reversal of Sadat's decision put an end to the riots. In the wake of the global financial crisis food prices soared and food riots again swept across cities of the Middle East. In Egypt, worries about the scarcity of flour and bread generated massive and deadly demonstrations, such as in the Nile delta town of Al-Mahalla Al Kobra where eleven people were killed in clashes and many more were arrested.[5] Similarly, the deprived parts of central Tunisia had been witnessing strikes and protests since January (Noueihed and Warren 2012: 24–25). In 2009 and 2010 a relaxing of speculative pressures on commodities and on oil meant that cereals' price inflation lowered from 10.2 per cent to –0.8 per cent,[6] but by 2011 food prices were increasing again.[7]

In 2011, global food prices were incredibly high, even higher than in 2008. Taking 2005 as the base year, in 2011 the real world food price index of the World Bank had achieved a level of 170 (see Figure 1.1 below).

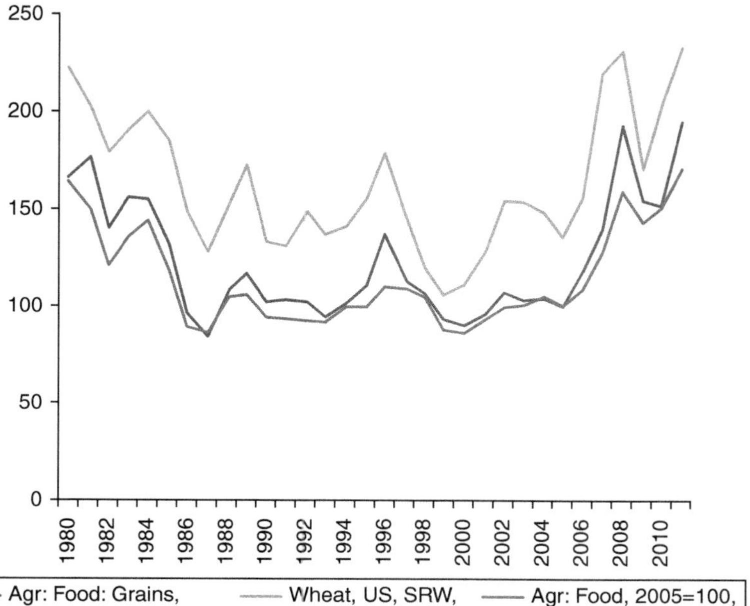

Figure 1.1 Real world food/wheat/grains price indexes, 1980–2011 (2005=100) 2005 US$

Source: World Bank

The spike in food prices of 2011 has been identified as a main determinant of the riots leading to the Arab Spring (Lagi et al. 2011). Correlating instances of social unrest with the UN Food and Agriculture Organization's (FAO) nominal global food price index between 2004 and 2011, a working paper by New England Complex Systems Institute, 'The Food Crises and Political Instability in North Africa and the Middle East' found that food riots were likely to occur when the index equalled or was greater than 210. When, in 2008, the FAO global food price index rose above 220, more than 60 food riots occurred in 30 different countries. This happened also in late 2010 and early 2011, allegedly triggering the Arab Spring uprisings. According to this study, there was less than a 6 per cent probability that the Arab Spring occurred by chance during an episode of high food prices (Lagi et al. 2011).

The main criticism leveraged against this thesis is that in countries like Egypt the prices of basic food staples were subsidised by the State, making price increases less dramatic (Noueihed and Warren 2012). In the case of Egypt, for example, it is estimated that the transmission of global food inflation to domestic food inflation is relatively low over the long term, lying between 13 per cent and 16 per cent, whereas in the short term, after 6 months, it is around 29 per cent. Moreover, international food price shocks explain only a small portion of domestic inflation shocks in both the short and long terms, and international price inflation has asymmetric effects on domestic prices (Al-Shawarby et al. 2012). This limits the applicability of models identifying a direct causal relation between global food inflation and the Arab Spring (Lagi et al. 2011; Jacks et al. 2011).

In this book it is argued that the increase in food prices is just one side of a broader underlying phenomenon represented by the marginalisation from globalization of the MENA region and the countries considered here.

The question this book will try to answer is to what extent the difficulties and inequalities plaguing the area at the onset of the uprisings were also a consequence of globalisation. The Arab Spring will thus be contextualised within the broader global political economy. To reference a well-known metaphor, it will try and find out whether the movement of a butterfly's wings elsewhere in the world, maybe in China, could eventually have led to the events of the Arab Spring.

However, the debate about globalisation is an ongoing one and the globalisation thesis does not come in a single, universally accepted version in the social sciences (Busch 2008: 5; Dicken 2007: 5). Before proceeding to the consequences of globalisation for the MENA area, it is therefore important to define what globalisation is from different perspectives in the field of international political economy (IPE), and to examine what the implications are of the different definitions of the concept on the capacity of the nation state to carry out relevant policy-making, which is the subject of this chapter.

What is globalisation?

As characterised by Anthony Giddens in a lecture entitled 'Globalisation: The state of the debate',[8] the globalisation debate has gone through three phases. The first phase saw opposition between the so-called 'sceptics', who questioned the very existence of the phenomenon, and 'globalists' who firmly asserted that its existence was undeniable. In the second phase, the idea that globalisation was a new phenomenon became consensual and the debate moved into the streets, where anti-globalists violently opposed its advent, commonly identifying it with the spread of political imperialism and economic neo-liberalism. In the third, and current, phase of this debate even the anti-globalists have come to terms with the inevitability of globalisation and discussions have shifted to tackle the question of how to govern globalisation so that it can be beneficial for everyone. Summing up, the debate moved from the questions, 'Does globalisation exist?' and 'What are the consequences of globalisation?' to 'How to govern globalisation?'

Giddens's characterisation is interesting, but reveals that the author is himself a globalist and adopts a neo-institutionalist perspective.[9] In fact, there is still not a widely agreed definition of what globalisation is, nor there is consensus on whether it is a completely original phenomenon, neither among the different disciplines in social sciences nor, more specifically, among the different approaches in IPE. In the next sections we will therefore try and answer Giddens's questions with reference mainly to theories of international political economy and to see what their relevance is for the study of the recent Arab uprisings.

Does globalisation exist?

Although in the general public discourse the question of whether globalisation exists may seem straightforward, in the academic debate the answer depends on the theoretical standpoint adopted. Limiting the analysis to IPE perspectives, scholars' positions on the subject can be classified into three broad groups (Dicken 1998: 5, 2007: 5). The first group includes those who continue to deny the existence of the phenomenon of globalisation and are often referred to as 'sceptics' (e.g. Hirst and

Thompson 1999a; Hirst et al. 2009). The second group is represented by the 'globalists' and is composed by those who support the globalisation thesis but provide a quantitative definition (e.g. Held and McGrew 2000; Holm and Sørensen 1995; Garret 1998). Finally the 'transnationalists' consider globalisation a structural phenomenon which requires a qualitative definition (e.g. Mittelman 2000; Dicken 1998, 2007; Hay and Marsh 2000).

Those who tend to deny globalisation rely on considerations underlying the historical recurrence of periods of increased international and cross-border interactions. Thus, the 'sceptics' refuse to characterise globalisation as a new, original phenomenon. In some cases, they might even deny any 'global', 'globalised' or 'globalising' nature to the current phase of capitalist development. This attitude is typical of realist approaches to IPE which see globalisation as a convenient myth in the hands of politicians in the most powerful states who spread it among public opinion with the aim of consolidating their hegemony. In essence, the notion of globalisation is much exaggerated in both the public and academic debate by those who demonise it as the mother of all evils as well as those who proclaim it to be the resolution to all problems. Realists would instead maintain that globalisation is hardly a new phenomenon and that even where the international political economy shows new trends these can easily be governed by traditional intergovernmental solutions (Gilpin 2000; Hirst et al. 2009).

The realist perspective draws on a quantitative definition of globalisation, one that is concerned about 'quantifying' globalisation through the identification of suitable measures for all of the elements which are generally included within its scope. Then (neo)-realist scholars have proceeded by comparing the ideal type of the 'globalised economy' with the ideal type of the 'internationalised economy', using data on the performance of the real economy to verify to what extent one or the other ideal type corresponds to the actual state of the world economy (Hirst and Thompson 1999a, b; Hirst et al. 2009).

Similarly, Gilpin (2000, 2001) demonstrates the extent to which the relevance of economic globalisation is grossly overstated. In fact, he argues, the world economy still fundamentally relies on the centrality of the nation state, the interests of which are increasingly catered for within integrated regional schemes. Starting always from a quantitative definition of globalisation, Gilpin identifies it with the increase in the integration of the world economy produced by a multiplicity of factors, such as increases in trade flows, in the developments of international finance and in the activities of multinational companies (Gilpin 2001).

Evidence allows the author to conclude that such an increase has been 'highly uneven, restricted to particular economic sectors and not nearly as extensive as many believe' (Gilpin 2001: 364). Indeed, there is no doubt in his mind that the level of economic integration was much higher during the period of the gold standard; in relative terms, the level of financial transactions and trade flows was greater even in the late 19th century (Gilpin 2001). Further, despite the fact that in the 20th century these flows were larger and faster in absolute terms, they were mainly concentrated within clearly defined regional economic areas dominated by regional hegemons.

With respect to financial globalisation, Gilpin notes how integration of financial markets is still limited to speculative and short-term investment. Yet if globalisation were a reality, he claims, the so called 'law of one price' would be respected. This is considered often the most important measure of economic integration, according to which identical goods would have identical prices in a perfectly integrated economy (Gilpin 2001: 368).

Hirst et al. (Hirst and Thompson 1999a, b; Hirst et al. 2009) are the main proponents of the thesis that globalisation is essentially a myth. In fact, for them, globalisation does not exist even as the 'end' of an ongoing process, whereas there is a clear trend towards regionalisation as the bigger and more powerful states seek to maximise their power. By contrasting the notion of a globalised economy with that of an 'internationalised' world economy (Hirst et al. 2009: Introduction) in which 'the principal entities remain national economies, or agents that continue to be primarily located in a definite national territory' (Hirst and Thompson 1999b: 140), these scholars come to the conclusion that the latter is still prevailing over the former.

This result is obtained by first identifying the main components of the two ideal types of world economy and then measuring them (Hirst et al. 2009). One way to measure the degree of integration of the world economy is, for example, the stock of foreign-owned productive capital. The data shows that until 1995, when the stock of inward foreign direct investment (FDI) as a percentage of GDP in the world was only 10.1 per cent, this figure did not seem dramatic enough to justify claims of the 'death' of the national economy. It is true that by 2005 this figure had more than doubled to become 22.7 per cent. However, Hirst et al. argue that many adjustments need to be made to make this really measure what it is intended to. For example, data on the contribution of inward FDI to domestic fixed capital formation show how unimportant they are (Hirst et al. 2009: 78). Moreover, if we take into consideration not only FDI flows, which identify the multinational companies which are lending to affiliated companies abroad, but also their investments in their home country, the picture changes dramatically. Taking the level of home sales and assets as a measure of the degree of globalisation of the world economy, the result is that multinational companies remain significantly 'home and regionally centred' (Hirst et al. 2009: 83–84). According to Hirst and Thompson (1999b: 152), the data showed that between two-thirds and three-quarters of multinational corporations' (MNCs) aggregate business activity continued to be home or regionally centred in the 1990s. If the degree of globalisation of the world economy is measured by the percentage of internationalisation of MNCs over total national output, given by the gross product of foreign affiliates as a percentage of national or regional GDP, it can be seen that this only increased from 5.1 per cent in 1982 to 5.4 per cent in 1994 in developed countries, from 6 per cent to 9.1 per cent in developing countries and from 5.2 per cent to 6 per cent for the world total overall (Hirst and Thompson 1999b: 152). Finally, looking at the debate about offshoring, Hirst et al. underline that, although some countries have seen a discernible increase in the outsourcing of production between 1995 and 2000, this is evidently less dramatic than often claimed and in some cases it has even declined (Hirst et al. 2009: 92, figure 3.6).

Similar considerations lead to the conclusion that 'international companies are still predominantly MNCs, with a clear home base to their operations, and not transnational companies (TNCs), which represent footloose, stateless companies' (Hirst and Thompson 1999b: 152).

Not dissimilarly, they also argued that the idea that financial markets are totally integrated in the global economy is a myth. First of all, if this were not the case, the correlation (R2) between domestic savings and investments, generally used to measure the degree of embeddedness of financial markets, should disappear. In fact, this has not unambiguously declined in the last years of the 20th century (Hirst and Thompson 1999a).

Moreover, if we look at the extent to which financial markets are still under the legal and institutional framework of nation states, realists note that financial markets are financial institutions with a clear national location and embedded in a clear national legal context; they raise assets within a national territory, extend credit to national customers, need to respect national macroeconomic policies and use nationally or regionally defined exchange rate systems and interest rates (Hirst and Thompson 1999a). This means that financial institutions are not uncontrollable, as they are subject to national legal, economic and political limits. Consequently, the best way to govern them is through intergovernmental agreements and cooperation (Hirst et al. 2009: ch.8).

In summary, for realists the idea of the globalised economy is a myth. They claim that the world economy is still concentrated in the hands of key nation states and therefore intergovernmental solutions to the problems of the world economy are the only feasible ones. In turn the myth of globalisation is utilised by those key hegemonic states to consolidate their power at both the international and regional level.

Ultimately this conclusion is the outcome of adopting a quantitative definition of globalisation. After realising that measures of globalisation do not confirm its existence or its relevance as a new phenomenon, they come to the conclusion that it is a convenient myth. However, the adoption of this quantitative definition of the phenomenon does not allow them to identify its salient and distinctive characteristics as a new phase in the development of capitalist economies.

If realists mainly adopt a sceptical approach to globalisation, liberal institutionalists are clearly 'globalists'. Thus, whereas for realists globalisation is mostly a convenient myth in the hands of the most powerful nation states to justify their hegemony, for liberal institutionalists globalisation is a fact that cannot be juxtaposed against any previous instances of international market integration (Held and McGrew 2000).

Despite adopting a definition of globalisation similar to the realists, the globalists maintain that the data does undeniably confirm the existence of the phenomenon. Moreover, they argue that this process of global integration is pretty advanced and brings with it a number of 'transformations' at all levels of governance, from the national to the local and the global, producing a total reshuffling of already existing and well-established institutional settings.

The definition of globalisation given by globalists is still a mainly quantitative one. According to Keohane, for example, globalisation is the intensification of transnational as well as interstate relations. For David Held, globalisation 'suggests a growing magnitude or intensity of global flows such that states and societies become increasingly enmeshed in worldwide systems and networks of interaction' (Held and McGrew 2000: 3), while in Phil Cerny's conceptualisation globalisation is brought about by interaction through denser economic relations amongst states (internationalisation) and denser relations cutting across states (transnationalisation) (Cerny 1999, 2010).

However, contrary to realist analyses, liberal institutionalist ones propose evidence showing the emergence of a completely new phase in the evolution of the global economy. This is characterised by an increase in the level of economic interactions between states and an increase in the number of economic activities overcoming national boundaries to acquire a global dimension. According to Held, this historically distinctive form of globalisation dates back to 1945. To distinguish this phase from previous historical waves of internationalisation, Held identifies four different types of globalisation according to four spatio-temporal dimensions: extensity, intensity, velocity, and reciprocity between local and global development. The argument states that all of these dimensions are quantifiable and need to be measured to know which phase of globalisation we are currently in (Coleman and Sajed 2013: 122–123).

The four types of globalisation identified by Held are: Thick Globalisation, characterised by high extensity, intensity, velocity and reciprocity; Diffused Globalisation, in which the first three dimensions are high, but reciprocity is low; Expansive Globalisation, where only the first two dimensions are high; and Thin Globalisation, when there is only an extensity of connections. Obviously for this scholar, the current phase is one of Thick Globalisation (Coleman and Sajed 2013: 122–123).

As noticed above, both sceptics and globalists start from a similar quantitative definition of globalisation defined as: 'The intensification of economic, political, social, and cultural relations across borders.' (Holm and Sørensen 1995: 12). However, it is precisely the insistence on measurable phenomena which leaves unsolved a number of questions. These relate first of all to the nature of the relationships existing between the economic, the political and the social dimensions of globalisation. Indeed, it does not even specify whether there is any relationship at all. Furthermore, insisting on quantitative elements does not help identifying the causes and consequences of globalisation, making it extremely difficult to relate it to other phenomena, such as the marginalisation of the MENA area. It is therefore necessary to deepen the perspective by adopting a qualitative definition.

From the qualitative point of view, globalisation is approached as an ongoing process of qualitative, structural transformation which is characterising the current historical phase of development of the capitalist economy (Dicken 2007; Mittelman 2000). Understood this way, there is no possibility of denying its existence. Moreover this perspective entails a number of elements which concur to identify it as a process, or, in the words of Mittelman (2000), a 'syndrome'. These elements tend to influence each other, not in a predetermined causal relation, but dialectically, allowing identification of the direction of change and, in some cases, enabling reaction. The components of this qualitative definition

Table 1.1 Dichotomies in the globalisation debate

	Sceptics	Globalists
Quantitative definition	Realists	Liberal institutionalists (Transformationalists)
Qualitative definition		Transnationalists (Hyperglobalists)

of globalisation are: technological development, spilling over into the transformation of both the financial and the productive structures through the geographical restructuring of production and the establishment of a new global division of labour and power. As a consequence of this structural transformation, the social and political systems also change, producing a polarisation of wealth, the subordination of politics to economics and the related decline of the nation state, and instances of commodification (Mittelman 2000; Overbeek 2000).

The table above (Table 1.1) shows the dichotomies identified so far in the debate about globalisation alongside the two dimensions of whether the IPE approaches considered are sceptical or believe in the existence of globalisation and whether they adopt a qualitative or a quantitative definition of it.

What are the consequences of globalisation?

As we have seen above, from the realist perspective the concept of globalisation is a convenient myth in the hands of politicians or public opinion-makers which can be used to justify the persistent hegemony of the most powerful nation states. If globalisation hardly exists, any new trends in the international political economy may be easily explained by making reference to the nation state (Gilpin 2000). It becomes therefore redundant, from this standpoint, to talk about the consequences of globalisation.

Instead, liberal institutionalists maintain not only that globalisation exists but also that it is rather different from any previous historical waves of internationalisation. From this perspective, the main consequence of globalisation is the transformation of both national and international institutional settings. This, in turn, is the consequence of the changes induced by globalisation on the nation state. However, contrary to the transnationalist perspective, from the liberal institutionalist point of view the nation state is able to survive globalisation, subject to changing substantially not only its role *vis-à-vis* its citizens, but also its position in the international system and even its functions (Cerny 2010).

To be precise, Cerny (1999) identifies the following two dimensions to the transformation of the state as induced by globalisation:

1. The state modifies the perception of its role in the economy and in the provision of 'public goods'.
2. States modify the way they interact economically with each other in the international system, creating interdependences and international linkages.

Related to the first aspect, the multiplication of international or transnational relations and interactions produces a new complex and multilayered institutional framework. On the one hand, this renders identification of which institution is responsible for which public good more difficult; on the other hand, it makes it more difficult to define what a public good is (Heritier 2002; Talani 2003).

In this context it is worth analysing with Cerny (1999) the impact of globalisation on the capacity of the state to provide the four main categories of public goods: regulatory, productive, distributive and redistributive.

Starting with regulatory public goods, these are defined as those goods providing for the establishment and application of rules for the operation and interactions of both market and non-market institutions. Globalisation has substantially impacted on the ability of national institutions to perform their regulatory function, undermining them from without and fragmenting them from within (Cerny 1999: 99). As a consequence, the regulatory function once guaranteed by the nation state needs now to be allocated to supranational institutions as they are the only ones able to provide regulatory public goods enforceable outside and above the national level. Overall, globalisation empowers international institutions and regimes, including international law (Held et al. 1999), and increases the constraints that they can impose on states.

Productive public goods are goods and services that were previously provided by the state for the existence of economies of scale, as in the case of energy production, for example. With the advent of globalisation and the increased dimensions and relevance of multinational companies, the state is no longer the only actor able to exploit economies of scale and there is therefore no need for the state to intervene in this context any more. Distributive public goods are defined as goods and services delivered by the state according to the collective nature of consumers (e.g. transport). In this case it is the individualisation of consumers through the process of commodification that has resulted in the loss of the raison d'etre of state provision (Cerny 1999; Heritier 2002).

The most dramatic impact of globalisation is, however, that experienced by redistributive public goods, which are those provided on the basis of a political rationale (e.g. welfare). Globalisation induced international pressure for wage restraint and flexibility of the labour market, thus impairing the power of trade unions, as well as the effectiveness of corporatist bargaining. This caused a substantial reduction in the provision of welfare state goods (Cerny 1999; Heritier 2002). The state has changed its profile from the 'welfare state' to the 'competition state' (Cerny 1999: 101). This is a state providing a dynamic competitive advantage in the international economy (as opposed to a static notion of 'comparative' advantage) (Cerny 2010: 32) and promoting a favourable investment climate to transnational economic actors. This happens by providing a new kind of public good, defined as 'immobile factors of capital' (Cerny 1999: 101), such as human capital, infrastructure, support for new technologies, protection of the environment and maintenance of the standard of living for the middle class.

Not only has the state transformed internally, with respect to its domestic role, from the welfare state to the externally oriented competition state, but it has also modified its position in the international system with respect to the way in which it interacts with the other states. Whereas before globalisation its interactions with the international system relied heavily on security and defence, now the state, both in the developed and in the underdeveloped world, has shifted its priorities to business, trying to attract it by, for example:

- Substituting the macro-level of policy-making with the micro-level (e.g. reduction of labour costs).
- Cultivating a 'dynamic competitive' advantage which requires a more flexible economic structure.
- Attracting foreign investment by adopting a neo-liberal macroeconomic agenda based on low inflation and a stable economy.
- Promoting profitability and efficiency in both the public and the private sector (Cerny 1999).

In contrast to the approaches analysed thus far, the transnationalist perspective puts emphasis on a definition of globalisation as a structural phenomenon, characterised by a number of qualitative transformations which have defined the current evolutionary phase of capitalism (Mittelman 2000; Overbeek 2000; Dicken 2011). Unlike quantitative definitions, the qualitative one adopted by transnationalists eliminates the necessity of measuring the different components of globalisation in order to prove its existence. In fact, it is the mere presence of a series of intertwined structural transformations that constitutes the ontology of globalisation. In Peter Dicken's words:

> Globalisation processes are qualitatively different from internationalization processes. They involve not merely the geographical extension of economic activity across national boundaries but also, more importantly, the functional integration of such internationally dispersed activities. (Dicken 1998: 5)

James Mittelman (2000, 2004: 6), famously dubbed globalisation a 'syndrome' of ontologically related phenomenana that acquire meaning by their coexistence in a given historical moment and by the relation that they bear with each other (similarly also Dicken 2007: 8).

Importantly, the relationships between the phenomena included within the scope of globalisation are not random. On the contrary, globalisation is defined within a precise framework. Therefore the accusations of 'vagueness' that are often leveraged against transnationalist scholars by mainstream ones (such as Hirst and Thompson 1999a) are unfounded.

For the purposes of this book, technological development is considered an exogeneous component of globalisation, although the debate about its sources is an important one (Overbeek 1995, 2000). Technological development is the engine of the process of globalisation and the factor determining transformations in the realms of finance and production (Dicken 2007, 2011), as well as in terms of socio-economic relations and political arrangements (Sassen 1988, 1991, 1996; see also Chapter 3).

To start with, technological progress is at the root of the extraordinary developments of financial markets that often go under the name of financial globalisation, defined by transnationalists as around-the-clock, 24 hours a day and seven days a week, access to financial transactions all over the globe (Cohen 1996: 269; Strange 1996). Paradoxically, however, the physical location of financial markets, instead of losing significance, becomes even more important. Indeed, the literature underlines how financial globalisation 'made geography more, not less, important' (Dicken 2003: 59). Not only did financial power not change location, but it became surprisingly even more concentrated in a handful of urban centres, such as London, New York and, to a lesser extent, Tokyo. This concentration is unparalleled in any other industries, despite the fact that financial markets are usually considered as extremely mobile (Dicken 2003: 462). This concentration of financial activities and services in specific urban centres resonates with Sassen's assessment of the role played by global cities in the intersection between the global and the local (Sassen 1991, 2000).

Furthermore, the role of domestic financial elites in financial globalisation has been enhanced, thanks to the fact that globalisation increases their bargaining power (almost blackmailing) within the national polity and *vis-à-vis* the national government. This leads to a shift in the power relations between the different domestic socio-economic groups that cannot be underestimated. Similar dynamics do not concern only the developed world, but also underdeveloped countries where the establishment of offshore markets has produced incredible transformations of the local economic structures and dramatically modified domestic power relations (Lilley 2000). Not that the definition of offshore refers only to the geographical location of financial activities; instead it mostly regards their juridical status. Indeed, a great number of offshore financial activities take place in the most established financial centres such as London, New York and Tokyo (Palan 2003: 2).

From this globalisation of financial markets there has also come an increase in the sensitivity of capital to interest rates, reducing, in the long run, the possibilities for nation states to adopt differentiated monetary and, consequently, macroeconomic policies. This decreases the state's capacity to control the national economy (Padoa-Schioppa 1994; Cohen 1996; Obstfeld and Taylor 2004).

The roots of the crisis of authority experienced by nation states both in the developed and in the less developed world can be found in these phenomena. The limitations posed by globalisation on the effectiveness of national macroeconomic policy action are indeed very significant and can lead to serious unrest. Contrary to institutionalists, in the minds of transnationalists the loss of the national level of economic governance is not compensated by the creation of multilayered systems of economic governance spanning from the local to the supranational level, if not partially and only in certain regions of the world, such as, most evidently, the European Union. In this way, the crisis of authority and legitimacy of the nation state induced by the loss of economic sovereignty within globalisation, as further elaborated below, is recognised as one of the most dangerous developments of this phase of capitalist development (Overbeek 1999, 2000; Van der Pijl 2011).

Technological progress is also the driving force behind the process of the global restructuring of production and its related geographical

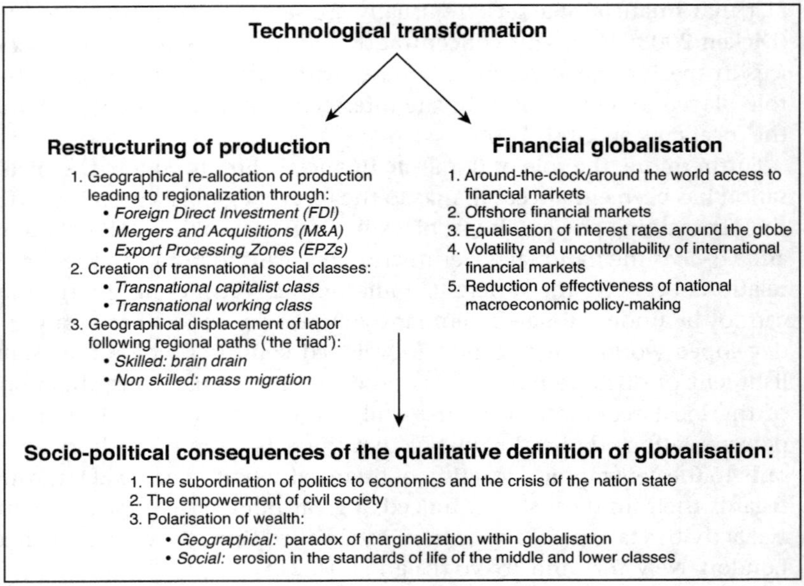

Figure 1.2 Components of the qualitative definition of globalisation

reallocation. This happens through foreign direct investment (FDIs), mergers and acquisitions (M&As), and the creation of export processing zones (EPZs). Indeed, technological development greatly improves the ability of transnational corporations to modify their productive chains to exploit geographically displaced cost reduction opportunities thanks to cheap transport, distant labour control or economies of scale in specific locations. Here, again, the capacity of the nation state to resist similar developments is greatly undermined by the increased bargaining power of transnational companies.

However this process is not happening evenly throughout the globe. On the contrary, one of the main characteristics of this global restructuring of production is the importance of regionalisation in the global political economy (Mittelman 2000: 41; Dicken 2007: 33). Here regionalisation is singled out as a step towards globalisation. There is not however a single pattern of regionalisation; not all regions are being integrated into the global political economy, and this gives rise to instances of geographical marginalisation (Mittelman 2000: 56; Dicken 2007).

Taken together, the dynamics referred to above lead to a new Global Division of Labour and Power (GDLP) (Mittelman 2000). This is characterised on the one hand by the geographical displacement of production alongside regional patterns to exploit, thanks to technological progress, cost reduction opportunities. On the other hand it is accompanied by a dramatic increase of brain-drain and mass migration from regions not included in the globalisation and regionalisation processes (Mittelman 2000). As a consequence, labour costs decrease not only in less developed countries, but also in industrialised ones. This new division of labour thus not only leads to lower costs of production by reallocating production abroad but also by hiring immigrants, especially illegal ones, in national economies. It also lowers the costs of production at home by increasing the pressure on trade unions and reducing their bargaining power, thanks also to consitutionalisation of disciplinary institutional arrangements at the national or at the regional level (Gill 1997; Gill and Mittelman 2011).

Furthermore, this restructuring of global production, together with the transformations induced by financial globalisation, also modifies social and political relations at all levels of organisation, from the local to the global (Mittelman 2000; Dicken 2011; Overbeek 2000). At the national level the most notable political consequence of globalisation, as further elaborated in the next section, is the subordination of politics to economics and the related crisis of the nation state. The state is unable to control economic forces and to guarantee prosperity, jobs and social protection to its citizens, thus producing tensions (Overbeek 2000). Among the social consequences of the processes described thus far, there is the empowerment of civil society thanks to technological development and its renewed propensity to challenge the state whose fading authority is less likely to be recognised as legitimate (Mittelman 2000).

More generally, in the academic literature it has been suggested that democratising consequences may also arise from the loss of power of the state, which needs to adapt to a new pluralism allowing for demands of political reform from civil society (Mittelman 2000: 27–28). Revolutionary pressures might also emerge as a consequence of the empowerment of civil society. However the notion itself of civil society needs discussion, especially in relation to the Middle East. First of all, it is worth noting that the notion of civil society does not coincide with that of the middle class/es.[10]

In a Gramscian conceptualisation (Gramsci 1975, 1999), civil society is one of the three realms where power is consolidated through force and/or consensus. These are the structural realm, that is the economic structure, and two super-structural ones, which are 'civil society', composed by private sector social actors, and 'political society', that is state institutions and public actors (Gramsci 1975, 1999). Thus, civil society is the level connecting the economic structure with the institutional level. According to Gramsci the role of civil society is to transform the corporate interests of economic groups, which derive from their position in the mode of production, into political demands through the identification of a suitable ideological framework. It is in the realm of civil society that economic groups form intermediate social associations, held together by an ideological framework which shapes their identity. This occurs thanks to the role played by intellectuals in helping the process of ideology and identity formation. In this way, civil society is the primary political realm, where political ideas are formed and the demands of groups to the political system are defined. It is also the realm in which economic groups gain consciousness of their interests and aspirations and first engage in political action. Finally it is in the context of civil society that groups form alliances with other contiguous groups with the aim of gaining hegemonic power by transforming their personal or corporate interests into universal ones (Gramsci 1975, 1999).

From this perspective, political society, understood as the ensemble of political institutions, is placed above civil society and coincides with what the realist would call the state and Gramsci calls 'the state proper'. To gain power, groups and alliances formed in the realm of civil society need to conquer the political institutions of the state proper, either using force, as in the case of violent regime change, or consensus, for example through democratic means.

However, Gramsci also distinguishes between the formal institutions of the state and what he refers to as the state in a wider, organic sense. This is the ensemble of the structure and the superstructure, the polity in its entirety, and in this sense it cannot be disentangled from civil society. The state in the organic sense is the articulation of political and civil society (Gramsci 1975, 1999). Although it is often claimed that the modus operandi of the state proper is force and that of civil society is consensus, Gramsci underlines that all three social realms can be ruled by either force or consensus. Moreover, they are also the context within which the battle for the consolidation of power through force and/or consent necessarily takes place to lead to supremacy (Cox 1981). The idea of civil society as proposed by Gramsci and its role in modifying consolidated institutional arrangements has been imported by transnationalist scholars of globalisation to frame the analysis of the disruptive impact of globalisation on social and institutional orders, such as through democratisation processes and revolutions (Mittelman 2000: 30).

A further consequence of globalisation from the transnationalist perspective is the polarisation of wealth in both geographical and social terms. In the first case this leads to the marginalisation of certain countries from the global political economy, as already underlined above. In the second case we can witness an increasing precariousness of the standards of living of the middle and lower classes (Mittelman 2000) as well as of the weakest groups in society, such as the elderly and women. The substantial erosion of secure employment following global restructuring processes as well as the crisis of the national welfare state brings to a head the marginalisation of entire sectors of society and brings the middle class to 'adjust speedily into poverty' (Mittelman 2000: 78).

This phenomenon is extremely relevant for an analysis of the events of the Arab Spring. In particular, Roccu (2012), applying Harvey's (2008, 2010) distinction between 'discontents' and 'dispossessed' from globalisation, identifies the Egyptian middle classes as the discontents and the lower classes as the dispossessed. This framework is used to demonstrate how both the middle and lower classes were progressively impoverished and marginalised in the age of globalisation, thus increasing their communality of interests and their mobilisation capacity (Roccu 2012: 73–75).

Using a Gramscian language, this alliance increased their potential to form a socio-economic bloc and to start battling for supremacy. As already underlined above, for Gramsci (1975, 1999) achieving supremacy requires the formation of alliances with other socio-economic actors. This is obtained by responding to their 'interests' (defined as their motivations stemming from their position in the mode of production) and to their 'ideal aspirations' which are formed and consolidated in the realm of civil society. As the interests of a group in modern capitalist societies are always economic ones, a leading or hegemonic socio-economic group can only be one with an essential role in the mode of production. In medieval societies, on the contrary, religious groups could also perform a leading moral and political role. It follows that in the case of the Arab Spring, the religious content of the leading socio-economic alliance must be read as an ideological framework, which conceals the role played by the groups in question in the mode of production. Indeed, for Gramsci (1975, 1999) it is precisely this essential role in the world of production that confers legitimacy to a socio-economic group, making its dominance socially and politically acceptable for other corporate actors.

The formation of a historical socio-economic bloc, however, is far more than a mere alliance. It is a dialectic unity between the structure and the superstructure, founded on a common ideology allowing the groups in question to overcome any contradictions between theory and practice, intellectuals and masses. The creation of such a cohesive bloc is no easy task and relies heavily on the role of 'organic intellectuals' in spreading a suitable ideology and achieving enduring hegemony. Nevertheless, the economic dimension is still essential; a bloc which is unable to guarantee the economic interests of its allies is doomed to lose its hegemonic power and, eventually, its supremacy (Gramsci 1975, 1999).

It is debatable whether in the wake of the Arab Spring this ideology was represented by Islam and it is even more debatable, as the events of the summer of 2013 in Egypt have shown,whether this emerging hegemonic socio-economic bloc can guarantee a performance of the economy consistent with consolidation of power. However as one Egyptian public servant interviewed by the author put it:

> When there is no more hope in society the only thing that is left is the skin, and the skin in Egypt is Islam. (Talani 2006)

Concluding, from the transnationalist perspective, the process of globalisation as defined to this point is not neutral in social and wealth terms, but entails new social cleavages and challenges, as well as new winners and new losers (Mittelman 2000, 2004).

Can globalisation be governed?

For realists the nation state remains firmly at the centre of the international system and its capacity to act is not altered in any significant way. Hirst and colleagues are critical of the generalised idea that the national level of governance has become obsolete and that it is time for more supranational systems of governance. The new political rhetoric which they term 'an anti-political liberalism' (Hirst et al. 2009: 225) is meaningless, when it is not dangerous (Hirst et al. 2009: 226). The idea that in a globalised economy markets and companies are now able to move freely from the intrusion of an interventionist state is a gift to the far right, which obviously exploits this myth to the maximum. It allows right-wing politicians to spread the idea that state-controlled workers' rights make national economies uncompetitive and in doing so it reduces the bargaining position of workers and workers' associations both in developed and less developed countries. To this extent, far from being a reality, globalisation is a convenient myth (Hirst et al. 2009: 226).

Given that this is the case, the authors prefer to 'ditch' the dangerous idea that globalisation has brought about new modes of governance and suggest that we concentrate on how to reinstate 'the state' in economic governance. From this perspective, the state remains the only actor which is able to govern (Hirst et al. 2009: 240). In sum:

> States remain 'sovereign', not in the sense that they are all powerful and omnicompetent within their territories, but because they police the borders of a territory and, to the degree that they are credibly democratic, are representative of the citizens within those borders. (Hirst et al. 2009: 239)

In the liberal institutionalists' view, instead, the state cannot govern globalisation alone, given the many transformations that it is subject to. The consequence is a shift in the level of governance from the national to the international realm and a multiplication of the sites of power. Thus, starting from the same quantitative definition of globalisation, the two mainstream schools of IPE reach opposite conclusions: for institutionalists the process of transnationalisation of the world economy is considerably advanced and brings about a number of transformations in the national and international governance structures which require completely different solutions to previous institutional arrangements. Needless to say, this multiplication of transnational linkages makes the national level of governance insufficient and inadequate, bringing calls for new forms of governance which transcend nation states. From this perspective the global economy appears as a web of interdependent and interconnected activities performed at different institutional levels by actors who are increasingly detached from the national level of governance.

Summing up, the globalisation process is happening within the yet-to-be-defined institutional terrain of the competition state at the national level and an increasingly fragmented international regime of undetermined institutions. Thus, this is still an ongoing process of institution building, but one which is both unavoidable and necessary. The contours of the process are still uncertain, as many of its outcomes will depend on the actors who will take its lead (Cerny 1999, 2010).

For institutionalists, a crucial role as agents of change is played by political institutions and political actors acting to integrate the national, the international and the transnational levels in a multi-level governance system. In addition, the competition state multiplies the number of layers and cleavages of the world economy, increasing the complexity and density of networks in an ever more interdependent and inter-penetrated global political economy (Keohane 2000).

According to Rosenau (2002: 71) globalisation brings about a fragmentation of authority which is increasingly associated with diverse spheres of governance. It follows that governance in the globalisation era can only happen in a multi-level/multi-centric fashion. Authority is thus not exercised only at the central level by the government, but is diffused in a multiplicity of formal and informal networks, thus becoming 'governance'. As he claims:

> While the rule systems of governments can be thought of as structures, those of governance are social functions or processes that can be performed or implemented in a variety of ways at different times and places (or even at the same time) by a variety of organizations. (Rosenau 2002: 72)

Rosenau identifies a multitude of institutional actors of change in the creation of this new governance system (Rosenau 2002: 80):

- Formal governmental institutions
- Formal international institutions
- NGOs, at all levels of governance, from local to transnational
- Transnational corporations
- Markets.

Consequently, globalisation can be governed by new governance systems, which are in turn categorised by Rosenau as six different types, according to two main variables: processes and structures (Rosenau 2002: 81).

In Cerny's analysis global political processes are characterised by 'transnational pluralism' (Cerny 2010). Globalisation multiplies the amount of international and transnational policy spaces, giving rise to a new form of pluralist politics. This new approach to politics is no longer under the exclusive control of the state. Instead, there is a sort of denationalisation of politics which is now increasingly stratified in a multilevel fashion according to different issue areas. This empowers new political actors and disempowers the state (Cerny 2010). As argued by Cerny, globalisation:

> strengthens the hands of transnationally linked interests and actors and shifts the balance of agenda setting, policy bargaining, and policy outcomes towards globalizing coalitions and protocoalitions. (Cerny 2010: 127)

Moving further along Cerny's and Rosenau's neo-institutionalist line of reasoning, David Held (1995, 2002, 2010) believes that the only way to govern globalisation is by establishing a 'cosmopolitan democracy'. Given that national autonomy and sovereignty have become obsolete in the Thick Globalisation era and that nation states are now irreversibly embedded in a broader legal and governance framework, what is needed is to build on them to achieve cosmopolitan values.

On the other hand, as already underlined, in the transnationalist perspective of globalisation it is technological change which represents the engine of transformation of both the productive and the financial structures. In political terms, the overcoming of national boundaries for the exploitation of global financial and productive opportunities modifies the existing balance of power between national political institutions and increasingly globalised economic elites. The global restructuring of production allows the latter to exert credible political pressure at the domestic level, asking for favourable macroeconomic policies in exchange for not moving economic activity abroad (Strange 1998; Mittelman 2004). This threat, in turn, acquires credibility thanks to technological development, which makes the possibility of easily moving capital across the border and displacing production truly effective (Overbeek 1995). As Mittelman puts it:

> No longer socially embedded in a national political economy, market forces are increasingly unaccountable and disembedded, less dependent on the social structures that gave rise to them. (Mittelman 2000: 56)

The debate is still open in academic and political circles about whether this leads to a total loss of power in national politics with respect to globalising capital, or if there is on the contrary still a margin for reaction from national political actors (Garret 1998). Some authors (Mittelman 2000: Introduction; 2004), advocate the activation of a 'double-movement', Polanyi style. After a phase of triumphant liberalism and of subordination of politics to economics, the losers of globalisation might react producing a counter-movement and allowing for a new social equilibrium to be established.

This is related to a further component of the qualitative definition of globalisation. Globalisation together with allowing for the emergence of a transnational capitalist class, creates the premises for the transnationalisation of the working class. This comes as a consequence of the restructuring of the international division of labour and the establishment of a new global division of labour and power (Mittelman 2000). Such developments could lead to the future reproduction of class struggle at the transnational level, although, obviously, there cannot be any certainty about its outcomes (Talani 2009).

What is clear, however, is that in the transnationalisation game there is a loss of control for parliamentary democracies (Overbeek 2000) in what Stephen Gill calls the New Constitutionalism, defined as:

> the move towards construction of legal or constitutional devices to remove or insulate substantially the new economic institutions from popular scrutiny or democratic accountability. (Gill 1992: 165)

The state is caught in the middle between globalising economic forces from the outside and social movements from within (Mittelman 2004: 15). Indeed, as already noted by Strange (1998) and underlined by Sassen (1996, 2006), one of the consequences of a similar approach to globalisation is the disempowerment of the national state political authority, or what Ruggie (1993) terms the unbundling of territoriality:

> In the modern international polity an institutional negation of exclusive territoriality serves as the means of situating and dealing with those dimensions of collective existence that territorial rulers recognize to be irreducibly transterritorial in character. Non-territorial functional space is the place wherein international society is anchored. (Ruggie 1993: 165)

Many in the transnationalist camp (Overbeek 1999; Cox 1996: 26–27) have come to the conclusion that the state is a victim of the global restructuring of capital which has nullified its capacity to perform its basic functions. Most importantly for the analysis carried out in this book, the state in the globalisation age is no longer in a position to guarantee social stability, income and employment to its citizens. As Overbeek states,

> if one of the essential functions of the modern state is to 'govern the economy' in order to guarantee the conditions for capital

> accumulation and the supply of sufficient employment and income opportunities to its population, then the process of global restructuring has made the state into a less and less effective guarantor. (Overbeek 1999: 11)

This loss of redistributive functions for the state may be slow in developed, OECD countries, but is much more repressive and painful in the less developed ones (Overbeek 1999). Moreover, the unbundling of territoriality as a consequence of globalisation, in the lack of any alternative governance systems, can result in a dangerous loss of control for the state over the national economy, which could in turn be at the roots of globalisation-induced social and ethnic instability and turmoil (Overbeek 1999; Cox 1996).

More explicitly, Van der Pijl (2011) links the Arab Spring to the crisis of the nation state in the context of globalisation. To start with, the political form of the nation state is an alien notion superimposed by the West on the reality of the region in the post-colonial order:

> the post-colonial state has had the task of domesticating and integrating pre-existing political processes: regulating and pacifying tribal, nomadic, sedentary or religious forms of authority and community. In the process, it has helped to shape – even as it has itself been shaped by – a specific mode of foreign relations. (Van der Pijl 2011: 30)

Moreover, in the age of globalisation, a generalised crisis of the nation state has impaired the capacity of the Arab State to act as a structure of social protection, thus making social unrest more likely.

> The unleashing of global capital, combined with post-Cold War pressure from the West to 'open up', has rendered sovereignty outside the Atlantic heartlands ever more commercialized and fractured, undermining the 'national containers' that the West once fostered. The upshot has been to create a generalized crisis of the nation-state on which Western dominion has rested for so long. (Van der Pijl 2011: 48)

Finally, it seems unlikely that any forms of alternative pan-Arabic or Islamic Umma project can substitute the state at the regional level (Van der Pijl 2011; Ayubi 1996; Chapter 4).

Similarly Sassen (1996, 2006) considers globalisation as the catalyst for the loss of power of the nation state over territory and people. However, contrary to the majority of transnationalists (e.g. Overbeek

2000; Dicken 2003; Mittelman 2000) who postulate the subordination of politics to economics in the global political economy, she proposes a more optimistic view of the capacity of local actors in big urban settings to react to the annihilation of politics and identify new forms of political empowerment and inclusion. She mostly refers to actors who are invisible to the formal political economy and manage to enter the political and economic stage through ICT. Thus, as already underlined in her seminal work on *The Global City: New York, London, Tokyo* (Sassen 1991), as well as her later interventions (Sassen 2006), global cities allow for the intersection between the global and the local and provide usually disenfranchised actors with the strength given by numbers to project their agendas in the global stage. This happens thanks to technological progress, which is the central notion of the qualitative definition of globalisation.

In conclusion, to answer the question posed by Giddens of whether globalisation can be governed, we need to distinguish again between different IPE approaches. For realists there is no doubt that the nation state is still in charge of the national and international political economy. For liberal institutionalists the state is being transformed by the globalisation process and a new multi-level institutional system is emerging as an alternative to govern an increasing complex and interdependent global political economy. Finally, according to transnationalists globalisation can hardly be governed as it entails an increasing subordination of politics to economics and a loss of power by the state to control internal and external economic processes. This incapacity of the state to react to global restructuring is at the roots of social instability.

Conclusion: the three paradoxes of globalisation

This book is firmly set within the traditional transnationalist approach to globalisation, adopting a distinctive qualitative definition of the phenomenon (Mittelman 2000; Sassen 1988, 1991, 1996; Dicken 1998, 2003). The process of globalisation is thus identified as qualitatively new, characterised by the dramatic increase of foreign direct investment (FDI), the marginalisation of certain geographical areas and the unprecedented loss of power by the nation state to govern the national economy, territory and people (Van der Pijl 2011; Overbeek 1999, 2000; Cox 1996; Sassen 1996; Mittelman 2000: 25–26). If in some regions of the world the creation of economically integrated regional schemes limits the disruptive potential of the global restructuring on the capacity of the nation state to control its economy and population, this is not the case in marginalised areas.

Technological transformation is a central component of the qualitative definition of globalisation, and it is the one factor that brings about transformation in terms of financial transactions and production (Overbeek 1995, 2000; Dicken 1998, 2003), as well as in the realm of socio-economic relations (Sassen 1988, 1991, 1996).

What is particularly relevant to frame the impact of globalisation on the MENA region is the geographical reallocation of production, which takes place through the creation of Export Processing Zones in developing countries, via a policy of Mergers and Acquisitions or through straightforward FDI (Mittelman 2000; Dicken 2003). As a consequence of the restructuring of production, the labour structure also changes, with a substantial reallocation of labour intensive production in less developed countries. However, this outcome is not happening evenly throughout the globe, but rather entails a process of regionalisation in some geographical areas, the so-called triad of the Americas, Europe and Asia, and marginalisation of the rest of the world, including the MENA area (Mittelman 2000; Overbeek 1999, 2000).

The MENA area is considered here as a clear example of lack of regionalisation, as Chapter 4 of this book will try to demonstrate. Moreover, the three countries undergoing a regime change after the Arab Spring – Tunisia, Egypt and Libya – are considered to have been progressively marginalised from the globalisation process and undergone a crisis of legitimacy rooted in the crisis of the nation state to govern the economy. Chapter 3 will address to what extent economic marginalisation produces, and in turn is produced also by, social and cultural marginalisation as well as the role played by civil society and social capital.

To sum up, the political economy consequences of globalisation that are relevant for the analysis in this book are:

- The regionalisation of the integrated areas of the globe through the constitution of a regional governance scheme, such as the EU.[11]
- A progressive marginalisation of the areas of the world which are not integrated in the globalisation process.
- The crisis of the state in marginalised countries and the resulting intensification of social and ethnic conflicts (Pellerin and Overbeek 2001).
- A precarisation of the standards of life of the middle and lower classes in both developed and less developed countries.

From the theoretical point of view, the following issues appear particularly relevant:

1. The paradox of regionalisation within globalisation.
2. The paradox of marginalisation within globalisation.
3. The paradox of the empowerment of civil society and social capital in the unfolding of the crisis of the nation state.

These three paradoxes will be addressed in detail in the next chapters of the book.

Notes

1. See R. Abouzeid, 'Bouazizi: The man who set himself and Tunisia on fire', TIME Magazine (21 January 2011) http://www.time.com/time/magazine/article/0,9171,2044723,00 as accessed on 11 January 2013; I. Watson and J. Karadsheh, 'The Tunisian fruit seller who kickstarted Arab uprising', CNN (22 March 2011) http://articles.cnn.com/2011–03–22/world/tunisia.bouazizi.arab.unrest_1_fruit-vendor-sidi-bouzid-abedine-ben-ali?_s=PM:WORLD as accessed on 11 January 2013.
2. See also Lagi et al. (2011); Arezki and Bruckner (2011); MacKenzie (2011); Fraser and Rimas (2011); Bellemare (2011).
3. At the beginning of 2008, after the massive losses that financial institutions had incurred on mortgage-backed securities and other derivatives, they started investing in commodity futures, especially the crude oil futures markets, giving rise to the fourth stage of the global financial crisis. As a consequence, NYMEX oil futures prices experienced almost a 100 per cent increase from US$ 75 per barrel in the beginning of October 2007 to their peak of US$ 147 per barrel on 11 July 2008.
4. A policy of 'opening', the Infitah was launched by Sadat in 1974 with the aim of reforming the Egyptian economy, moving away from a planned towards a market economy and increasing the role played by the private sector. See Roccu (2012).
5. See Lynch (2008); also 'Egyptian court convicts 22 for food riots', The Hindu (15 December 2008) http://www.hindu.com/thehindu/holnus/003200812151875.htm as accessed on 11 January 2013.
6. Based on food consumer price index (CPI). See US department of agriculture website: http://useconomy.about.com/gi/o.htm?zi=1/XJ&zTi=1&sdn=useconomy&cdn=newsissues&tm=3836&gps=239_367_1525_751&f=00&su=p284.13.342.ip_&tt=12&bt=1&bts=1&zu=http%3A//www.ers.usda.gov/Briefing/CPIFoodAndExpenditures/consumerpriceindex.htm as accessed on 10 January 2012.
7. See World Bank database website: http://databank.worldbank.org/Data/Views/Reports/Chart.aspx as accessed on 10 January 2012.
8. UCLA, 7 November 2005.
9. For more about Giddens's perspective on Globalisation see Giddens (1999).

10. For a competent discussion of the definition of the Middle class in the Middle East and in Egypt in particular see Roccu (2012).
11. See, for example, the relations between ETUC and the European Round Table or UNICE at the European level.

References

Al-Shawarby, S., and Hoda, S. (2012). *Are International Food Price Spikes The Source Of Egypt's High Inflation?* Economic Research Forum, Working Paper 714, Cairo: October 2012 website: http://www.erf.org.eg/CMS/uploads/pdf/714.pdf as accessed on 15 January 2013.

Arezki, R., and Bruckner, M. (2011). *Food Prices and Political Instability*. IMF Working Paper 11/62, website: http://www.imf.org/external/pubs/ft/wp/2011/wp1162.pdf as accessed on 11 January 2013.

Ayubi, N. (1996). *Over-stating the Arab State*. I.B.Tauris, London.

Bellemare, M. F. (2011). *Rising Food Prices, Food Price Volatility, and Political Unrest.* SSRN (28 June 2011) http://ssrn.com/abstract=1874101 as accessed on 11 January 2013.

Busch, A. (2008). *Banking Regulation and Globalisation*. Oxford University Press, Oxford.

Cerny, P. (1999). 'Reconstructing the Political in a Globalising World', in Buelens, F. (ed.) *Globalisation and the Nation State*. Edward Elgar, Cheltenham.

Cerny, P. (2010). *Rethinking World Politics: A Theory of Transnational Neo-pluralism.* Oxford University Press, New York.

Cohen, B.J. (1996). 'Phoenix Risen: The Resurrection of Global Finance', *World Politics*, 48(2), 268–296.Coleman, W.D., and Sajed, A. (2013). *Fifty Key Thinkers on Globalisation*. Routledge, London.

Cox, R.W. (1981). Social Forces, States, and World Orders: Beyond International Relations Theory. *Millennium*, 10, 127–155.

Cox, R.W. (1996). *Approaches to World Order.* Cambridge University Press, Cambridge.

Dicken, P. (1998). *Global Shift, Transforming the World Economy*, (3rd ed.). Paul Chapman Publishing, London.

Dicken, P. (2003). *Global Shift: Reshaping the Global Economic Map in the 21st century*, (4th ed.). Sage Publications, London.

Dicken, P. (2007). *Global Shift: Mapping the Changing Contours of the World Economy*, (5th ed.). Sage Publications, London.

Dicken, P. (2011). *Global Shift: Mapping the Changing Contours of the World Economy*, (6th ed.). Guilford, New York.

FAO (2011). *North Africa Brief.* FAO/GIEWS Global Watch. March 2011. Available on: http://www.fao.org/giews/english/shortnews/nafria110311.pdf as accessed on 28 July 2013.

Fraser, E., and Rimas, A. (2011). *The Psychology of Food Riots*, Foreign Affairs, 30 January 2011, http://www.foreignaffairs.com/articles/67338/evan-fraser-and-andrew-rimas/the-psychology-of-food-riots as accessed on 11 January 2013.

Garret, G. (1998). *Partisan Politics in the Global Economy.* Cambridge University Press, Cambridge.

Giddens, A. (1999). *Runaway World: How Globalisation is Reshaping Our Lives.* Routledge, New York.

Gill, S.R. (1992). 'The Emerging World Order and European Change', in Miliband, R., and Panitch, L. (eds) *Communist Regimes: The Aftermath. The Socialist Register 1992*. Merlin Press, London.
Gill, S. (1997). 'An EMU or an Ostrich?: EMU and Neo-liberal Globalisation; Limits and Alternatives', in Minkkinen, P., and Potomaki, H. (eds) *The Politics of Economic and Monetary Union*. Kluwer Academic Publishers, The Hague.
Gill, S., and James H. Mittelman, (ed) (2011) *Innovation and Transformation in International Studies*. Cambridge University Press, Cambridge.
Gilpin, R. (2000). *The Challenges of Global Capitalism: The World Economy in the 21st Century*. Princeton University Press, Princeton.
Gilpin, R. (2001). *Global Political Economy: Understanding the Global Economic Order*. Princeton University Press, Princeton and Oxford.
Goldstein, J., and Keohane, R.O. (1993). *Ideas in Foreign Policy*. Cornell University Press, Ithaca, New York.
Gosh, B. (1999). *Challenges and Opportunities of Economic Globalisation: Some Implications for Labour, Industry and Nation States*. Paper prepared for the Bundesanstalt fur Arbeit workshop on 'Internationalisierung der Arbeitsmarkte', 27–28 April, Frankfurt a/M.
Gramsci, A. (1975). *Quaderni dal carcere*. Einaudi, Torino.
Gramsci, A. (1999). *Selections from the Prison Notebooks of Antonio Gramsci*. Elecbook electronic books, London.
Harvey, D. (2008). The Right to the City. *New Left Review*, 53, September–October 2008.
Harvey, D. (2010). *The Enigma of Capital and the Crises of Capitalism*. Profile Books, London.
Hay, C., and Marsh, D. (eds) (2000). *Demystifying Globalisation*. Palgrave MacMillan.
Held, D. (1995). *Democracy and the Global Order: From the Modern State to Cosmopolitan Governance*. Stanford University Press, Stanford, CA.
Held, D., McGrew, A., Goldblatt, D., and Perraton, J. (1999). *Global Transformation*. Polity Press, Cambridge, UK.
Held, D., and McGrew, A. (2000). *The Global Transformations Reader*. Polity Press, Cambridge, UK.
Held, D. (2002). Law of States, Law of Peoples. *Legal Theory*, 8(1), 1–44.
Held, D. (2010). *Cosmopolitanism: Ideas and Realities*. Polity Press, Cambridge, UK.
Heritier, A. (ed.) (2002). *Common Goods: Reinventing European and International Governance*. Rowman and Littlefield Publishers, Lanham, MD.
Hirst, P., and Thompson, G. (1999a). *Globalisation in Question*, (2nd ed.). Polity Press, Cambridge, UK.
Hirst, P., and Thompson, G. (1999b). 'The Tyranny of Globalisation: Myth or Reality?', in Buelens, F. (ed.) *Globalisation and the Nation State*. Edward Elgar.
Hirst, P., Thompson, G., and Bromely, S. (2009). *Globalisation in Question, The International Economy and the Possibilities of Governance*, (3rd ed.). Polity Press, Cambridge, UK.
Holm, H.H., and Sørensen, G. (1995). *Whose World Order? Uneven Globalisation and the End of the Cold War*. Westview Press, Boulder, CO.
Jacks, D.S., O'Rourke, K.H., and Williamson, J.G. (2011). Commodity Price Volatility and World Market Integration since 1700. *The Review of Economics and Statistics*, MIT Press, 93(3), 800–813.

Keohane, R.O. (2000). 'Sovereignty in International Society', in Held, D., and McGrew, A. (eds) *The Global Transformations Reader*. Polity Press, ch. 9.
Lagi, M. (2012). *Economics of Food Prices and Crises*. Necsi.edu, website: http://www.academia.edu/1399884/Economics_of_Food_Prices_and_Crises as accessed on 11 January 2013.
Lagi, M., Bertrand, K. Z., and Bar-Yam, Y. (2011). *Food Crises and Political Instability in North Africa and the Middle East*, New England complex system Institute, website: http://necsi.edu/research/social/food_crises.pdf As accessed on 10 January 2013.
Lilley, P. (2000). *Dirty Dealing: The Untold Truth about Global Money Laundering*. Kogan Page, London.
Lynch, D. (2008). *Tension in Egypt Shows Potency of Food Crisis*, USA Today (30 April 2008) http://www.usatoday.com/money/world/2008–04–29-egypt-food-shortage_N.htm, as accessed on 11 January 2013.
MacKenzie, D. (2011). *Can Complexity Theory Explain Egypt's Crisis?*, New Scientist (3 February 2011) http://www.newscientist.com/article/dn20082-can-complexity-theory-explain-egypts-crisis.html, as accessed on 11 January 2013.
Maloney, S. (2011). 'The Economic Dimension: The Price of Freedom', in Pollack, K. (ed.) *The Arab Awakening*. The Brookings Institution, Washington, pp. 66–76.
Mittelman, J.H. (2000). *The Globalisation Syndrome: Transformation and Resistance*. Princeton University Press, Princeton.
Mittelman, J.H. (2004). *Whither Globalization? The Vortex of Knowledge and Ideology*, Routledge,
Noueihed, L., and Warren, A. (2012). *The Battle for the Arab Spring*. Yale University Press, New Haven, CT.
Obstfeld, M., and Taylor, A.M. (2004). *Global Capital Markets: Integration, Crisis and Growth*. Cambridge University Press, Cambridge, UK.
Orlowski, L.T. (2008). *Stages of the 2007/2008 Global Financial Crisis: Is There a Wandering Asset-Price Bubble?* Economics Discussion Papers, No 2008–43, http://www.economics-ejournal.org/economics/discussionpapers/2008–43 as accessed on 18 May 2009.
Pellerin, H. and Overbeek, H.W. (2001). 'Neoliberal Regionalism and the Management of People's Mobility', in Bieler, A., and Morton, A.D. (eds) *Social Forces in the Making of the 'New Europe'*. Palgrave MacMillan.
Overbeek, H.W. (1995). 'Globalisation and the Restructuring of the European Labor Markets: The Role of Migration', in Simai, M. (ed.) *Global Employment. An International Investigation into the Future of Work*. Zed Books and United Nations University Press, London/Tokyo.
Overbeek, H. (1999). *The Budapest Process: Internationalization of Migration Control*, Paper presented to the 40th Annual Conference of the International Studies Association, 16–20 February 1999, Washington D.C., Mimeo.
Overbeek, H. (2000). 'Globalisation, Sovereignty and Transnational Regulation: Reshaping the Governance of International Migration', in Gosh, B. (ed.) *Managing Migration: Time for a New International Regime*, Oxford University Press, Oxford.
Padoa-Schioppa, T. (1994). *The Road to Monetary Union in Europe: The Emperor, the Kings and the Genies*. Clarendon Press, Oxford.
Palan, R. (2003). *The Offshore World*. Cornell University Press, Ithaca, NY.

Roccu, R. (2012). 'Of Middle Classes, Economic Reforms and Popular Revolts: Why Democratization Theory Failed, Again', in Panebianco, S. (ed.) *Winds of Democratic Change in the Mediterranean.* Rubbettino, Soveria Mannelli, pp. 61–82.

Rosenau, J. (2002). 'Governance in a New Global Order', in Held, D., and McGrew, A. (eds) *Governing Globalisation: Power, Authority and Global Governance.* Polity Press, Cambridge, UK.

Ruggie, J. G. (1993). Territoriality and beyond: Problematizing Modernity in International Relations. *International Organization*, 47(1), 139–174.

Sassen, S. (1988). *The Mobility of Labour and Capital.* Cambridge University Press, Cambridge, UK.

Sassen, S. (1991). *The Global City: New York, London, Tokyo.* Princeton University Press, Princeton, NJ.

Sassen, S. (1996). *Losing Control? Sovereignty in the Age of Globalization.* Columbia University Press, New York.

Sassen, S. (2006). *Territory, Authority, Rights: From Medieval to Global Assemblages.* Princeton University Press, Princeton NJ.

Smith, A.F. (2011). *Starving the South.* St. Martin's Press, New York.

Strange, S. (1996). *The Retreat of the State.* Cambridge University Press, Cambridge.

Strange, S. (1998). *Mad Money.* Manchester University Press, Manchester.

Talani, L.S. (2003). *Avoiding the 'G' Word in Reinventing European and International Governance.* International Studies Review, March 2003.

Talani, L.S. (2006). Interview with an Anonymous Functionnaire of the Egyptian Ministry for Migration and Manpower, unpublished.

Talani, L.S. (2009). *From Egypt to Europe.* I.B.Tauris

Talani, L.S. (2013). *European Political Economy: An IPE Perspective.* Ashgate, London.

Van der Pijl, K. (2011). *Arab Revolts and Nation-State Crisis*, NLR 70, July–August 2011.

2
The Paradox of Regionalisation within Globalisation: Some Theoretical Concerns

Globalisation and regionalisation

Despite there being no consensus on how to define globalisation or, as we have seen in the previous chapter, even on whether it exists, scholars of IPE from a variety of different academic standpoints are somewhat paradoxically in agreement that regionalisation is indeed happening. What is more controversial is however its relation with globalisation.

Realism: the enduring hegemony of the state within the 'triad'

In the realist camp, as already discussed, Hirst and colleagues (Hirst and Thompson 1999a, b; Hirst et al. 2009) maintain that globalisation is essentially a myth, a phenomenon the existence of which is highly debatable even as the 'end' of an ongoing process. There is however no doubt that regionalisation processes are taking place as a consequence of regional hegemonic states seeking to maximise their power.

In sum, if there is no global political economy, there is, nevertheless a clear trend toward a regional one. This is happening *de jure*, through the establishment of formal regional institutional and free trade arrangements (regionalism), and *de facto,* through the emergence of economically integrated blocks whose boundaries do not necessarily coincide with their formal definition (regionalisation) (Hirst et al. 2009: 159). Moreover, although it is true that in some areas of the world, especially Europe, formal regionalism is pretty advanced, this cannot be taken for granted or assumed to be happening everywhere and in a steady way, as the intergovernmentalist/realist theories of integration that are analysed below will make clear. In any case, formal institutionalised regionalism is always a consequence of *de facto* economic regionalisation (Hirst et al. 2009: 159; Moravscik 1991, 1993a, 1993b).

Already in the 1990s the clustering of the global economy into three major economic blocks, on the basis of firms' decisions about where to trade and invest, was manifest. At that stage, Hirst and Thompson (1999a, 1999b) identified the triad of the USA, the EU and Japan, which tended to direct its FDI flows and stock toward a fixed cluster of countries, forming three clearly distinguishable groupings. These were regionally specific and dominated by one or more of the members of the triad (see Figure 2.1).

Thus, the process of regionalisation is for realists the consequence of the increased power of bigger states over small ones in a clearly defined regional context. As such, instead of being a step toward globalisation, as for institutionalists and transnationalists, it is rather the contrary. In fact, the direction of FDI is first between the triad leaders and then between the dominant country and its cluster rather than among the countries within the cluster (Figure 2.1) (Hirst and Thompson 1999a: 120).

In the last couple of decades this equilibrium has been altered by the impressive economic growth of economies in East Asia, most evidently China (Hirst et al. 2009: 131). As a consequence of the unprecedented industrialisation of Asia, the region has come to account for over 35 per cent of world output and over 25 per cent of world exports. Asia has accounted for over 50 per cent of total global economic growth since the beginning of the millennium (Hirst et al. 2009: 140). This was accompanied by a clear trend towards regionalisation with China emerging as the leader of this process, and potentially India following suit. The level of intra-regional trade in Asia is comparable to that of the NAFTA and production processes have been organised in regionally integrated supply chains. China is rising to the role of new hegemon of a region in expansion: from 1979 onwards, China had the fastest rate of total GDP growth (9.4 per cent), its per worker GDP growth was 7.7 per cent and its per capita GDP growth was 8.1 per cent (Hirst et al. 2009: 142). As Hirst et al. put it, China is the:

> dominant part of a general shift in the historical geography of industrial capitalism to emerging Asia. (Hirst et al. 2009: 143)

The success stories of some Asian countries converging towards US levels of productivity is compounded by the relative divergence of other regions of the globe, most notably Africa, parts of the Middle East and central and western Asia (Hirst et al. 2009: 148). This phenomenon, recognised by realists, foreshadows the paradox of marginalisation within globalisation, the determinants of which are discussed in more detail by transnationalists.

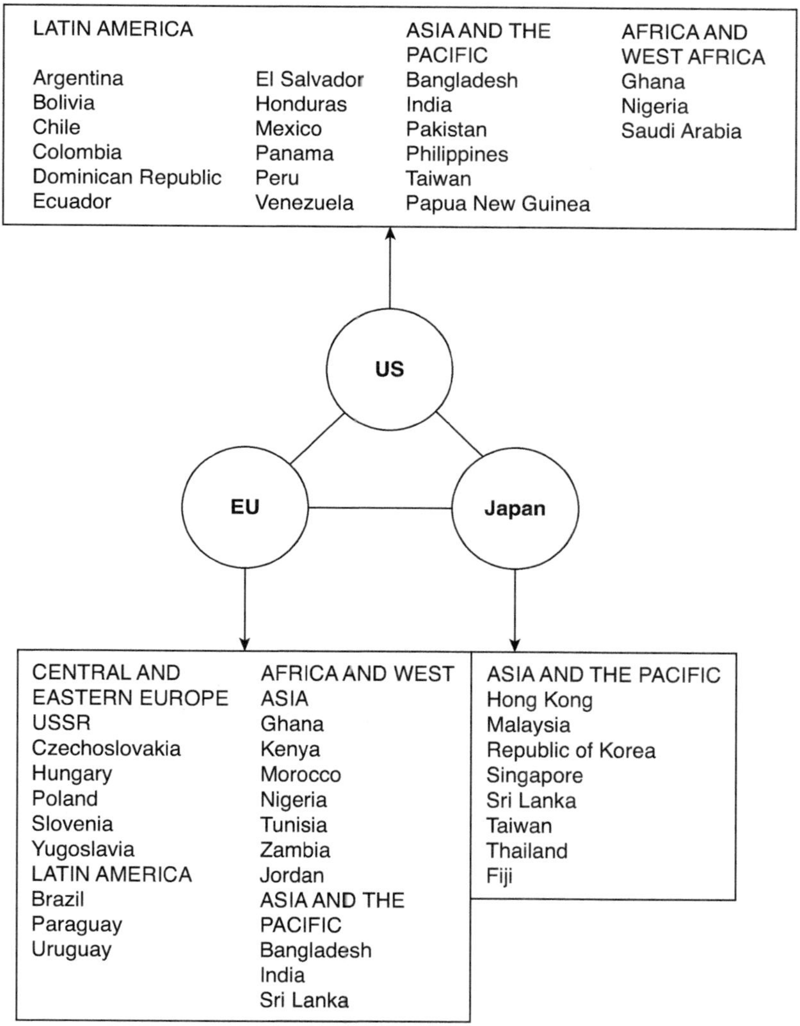

Figure 2.1 Foreign direct investment cluster of triad members (economies in which triad members dominate inward foreign direct investment stocks/flows), 1990

Source: See Hirst and Thompson (1999a: 120)

Summing up, given the pattern of industrialisation of the Asian region, including India, Hirst et al. (2009: 156–157) foresee a trend towards the convergence of the Asian economies and the economies of advanced capitalist countries. However they do not see this as a process leading to globalisation. Instead, they recognise a trend in the international economy towards what they call 'supranational regionalisation', defining a region as 'a geographically contiguous area composed of the territories of nation states that have either combined in an integrative economic or monetary union, or whose economies have evolved into a closely interdependent entity, or who can empirically be shown to be advancing along those routes' (Hirst et al. 2009: 159).

Instances of similar trajectories are represented most obviously by the European Union (EU) which, as further discussed below, presents the most advanced form of *de jure* regionalism and *de facto* regionalisation. There are other examples of this process of 'supranationational regionalisation', such as the North American Free Trade Agreement (NAFTA), Mercosur (including Argentina, Brazil, Paraguay, Uruguay and Venezuela), the Association of South-East Asian Nations (ASEAN) and the West African Economic and Monetary Union, among others. It is noteworthy indeed that in 2004 most export flows were still taking place at the intra-regional level (Table 2.1).

The creation of supranational regional economic blocks, in the conceptualisation of these authors, does not coincide with the intensification of globalisation processes. They suggest that the international system is showing strong tendencies towards forming supranational blocks of these kinds rather than intensifying globalisation processes. Indeed, they claim, 'under current conditions, the supranational regionalism/regionalisation process looks to be more convincing than full globalism/Globalisation' (Hirst et al. 2009: 189). This is in contrast with the interpretation given to the same phenomenon by other scholars (Amin 2006; Gamble and Payne 1996: 16; Cox 1987; Held and McGrew 2007) who

Table 2.1 Share of inter-regional merchandise export flows in each region as a percentage of total merchandise exports, 2004

	Destination			
Origin	**North America**	**Europe**	**Asia**	**Total**
North America	56	16	9	81
Europe	9	74	8	91
Asia	22	18	50	90

Source: Hirst et al. (2009: 164)

seem to see it as a part of globalisation, rather than being distinct from it. To them we turn in the next two sections.

Liberal-institutionalism: regionalism as a step towards cosmopolitanism

In the liberal-institutionalist context, the process of regionalisation is not interpreted as a barrier to globalisation, but as a moment within this process, institutionalising new forms of trans-boundary and supranational governance at the regional level which are by no means inconsistent with the emergence of a new global regime (Held and McGrew 2000: 12, 2007: 78–81).

From the political economy point of view, although it cannot be denied that most trade happens within clearly defined regions (as seen with the triad above), regional and multilateral liberalisation have gone hand in hand since at least 1947 (Held and McGrew 2007: 80 quotes Baldwin 2006: 24). Liberalisation renders trade blocks unsustainable, and this is demonstrated by the fact that there is a trend towards price convergence in the global political economy. Moreover, regionalism in trade does not translate into a regional segmentation of world markets (Held and McGrew 2007: 81). Even more importantly, global trade is regulated by a global institution, the WTO, which defines the global regulatory framework within which markets have to act. Thus, global markets are not totally free but organised according to a global legal framework defined by the WTO, as well as by a growing body of transnational private merchant law (Held and McGrew 2007: 81).

In sum, even if some regional trends in trade may be recognised, there is no doubt for institutionalists that

> trade globalisation is not simply about trends in world trade but also the critical importance of global and transnational trade authorities in the construction of global markets. (Held and McGrew 2007: 81)

Similarly, despite the vagaries of financial markets and some regional trends in financial flows, there is no way of denying that global financial markets have become increasingly integrated since the 1980s (Held and McGrew 2007: 86). Full capital mobility and openness are demonstrated by increasing convergence of interest rates and even the savings-investments correlation appears to have decreased from the 1990s (Held and McGrew 2007: 86–87).

Most importantly, again, the institutional dimension of globalisation is undeniable. First, it is unquestionable that legal restrictions to capital flows have substantially decreased since the 1970s. This means that the liberalisation of capital movements has substantially increased and with it so too has financial globalisation, as defined in quantitative terms (Cohen 1996, 2001; Talani 2012). Moreover, there is an increasing trend towards the constitution of private or public agencies in charge of regularising and organising trans-border finance. Amongst these institutions there are multinational banks, as well as regulatory and surveillance bodies such as the IMF, the Bank for International Settlements (BIS), the Financial Action Task Force (FATF) or the International Accounting Standards Board (IASB) (Held and McGrew 2007: 89).

Effectively, institutionalists do not recognise any specificity to the process of regionalisation as they view it as a step in the creation of a truly global economy and governance system. Regional institutional projects, such as Mercosur or the EU, alongside global institutions, contribute to the creation of a new multi-layered global system of economic governance (Held and McGrew 2007: 115; Rosenau 1990, 1997). The conceptualisation of the global economy as 'triad-isation' or regionalisation is therefore misleading. Indeed:

> It is the very clustering of FDI around the three major economic regions, combined with the intensity of interregional flows, that reinforces the dynamic of global economic integration. (Held and McGrew 2007: 92)

Thus, regionalisation is a complementary tendency to globalisation, not a competing one (Held and McGrew 2007: 108). This is so much the case that generally, starting from neo-functionalists and their conceptualisation of the supranationalisation of Europe (as detailed below), neo-institutionalists prefer to focus on the end of the process: the creation of a truly global institutional system of governance based on cosmopolitan values.

Many are the prominent neo-institutionalists auspicating the advent of cosmopolitanism as an end of the global restructuring of the governance system (Held 1995, 2002, 2010a; Beck 2005, 2006, 2009; Archibugi 2010; Kaldor 2010). According to Held, cosmopolitan values need to be expressed as a set of principles:

> These are principles that can be universally shared and can form the basis for the protection and nurturing of each person's equal significance in the moral realm of all humanity. (Held 2010a: 230)

Importantly, for Held cosmopolitan principles need to be adopted by cosmopolitan institutions, including cosmopolitan law and cosmopolitan democracy (Held 2010a: 240–241; Held 2010b: 306).

Cosmopolitan law implies the subordination of national, regional and international sovereignties to it. As a consequence, authority should also be recast at the cosmopolitan level by adopting a cosmopolitan democracy. This would form a political system which could coexist with the state system, but also override it when dealing with international and transnational activities (Held 2010a; Held 2010b: 306). In this view, globalisation has furthered the need to embed the fundamental rights of human beings at a cosmopolitan level of governance (Held 2010b). Indeed, in the period after the Second World War there was a progressive disembedding of sovereignty and authority from the national level and the building of a 'liberal international sovereignty' regime. These changes helped relegitimise the state by reconstructing the necessary legal and democratic forms of governance at supranational levels, including the regional one (Held 1995, 2010c; Held and McGrew 2007).

However these international/regional forms of governance are becoming increasingly obsolete in the age of globalisation. This happens because they still rely on state-centric institutional structures and therefore cannot accommodate the new multi-centric forms of political organisation brought about by globalisation. In particular Held underlines how globalisation has created new 'overlapping communities of fate' (Held 2010a: 244). These are political communities held together by processes which totally transcend national and even regional boundaries, for example, those affected by environmental problems, by the modalities of regulation of the global financial system or by the global spread of diseases such as HIV/AIDS. Therefore, the needs of those belonging to similar communities cannot be catered for by any single state at the centre of international or regional institutional arrangements. The argument follows that what is needed is a new cosmopolitan democracy able to protect the rights of this multitude of overlapping communities. Cosmopolitanism should thus build upon already existing international/regional institutional schemes and bring forward the process of globalisation of governance (Held 2010b, 2002).

Similarly, in Beck's conceptualisation the 'cosmopolitanisation' of society is a sort of unintended consequence of the increase in cross-border interactions between actors who are more and more threatened by the catastrophic consequences of globalisation, such as financial and ecological risks (Beck 2010: 219; Beck 2005, 2006; similarly Giddens 1990). Again, the survival of humankind rests on the building of a sort of Kantian Cosmopolitan Res-publica (Wallace Brown and Held 2010: 45). Cosmopolitanism is understood here, as in the Greek etymology, as dual citizenship: citizenship of the Cosmos (world/globe) and citizenship of the polis (city/state) (Wallace Brown and Held 2010: 4; similarly Beck 2005, 2006).

The notion of universal citizenship is indeed recurrent in neo-institutionalist thinking. In Soysal's analysis, for example, post-national citizenship derives from international human rights standards granted on the basis of universalistic notions of personhood. This makes the idea of national citizenship obsolete (Soysal 1998, 2000). In fact, contemporary citizenship transcends national definitions as it is based on two fundamental paradoxes:

1. First, the tendency towards decoupling of the two main elements of citizenship: rights and identities.
2. Second, the fact that universalistic conceptions of personhood legitimise claiming particularistic rights in the public sphere (Soysal 2000).

This emphasis on the almost automatic, necessary (Beck 2010) entrenchment of fundamental rights from the state to the cosmos found in cosmopolitan democracy is, however, not shared by transnationalists who instead underline the contradictions of globalisation and their potential to create tensions and crises.

Transnationalism: the regional dimension of the global restructuring of production

If institutionalists stress the importance of the regionalisation of the governance system within a multi-layered reorganisation of power, transnationalists underline how the global restructuring of production favours some regions over others (Overbeek 1995, 1999, 2000).

From the transnationalist perspective, as noticed above, the process of globalisation entails a number of paradoxes and contradictions. In particular, globalization emphasises the local within the global, empowering local, subnational actors, especially in urban contexts as underlined by Sassen (1981, 1988, 1991). It also favours other localising tendencies which produce instances of regionalisation in core regions. Overbeek refers to this phenomenon as the restructuring of the global political economy into macro-regions (Overbeek 2000). The underlying dynamic of this conception of regionalisation is neo-liberal restructuring which, together with the establishment of new forms of open regionalism, leads to what transnationalists term 'neo-liberal regionalism' (Overbeek 2000; Pellerin and Overbeek 2001).

In the context of the crisis of the nation state deriving from the subordination of politics to economics (Strange 1991, 2002), market forces reorganize their mobility/fixity nexus at the regional level by enforcing 'open regionalism' (Pellerin and Overbeek 2001). This is defined by transnationalists as:

> forms of regional integration aimed at combining further liberalisation of the flow of goods and capital with a revival of certain structures of governance of the market. (Pellerin and Overbeek 2001: 7 mimeo version)

Instances of neo-liberal regionalism projects are represented by the EU, NAFTA, Mercosur and any other similar regional free trade initiatives (Gamble and Payne 1996; Hettne et al. 1999).

Also for Mittelman (2000: 112) the prevailing model of regionalism in the current phase of capitalism is the neo-liberal one. This is different from the forms of regionalism prevailing in the 1930s, defined as 'autocentric regionalism' (Mittelman 2000: 112), which were characterised by strong protectionist tendencies. It is also different from the essentially failed 'development regionalism' which would put more emphasis on redistribution (Mittelman 2000: 117). This neo-liberal form of regionalism is extrovert, being open to the global political economy through three different layers of interaction: the macro-regional level, the national level and the micro-regional level. It is thus multifaceted and open to the wider economy by a constant movement to higher degrees of 'regioness' (Hettne 1994: 7–8). As such, it is a dimension of the globalisation process.

The rationale for the formation of similar regional schemes in the core of the global political economy is that for capital to be mobile it is necessary to have some political and economic stability in the regions where it wants to move to (Gamble and Payne 1996). This is what Harvey defined as 'the spatial fix' (Harvey 2005). Deducing *a contrario* from this logic, the regions where capital mobility is limited and relatively decreasing, have a lower incentive to 'fixity' and to the formation of regional economic institutional schemes. This, as elaborated further in this book, is the case of the MENA area.

Overbeek and Pellerin refer to the 'mobility–fixity nexus', which is defined as 'the logic determining both instances and places of mobility and fixity of global capitalism' (Pellerin and Overbeek 2001). Whereas in the period of embedded neo-liberalism, in the aftermath of the Second World War, capital accumulation processes took place almost exclusively at the level of the nation state, with the subsequent advent of globalisation and the global restructuring of production alongside regional patterns, the mobility–fixity nexus has tended to become more regional in nature (Pellerin and Overbeek 2001; Dicken 2011; Mittelman 2000).

The establishment of neo-liberal regions is coincident with the formation of regional productive structures, with their own integrated regional chains of production, their regional markets and their regional divisions of labour both among countries and within regions (Mittelman 2000: 123; Gamble and Payne 1996).

Capital mobility is indeed increasingly following regional patterns. As a consequence, regions emerge as the logical spatial level of organisation of production (Overbeek 2000). Transnationalists (Overbeek 2000; Pellerin and Overbeek 2001; Mittelman 2000; Dicken 2011) note how the majority of economic activities of Transnational Corporations (TNCs), both in the sphere of production and in the financial one, is indeed concentrated in the three core regions of the world. These coincide with the realist 'triad' and are North America (NAFTA), Western Europe (EU) and East Asia.

Thus both realists and transnationalists recognise an established trend towards the regionalisation of the three core areas of the global political economy. For realists the engine of this process continues to be the nation state, or, more precisely the most powerful states within a region (Hirst et al. 2009). On the contrary, transnationalists remark how foreign direct investment is not undertaken by countries but by transnational corporations (TNCs) (Mittelman 2000: 123; Overbeek 2000; Dicken 2011: ch. 7; Strange 1991, 2002). Moreover, the explosion of mergers and acquisition (M&As) which are mainly concentrated in the developed world, reinforces the power of TNCs tremendously. Finally, TNCs are able to increase their control of the economy through other means which are less easily detectable, such as strategic alliances and other non-equity arrangements (Overbeek 2000).

This process of concentration of capital by TNCs is not, however, occurring globally, but rather taking place in clearly defined regional contexts. Indeed, TNCs increasingly locate their integrated productive networks within the three most important regions, that is North America, Western Europe and East Asia / Pacific, the afore-mentioned triad. Amin (2006) identifies in the triad a new collective imperialism which has emerged to oversee the spreading of globalisation led by transnational corporations. Neo-liberal globalisation is dominated, *de facto*, by the triad and this leaves the rest of the globe marginalised from its dynamics (Amin 2006).

The reasons for this happening have been traced by Overbeek (2000). First of all, in the sphere of production capital is not totally mobile. Indeed, some barriers to full mobility of productive capital still exist (technological, logistical or skill-related), and these vary from industry to industry, rendering some industries more mobile than others (Dicken 2011). Furthermore, some elements of the competition state (Cerny 1999) have been noted by transnationalists who underline how states compete with each other to attract TNCs by adopting appropriate macroeconomic policies (Overbeek 2000).

Moreover, the incentive for TNCs to fix their organisation of production spatially at the regional level is strong because globalisation increases uncertainties, for example in terms of exchange rate fluctuations or volatility of financial markets. Such uncertainties are detrimental to capital accumulation, but cannot be handled by the nation state because technological progress has made possible the exploitation of economies of scale overcoming national territories and mostly coinciding with regional ones. This is why in the age of globalisation capital increasingly needs regional schemes of integration in the core areas of globalisation, such as the European Single Market and European Economic and Monetary Union (Overbeek 2000; Talani 2014). In the core of the global system, these processes of regional institutional integration are compounded by the enforcement of a neo-liberal agenda focusing on deregulation, liberalisation, flexibilisation and, more recently, austerity (Cafruny and Ryner 2007; Van Apeldoorn et al. 2003; Mittelman 2000; Talani 2014). This is what Gill refers to as 'new constitutionalism' which clearly contains a disciplinary aim (Gill 1997).

Again, contrary to realists, transnationalists do not consider the process of regionalisation as negating globalisation. They are the two sides of the same coin, two elements of the structural transformations induced by globalisation, as defined in qualitative terms (Pellerin and Overbeek 2001; Overbeek 2000; Mittelman 2000).

As further analysed below, however, this spatial reorganisation of the mobility–fixity nexus at the regional level is not without contradictions. Callinicos, for example, underlines how in regional integration processes major issues remain unresolved in the relation between states and regional institutions, as well as between different fractions of capital which have contradictory interests and needs in terms of regionalisation.

Moreover, Overbeek observes how fundamental tensions also arise between people (citizens, workers and migrants) and capital (Overbeek 2000).

Most importantly for this book, there is an increasing contradiction between the core area of the global restructuring of production, and the peripheries. In fact, the spatial reorganisation of the 'mobility–fixity' nexus does not involve peripheral regions of the globe (e.g. Africa and the Middle East). In fact, as noted by Dicken (2011: 25), there is a continuing geographical concentration within the global economy. This is accompanied by an increasing peripherisation of some areas, most notably Africa, including Northern Africa to which the three countries analysed here belong.

Concluding, the 'unbundling of territoriality' (Ruggie 1993) creates new sites of organisation of the political and economic functions of the state amongst which regional forms are prevailing, but this happens mainly in the core of the global political economy. The European Union is the region where unbundling is most advanced and it is therefore the focus of much theory of regional integration, as further discussed in the next section (similarly Hettne 1994: 12; contra Mittelman 2000: 115).

How does regionalisation take place? The mechanisms of integration in the IPE theoretical debate

If all IPE theoretical approaches recognise that regionalisation in the global political economy is taking place, it is worth asking how they answer the question of how it happens. Therefore, in this section the mechanisms of regional integration will be analysed from the different IPE perspectives. In the theoretical debate in IPE there is a clear divide between orthodox approaches, more and more influenced by rational choice, and critical IPE perspectives. The latter, as further elaborated below, are varied in their philosophical foundations and methodologies, but are united by some fundamental criticisms to the mainstream ontology (Murphy and Tooze 1991: 29). Given that the most developed regionalisation process is that of European Union integration, it should not come as a surprise that the theories of regional integration referred to below are mostly concerned with it.

Mainstream theories of regional integration

Mainstream approaches in international political economy are traditionally represented by neo-realist and liberal institutionalist perspectives. In the debate about regional integration, with specific reference to the case of European integration, this translates into the established dichotomy between intergovernmentalism and neo-functionalism. While the first originates from the realist tradition, the latter is very strongly related to the liberal institutionalist, Kantian philosophical tradition.

Although, as further detailed below, the debate has moved on from this dichotomy, these two schools of thought are still too important not to be considered here. Therefore we turn below to the most relevant tenets of these two approaches on the subject of regional integration.

Intergovernmentalist explanations

As in the case of any other version of realism in international relations (IR), the intergovernmentalist approach to regionalisation in general and to European economic integration in particular postulates that nation states dominate decision-making processes and their outcomes reflect the relative power and interests of the member states.

However, contrary to realism in IR, intergovernmentalists stress the importance of 'low politics', especially the economic interests pursued by nation states in the international/regional arena, as opposed to geopolitical considerations (Moravcsik 1998: 26). Whereas realist accounts of international economic decision making and agreements would assume that security or geopolitical strategic considerations define states' economic choices,[1] intergovernmentalists emphasise economic interests as the basis for state preferences in regional economic integration (Moravcsik and Schimmelfennig 2009: 70).

Thus, in the intergovernmentalist conceptualisation, the process of regional economic integration is the result of rational strategies pursued by governments acting to maximise their preferences and power (Moravcsik and Schimmelfennig 2009). Hence the emphasis of many intergovernmentalists/rationalists on the use of rational choice language and/or models (Pollack 1996, 1997, 2010).

Moreover, in more recent contributions, intergovernmentalists introduce an explicit theory of domestic politics to identify states' economic interests and preferences in the international/regional integration process. They also add an explicit theory of bargaining in international negotiations.

The seminal work in intergovernmentalist theory is Moravcsik's 'Negotiating the Single European Act', (1991) in which he proposes an intergovernmental institutionalist approach to regional economic integration.

Taking the case of regional integration in Europe, Moravicsik proposes evidence supporting the hypothesis that the mechanism of regional integration is represented by the economic interests of the states and by the power relations between them. In this context, international institutions play a role in facilitating and consolidating existing inter-state agreements.

Thus, the three most fundamental principles of intergovernmentalism are:

- Intergovernmentalism
- Lowest common denominator bargaining
- Strict limits on future transfers of sovereignty.

A later version of Moravcsik's intergovernmentalism is represented by his new 'liberal intergovernmentalism'. Based on a liberal conceptualisation of domestic politics, this new version of intergovernmentalism proposes an explicit theory of national preference formation which is added to the systemic level analysis of inter-state bargaining (Moravcsik 1993a: 474; Moravcsik and Schimmelfennig 2009).

Liberal intergovernmentalism is based on three essential assumptions:

- State behaviour is assumed to always be rational.
- National preferences are assumed to be formed according to a liberal understanding of their dynamics.
- Intergovernmentalism is assumed to explain inter-state negotiations (Moravcsik 1993a: 474; Moravcsik and Schimmelfennig 2009).

The final stage in this shift towards a two-level game conceptualisation of international relations and regionalisation processes is completed by Moravcsik in the introduction to Evans, Jacobson and Putnam's 'Double edged diplomacy: international bargaining and domestic politics' (Moravcsik 1993b). Here there is the acknowledgment that international and regional integration theorists can no longer afford to ignore the domestic level of analysis and need to integrate it to the systemic level in a theory of double-edged diplomacy. To better achieve this result Moravcsik devises a rationalist framework of international cooperation. He does this through an integrated domestic/international theorisation of regional integration from the intergovernmentalist perspective in 'The Choice for Europe' (1998). Very importantly, in this book regional integration is conceptualised as a series of choices made by rational national decision makers. These choices are in response to the limits imposed and the requests made by powerful domestic economic groups aiming at maximising their economic interests, by power relations in the international/regional system, and by the capacity of international institutions to bolster the credibility of inter-state commitments (Moravcsik 1998: 18).

As such, the process of regional integration can be understood only by using a rationalist framework of international cooperation, within which major negotiations are conceptualized as comprising three stages. The first stage is the domestic bargaining process. Here states identify a specific set of policy preferences. Preferences are intended not only as policy goals but also as a set of underlying national objectives independent of the international system. The second stage entails the analysis of international negotiations, where states bargain with each other in the international system to maximise their chances of achieving their preferences. In the third stage the decision to create supranational institutions is taken. It is at this point, and on the basis of the outcomes of international negotiations, that states decide whether or not to delegate sovereignty to an international institution.

Thus, in the author's theorisation the three stages are:

1. National preferences formation
2. Interstate bargaining
3. The choice to delegate sovereignty to international institutions.

In summary, this approach to regional integration identifies states as the main actors of international negotiations. They are conceptualised as rational actors entering international/regional agreements to maximise the economic interests of powerful domestic groups and accepting the creation of international/regional institutional settings only to ensure compliance to agreements by the other sovereign states.

A number of assumptions are made for this tripartite framework to work. In the words of the author: 'The framework assumes above all that the primary political instrument by which individuals and groups in civil society seek to influence international negotiations is the nation state which acts externally as a unitary and rational actor on behalf of its constituents' (Moravcsik 1998: 22). For the purposes of our discussion, the most important assumptions made by intergovernmentalists are that, in deciding whether or not to enter regional institutional arrangements, states are a) *unitary*, that is they act in the international context with a single voice, and b) *rational*, that is in international negotiations they seek to maximise the achievement of a ranked set of preferences. Both assumptions, as we will see further on, are strongly criticised by critical theorists.

Neo-functionalist explanations

Contrary to the intergovernmentalist interpretation of regional integration processes, which can be applied to any region of the globe, neo-functionalist integration theory, as devised by E.B. Haas in his study 'The Uniting of Europe' (Haas 1968), was directly aimed at addressing the origins and evolution of the European Community because it was the community itself in its early stage that inspired the original form of this thesis.

However, the neo-functionalist interpretation of regional integration is clearly in line with the liberal institutionalist (later known as neo-institutionalist) school of international relations/international political economy. Specifically, they both rely on a Kantian understanding of the underlying rationality of cooperation in the international system and of the creation of a supranational, maybe cosmopolitan, political community. Indeed, the conceptual origins of the approach are identifiable in classical functionalist theories of international integration and cooperation.[2] Moreover, both perspectives put emphasis on the proactive role played by institutions and institutional actors in the process of international/regional integration. This contrasts with the classical realist/neo-realist conceptualisation of the nation state as the 'principal' of the international arena.[3]

The following conceptual propositions define neo-functionalist explanations of integration:

- The process of regional integration leading to the creation of a supranational political community is approached using the tools of ideal type analysis.
- Society is conceptualised in a liberal–pluralist way in which interest groups/political parties and other national actors progressively shift their loyalty from the national to the supranational level.
- The mechanism of regional integration relies on the notion of spillover.

To start with, neo-functionalist analyses of regional integration identify the ideal type of the 'political community', the approximation to which defines success in the process of integration. The notion of the supranational political community, however, does not necessarily take any specific constitutional form, such as, for example, that of the federal state, although this could be a possibility. Unitary state, a federal state, or even, in certain circumstances, confederate arrangements, are all possible constitutional solutions once the supranational political community has been achieved (Haas 1968: 8).

In turn, the assessment of whether and to what extent such a supranational political community has been formed does not rely so much on objective criteria, but on the conduct of groups, individuals and governments: it requires their shift of loyalty from the central authorities of the nation state to supranational political institutions. Thus, in the neo-functionalist conceptualisation, the definition of 'political integration' coincides with that of a process in the course of which this shift of loyalties gradually takes place.

Neo-functionalism, as intergovernmentalism, is an IPE theory to the extent that it recognises the primacy of the process of economic integration over the process of political integration. In regional integration, the economic always precedes the political. Moreover, the level of *de facto* economic integration does not necessarily translate into *de jure* institutional integration, although the final aim is always the creation of a supranational political community (Rosamond 2000: 60).

As far as the dynamics of the integration process from the neo-functionalist perspective are concerned, the neo-functionalist approach to integration is based on the notion of spillover. This is the idea that integration in one issue area is functionally related to integration in another realm. Thus, the need to fully gather the benefits of integration in the first area leads to pressures to integrate further in other areas.

Early neo-functionalists, such as Haas, pointed to the existence of two sorts of spillover. Functional spillover is defined as the economic necessity to integrate in other, linked policy areas as a consequence of the steps taken in integrating in one particular issue area. Political spillover is linked to the fundamental role of existing supranational institutions in giving impetus to a self-reinforcing process of institution building.

Both sorts of spillovers produce further steps in the process of integration, working through interest group pressure, public opinion, elite socialisation, or other domestic actors and processes. In particular, in Haas's conceptualisation, pressure groups and political parties are 'singled out as significant carriers of values and ideologies whose opposition, identity or convergence determines the success or failure of a transnational ideology' (Haas 1968: 5). Moreover, for Haas interest groups are more important than political parties because they represent the most dynamic component of the political process in advanced pluralist democracies. This is particularly true of economic interest groups. Specifically, he argues that 'almost universally economic groups seem to be in the forefront of those who clamour for the recognition of common needs' (Haas 1968: 5). Contrary to neo-constructivist approaches to regional integration, early neo-functionalism does not attribute any particular importance to the ideological connotation of groups which may or may not be ideologically oriented (Haas 1968: 287–289).

Pressures in favour of more integration would initially be exerted by pressure groups and political parties at the national level. However, with more integration the power and functions of regional institutions increases, and so the demands, expectations and loyalties of groups and parties will gradually shift to the regional level. Supranational institutions will then become a powerful engine of integration and of community development. Thus, integration will be fostered by both national political actors recognising that their interests are better served at the regional institutional level and also by supranational institutions acting in response to the political expectations of groups wanting greater supranationalism.

Concluding, early neo-functionalists were genuinely interested in the evolution of new supranational institutions, rather than specific policy developments. Similarly, their intellectual heirs, liberal institutionalists such as Nye and Keohane focused on the analysis of international interdependence and the creation of a multi-level system of governance (Keohane and Nye 1977). However, evidence about the failure of the European integration process to move steadily towards the final goal of the supranational political community undermined the neo-functionalist faith in spillovers.[4] As a consequence, neo-functionalism was revised by later scholars (Schmitter 1970; Lindberg and Scheingold 1970). Despite the array of criticisms that even this modified version of neo-functionalism provoked (e.g. Hoffmann 1995: 84ff; Moravcsik 1991, 1993a, b; Milward 2000: 11–12; Risse-Kappen 1996: 56ff) in the opinions of some scholars this approach continues to be capable of addressing the success of regional economic integration since the 1980s (Leibfried and Pierson 1995; Marks and McAdam 1996, Taylor 1990 Tranholm-Mikkelsen 1991).

Critical approaches to regional economic integration

Within the field of international political economy, regional economic integration has also been studied by scholars using the conceptual, analytical and theoretical tools provided by critical approaches to international political economy.

Critical scholars differ from mainstream ones on methodological, epistemological and substantive grounds in their conceptualisation of the process of regional economic integration. In substantive terms, critical theorists shift the focus from the mere consideration of formal institutions such as nation states or international organisations, to other actors, including socio-economic interest groups, MNCs, NGOs, political parties, ideologies and public opinion. Epistemologically, critical theories, especially neo-constructivism and neo-Gramscian approaches, tend to overcome the subject–object distinction that is typical of positivist analysis, thus rejecting the objectivity of social reality and recognising in the scholar the possibility of subjective interventions to modify it. In methodological terms this means that critical analyses discard causal explanations in favour of contextual social or historical ones. The social reality under scrutiny is 'reconstructed' within a specific ideological, historical or social context, hence the label 'constructivism'. A social event is not given, is not a *datum*, but is constructed, a *factum*.

As a consequence, methodological individualism based on the rational actor model is rejected and the analysis focuses on 'the situation' in which a particular event takes place. Obviously different critical approaches would reconstruct the situation differently according to their different philosophical assumptions about which are the most important explanatory variables. Indeed, there are critical theorists who stress the role of explanatory variables such as material interests, whereas others are more interested in the role played by ideas or shared beliefs to explain why certain social events take place.

Neo-Gramscian approaches: a transnational historical materialist theory of regional integration[5]

The process of regional integration is understood by neo-Gramscian scholars in historical terms. It coincides with the progressive institutionalisation of the neo-liberal project at the regional level, fostered by the social and economic actors gaining the most from it (Cafruny and Ryner 2007: 5).

Cafruny and Ryner (2007) identify two phases in the establishment of the European regional integration process. In the first phase, after the Second World War, the regional integration project was aimed at consolidating European national capitalisms through the institutionalisation of supranational economic cooperation (Cafruny and Ryner 2007: 3). In the second phase, from the beginning of the 1980s, regional economic cooperation was the consequence of the failure of national Keynesianism to ensure enduring prosperity to national hegemonic socio-economic blocs and of the realisation that only a neo-liberal project could achieve a similar objective. Given the inherently contradictory nature of this process, however, and the fact that European capitalist elites are subordinated to US ones, the process of European economic integration is in constant crisis (Cafruny and Ryner 2007: Introduction).

One of the most successful attempts to translate neo-Gramscian approaches to international political economy into a fully-fledged theory of regional integration is represented by Ryner, Van Apeldoorn and Overbeek's transnational historical materialist theory (Van Apeldoorn et al. 2003). This theory rotates around three concepts: *historical materialism, transnationalism,* and *neo-Gramscianism.*

In the conceptualisation of these scholars, the historical materialist approach to regional integration includes:

- A materialist conception of history. This means a conception of history in which the material forces of production as well as the relations of production represent the determinants of social action and change.
- A rejection of the separation between the subject and object and its substitution with a dialectic understanding of reality as a dynamic totality.
- A rejection of the rational actor model and its substitution with the so-called 'method of abstraction', consisting in the reconstruction of the social phenomenon under analysis within its historical and social context. (Van Apeldoorn et al. 2003: 33)

In this context, the process of regional integration stems from historically defined power relations in the structure of production. As such, it is understood as a relatively autonomous regional expression of an emerging capitalist global political economy (Cox 1987; Rupert 1995; Van der Pijl 1984, 1988, 1989, 1998).

More in general, social reality cannot be interpreted by making reference to universal rules. It must be studied within its socio-economic context, the so called 'situation', as historically determined and produced by the contradictory dynamics of capitalism (Van Apeldoorn et al. 2003: 34).

This version of historical materialism relies on a transnational interpretation of the dynamics leading to the formation of social relations in contemporary capitalism. The transnational context, in turn, is the one transcending national boundaries. Therefore, social relations, especially class relations, are formed neither 'outside' national boundaries, in the 'international' arena, nor inside them, in the 'domestic' arena. Instead, they happen at the same time in both realms. Thus, reverting to the notion of transnationalism allows neo-Gramscian theorists to discard the dichotomy between the national and the international levels of analysis (Van Apeldoorn et al. 2003: 36). Indeed, only a dialectical understanding of the dynamic relations between domestic and external factors can make sense of the true nature of the international system and of any process of regional integration (Van Apeldoorn et al. 2003: 36).

The most important characteristic of this critical approach to regional integration is, however, its reliance on Gramsci's sociology of power. This is based on Macchiavelli's distinction between rule by 'force' and rule through 'consensus'. However, in Gramscian theory this distinction characterises two ideal-type aspects of supremacy. When supremacy is obtained and exercised without the conscious consent of the ruled, it becomes 'domination'. If, on the contrary, it is characterised by moral and intellectual direction, it is understood as 'ethical hegemony'. Thus, although true, conscious 'consensus' is necessary to have ethical hegemony, domination does not require force as in Machiavelli, but can be based on consensus obtained through fraud and deception. Moreover, in the Gramscian conceptualisation, power in the real world is often exercised using a mixture of force and consensus. This does not allow for a clear distinction in practice between domination and hegemony (Gramsci 1975, 1999).

Neo-Marxist interpretations of regionalisation

Marxist critiques of mainstream accounts of regional integration, as Gramscian ones, underline their ahistorical nature and an inability to identify the roots of present political arrangements.

With the global financial crisis and the crisis of the Eurozone, neo-Marxist approaches have experienced a revival as these two events seem to have vindicated Marxism's most traditional predictions about the inherent instability of capitalist systems (e.g. Cafruny 2010; Callinicos 2010; Gamble 2009; Nousios et al. 2012). Here, however, we focus on Marxist conceptualisations of regionalisation.

Peter Cocks (1991) proposed one of the most systematic neo-Marxist interpretations of regional integration processes. Making reference mainly to the European case, the author underlines how European political integration already started in the 16th century as an element of the process of state-building at both the national and the international level. This statement is based on the traditional Marxist conceptualisation of the state as the instrument for the exercise of power by the dominant capitalist class. Within the Marxist paradigm the whole process of nation state-building is interpreted as a process of legitimating the power of the capitalist class. State institutions are, in turn, viewed as the instruments allowing such a power to be imposed on the rest of society.

As a consequence, regional integration processes found their *raison d'être* in the need to address the problems arising from the growth of capitalism. Capitalism's extension beyond the borders of the nation state, as a natural outcome of the process of capital accumulation, means that the capitalist class needs to create new institutions at the regional level able to fulfil the functions previously performed by the state. Thus, the process of regional institution building is simply a function of the need of the capitalist class to identify a political infrastructure for the expansion of productive forces outside national boundaries and to legitimise its power: it is a function of the need to identify a new mobility–fixity nexus. As Cocks puts it:

> Political and economic integration are methods of providing the institutional conditions for the expansion of capital, while social integration is the process of legitimising the new institutions. (Cocks 1991: 36)

In summary:

> Integration refers to the geographical spread of state functions in response to the exigencies of capital accumulation and the realisation of surplus value on the one hand, and their associated legitimation problems, on the other. (Cocks 1991: 37)

Concluding, in Cocks' understanding the notion of regional political integration is contiguous to the notion of state-building. Here state-building is essentially conceptualised as the mechanism reproducing the conditions for the survival of the capitalist class and its legitimation at the social level.

Similarly, Callinicos (1997) proposes a reading of the process of European integration in the light of the competition between advanced capitalist states, both within the European context and globally. Based on Harman's original contribution (Harman 1971, 1991), Callinicos argues that while capitalism had overcome national boundaries, no single state, not even Germany, France or the UK, could yet compete at the global level. Therefore, regional integration schemes, like the European Economic Community, must be interpreted as an attempt to allow national capitalisms to thrive at the regional level without having to address global competition. This attempt, however, is not without contradictions, especially between nation states and multinational capital. Indeed, these contradictions, even in the case of Europe, are still outstanding and have not been resolved by building truly supranational institutions (Callinicos 1997).

Hazel Smith (2002) addresses the process of regional integration from a totally different Marxist standpoint. Starting from Marx's criticism of liberal constitutionalism as expressed in his pamphlet 'On the Jewish Question' (Marx 1978), this author proposes the idea that political emancipation, as provided by liberal constitutionalism, or by liberal democracy today, does not coincide with human emancipation and is indeed functional to the needs of capitalism. This is in stark contrast to what neo-institutionalists, *a la* Held, have been advocating for the future of global governance.

Indeed, political emancipation is based on the individualisation of rights and the attribution to all human beings, conceptualised as selfish monads, of equal rights to participate in the political process. However, human beings are not equal in substantive terms. Therefore this form of equality is not substantial, in that it does not tackle real inequalities, which are of a socio-economic nature. Real human emancipation can be obtained only by eliminating socio-economic inequalities but this is totally outside the scope of liberal democracy. Effectively, the kind of political emancipation advocated by liberal institutionalists is functional to the need of capital to give all individuals equal rights to enter into contractual relationships both as consumers and as workers. This is a form of 'commodification' of human beings, a commodification which is necessary for capitalism to thrive. Concluding, from this standpoint the increasing political liberalisation and expanding attribution of rights from the national to the supranational level is necessary for capital to extend capitalist relations of production beyond the boundaries of the nation state.

Neo-constructivism as a critical approach to regional integration

Neo-constructivism is critical of the mainstream assumptions relating to the rationality of social action, state-centrism and the distinction between integration in 'low politics' and integration in 'high politics' (e.g. Börzel and Risse 2000; Christiansen et al. 1999, 2001; Risse 2009).

To criticise the rational actor model neo-constructivists revert to social constructivism which is based on the idea that social reality is a human construct and as such it is reproduced through daily practices. They adopt a 'social ontology', which implies that human beings are embedded in and ontologically 'defined' by their social relations, ideas and value systems. Consequently, the only way to make sense of human action is by analysing its social context and systems of values (Risse 2009).

More specifically, social action does not follow an 'instrumental rationality', that is, it does not strive to maximise a utility function. On the contrary, it is informed exclusively by ideas and shared beliefs. Thus neo-constructivist scholars reject completely the logic of instrumentality in favour of what March and Olsen call 'the logic of appropriateness' (March and Olsen 1989: 151). In other words, in their decision making social actors 'try to do the right thing' (Risse 2009: 148). Their actions are justified by their values, beliefs and their views of the world and not by material interests rationally ranked according to their utility functions. Thus, understanding why actors take specific decisions requires understanding the values or ideas pursued by them, how these are communicated and how the actors communicate them to others (this is the analysis of communicative action).[6]

To criticise state-centrism, neo-constructivists revert to the notions of transnationalism and transgovernmentalism (Risse-Kappen 1995). Transnational relations are defined as 'transboundary relations that include at least one non-governmental actor' (Risse-Kappen 1996: 57). Transgovernmental relations are instead defined as 'cross-boundary relations among sub-units of national governments in the absence of centralised decisions by state executives' (Risse-Kappen 1996: 57). Using these two concepts neo-constructivists discard the notion of the state as the only actor in the international arena (transnationalism) and of the state as a unitary, monolithic actor (transgovernmentalism).

Finally, neo-constructivists' conceptualisations of regional integration reject the mainstream proposition that integration in low politics (economic issues) is easier than integration in high politics (foreign, defence and security policy). This is mainly due to the recessive role they assign to material interests in explaining social action in general (Risse 2009: 150). From this theoretical standpoint the vectors of integration are represented by the profound beliefs of policy-makers and by the degree of transnationalisation and transgovernmentalism of the issue to be integrated, rather than by the maximisation of an economic or material interest. Therefore, the distinction between low and high politics becomes irrelevant.

Conclusion

At the end of this excursion into regionalisation it is worth asking, does regionalisation exist?

It seems evident from everything discussed in this chapter that from whichever perspective we analyse this question there is one consensual answer: yes, regionalisation exists. However it is also clear that it is mainly happening in the core countries of the global political economy.

This is indeed at the core of the realist analysis of this issue, in so far as the scholars sharing this view deny the existence of globalisation and emphasise the phenomenon of the creation of three macro-regions in Europe, the Americas and Asia, dominated by hegemonic nation states. In turn, a similar perspective on the mechanisms of integration is typically found in the intergovernmentalist approach. This identifies the interests of the most powerful states, especially their economic interests, as the only engine of integration. It follows that, not only are integration processes not necessary, but they are also by definition creating more divergence than convergence as they are the expression of power relations with the weakest countries' interests subordinated to the ones of the hegemonic nation states.

On the opposite side of this argument, liberal institutionalists consider the process of regionalisation not as competing with globalisation, but as complementary to it. It is true that the global political economy shows a tendency towards the creation of macroeconomic regions and that these coincide with the realist triad. However on the one hand this is just a step towards further global integration as the liberalisation processes enshrined in a quantitative definition of globalisation are at odds with the creation of protectionist trade and institutional regional blocs. On the other hand, existing international institutions are increasingly inadequate to cater for the needs and fundamental rights to equity and justice of the entirety of humanity, especially peripheral and marginalised geographical areas and social sectors. Therefore there is a sort of neo-functionalist need to create a new global governance system based on cosmopolitan values embedded in cosmopolitan law and institutions. This would form a universal, cosmopolitan political community, which would guarantee equality and social justice for everyone.

The transnationalists, on the contrary, tend to discard as utopian the projections of a cosmopolitan supranational political community to come and to identify in the neo-liberal regionalisation process the restructuring of a mobility–fixity nexus. This is necessary for capital accumulation to take place both at the national and at the regional level. They propose a more contradictory picture of the consequences of globalisation, amongst which the most relevant for our analysis is the progressive marginalisation of the MENA area and its lack of regionalisation. This happens amid the crisis of the nation state as the locus of organisation of production and of control of territory and, most importantly, people.

So where does this leave our study of the integration of the MENA area in the global political economy?

It appears that again, from any of the possible theoretical standpoints, the Middle East and Northern Africa is one of the areas of the world where regionalisation is not taking place. This conclusion needs, of course some empirical backing, which will be attempted in Chapter 4 of this book. However we can already conclude that the dynamics of globalisation as analysed so far do not leave many hopes that the area will be easily integrated in the future.

Indeed, the mechanisms of regional integration as identified by the main theories reflecting on this subject do not seem to have been activated in the area. In turn, as states in the post-colonialist MENA area took over the role of providing for the economic development of society to provide shelter from the vagaries of the markets (van der Pijl 2011; Dodge and Higgot 2002), the subsequent marginalisation of the area from globalisation and its lack of *de facto* and *de jure* regionalisation have come together with the crisis of the nation state to leave civil societies alone and unprotected.

The next chapter is devoted to the analysis of the sources of marginalisation and its impact on the civil societies of the countries considered, including the rise and radicalisation of Islam.

Notes

1. For realist interpretations of the process of European integration see Hoffman (1966); also Milward (2000).
2. See Taylor (1994). For a thorough discussion of the differences and affinities between classic functionalist approaches to international integration and neo-functionalism see Rosamond (2000) and also Niemann and Schmitter (2009).
3. The principal–agent model originated in the new economics of organisation. It has been applied to the study of European integration within the intergovernmentalist tradition by Moravcsik (1993a, b, 1998) and Pollack (1996, 1997) amongst others; see also Pollack (2010).
4. For a neo-functionalist account of the up and downs of European Integration see Lindberg and Scheingold (1970).

5. For some surveys of similar approaches to the study of European integration, see Bieler and Morton (2001). For a general overview of critical approaches to European Integration see Cafruny and Ryner (2009). For an application of critical approaches to the case of Europe see Cafruny and Ryner (2007).
6. See Risse (2009: 149); see also Risse (2000). The emphasis on communicative action sparked the development of a thriving meso-approach to international relations/European integration based on 'Discourse analysis'. See also Waever (1996, 2009), Diez (1999, 2001).

References

Amin, S. (2006). *Beyond US Hegemony? Assessing the Prospects for a Multipolar World.* Zed Books, London.

Archibugi, D. (2010). 'The Architecture of Cosmopolitan Democracy', in Wallace Brown, G., and Held, D. (eds) *The Cosmopolitanism Reader.* Polity Press, Cambridge, pp. 312–333.

Beck, U. (2005). *Power in the Global Age: A New Global Political Economy.* Polity Press, Cambridge, UK.

Beck, U. (2006). *The Cosmopolitan Vision.* Polity Press, Cambridge, UK.

Beck, U. (2009). *World at Risk.* Polity Press, Cambridge, UK.

Beck, U. (2010). 'The Cosmopolitan Manifesto', in Wallace Brown, G., and Held, D. (eds) *The Cosmopolitanism Reader.* Polity Press, Cambridge, pp. 217–228.

Bieler, A., and Morton, A.D. (eds) (2001). *Social Forces in the Making of the New Europe: The Restructuring of European Social Relations in the Global Political Economy.* Houndmills: Palgrave.

Börzel, T.A., and Risse, T. (2000). 'Who is Afraid of a European Federation? How to Constitutionalise a Multi-Level Governance System'. Part of contributions to the *Jean Monnet Working Paper No.7/00, Symposium: Responses to Joschka Fischer,* http://www.jeanmonnetprogram.org/papers/00/00f0101.html

Cafruny, A. (2010). 'The Global Financial Crisis and the Crisis of European Neo-liberalism', in L. S. Talani. (ed.) *The Global Crash: Toward a New Global Financial Regime?* Palgrave, Basingstoke.

Cafruny, A., and Ryner, M. (2007). *Europe at Bay.* Lynne Rienner Publishers.

Cafruny, A., and Ryner, M. (2009). 'Critical Political Economy', in Wiener, A., and Diez, T. (eds) *European Integration Theory* (2nd ed.). Palgrave, Basingstoke, pp. 221–241.

Callinicos A. (1997). Europe: The Mounting Crisis. *International Socialism,* 75(2).

Callinicos, A. (2010). *Bonfire of Illusions.* Polity Press, London.

Cerny, P. (1999). 'Reconstructing the Political in a Globalising World', in Buelens, F. (ed.) *Globalisation and the Nation State.* Edward Elgar.

Christiansen, T., Jorgenson, K.E., and Wiener, A. (1999). The Social Construction of Europe. *Journal of European Public Policy,* 6(4), 528–544.

Christiansen, T., Jorgenson, K.E., and Wiener, A. (eds) (2001). *The Social Construction of Europe.* Sage. London.

Cohen, B.J. (1996). Phoenix Risen: The Resurrection of Global Finance. *World Politics,* 48(2), 268–296, p. 269.

Cohen, B.J. (2001). Electronic Money: New Day or False Dawn? *Review of International Political Economy,* 8, 197–225.

Cocks, P. (1991). 'Towards a Marxist Theory of European Integration', in Frieden, J.A., and Lake, D.A. (eds) *International Political Economy: Perspectives on Global Power and Wealth* (2nd ed.). Unwin Hyman, London.
Cox, R.W. (1987). *Production, Power, and World Order: Social Forces in the Making of History.* Columbia University Press, New York.
Dicken, P. (2011). *Global Shift: Mapping the Changing Contours of the World Economy* (6th ed.). Guilford.
Diez, T. (1999). Speaking 'Europe': The Politics of Integration Discourse. *Journal of European Public Policy*, 6(4), 598–613.
Diez, T. (2001). Europe as a Discursive Battleground: Discourse Analysis and European Integration Studies. *Co-operation and Conflict*, 36(1), 5–38.
Dodge, T., and Higgot, R. (2002). *Globalisation and the Middle East.* The Royal Institute of International Affairs, London.
Gamble, A., and Payne, A. (1996). *Regionalism and World Order.* Macmillan.
Gamble, A. (2009). *The Spectre at the Feast.* Palgrave, London.
Giddens, A. (1990). *The Consequences of Modernity.* Stanford University Press, Stanford, CA.
Gill, S. (1997). 'An EMU or an Ostrich?: EMU and Neo-liberal Globalisation; Limits and Alternatives', in Minkkinen, P., and Potomaki, H. (eds) *The Politics of Economic and Monetary Union.* Kluwer Academic Publishers, The Hague.
Gramsci, A. (1975). *Quaderni dal carcere.* Einaudi, Torino.
Gramsci, A. (1999). *Selections from the Prison Notebooks of Antonio Gramsci.* Elecbook electronic books, London.
Haas, E.B. (1968). *The Uniting of Europe: Political, Social and Economic Forces.* Stanford University Press, Stanford, CA.
Harman, C. (1971). The Common Market. *International Socialism* (old series), 49.
Harman, C. (1991). The State and Capitalism Today. *International Socialism*, 51.
Harvey, D. (2005). *A Brief History of Neo-liberalism.* Oxford University Press, Oxford.
Held, D. (1995). *Democracy and the Global Order: From the Modern State to Cosmopolitan Governance.* Stanford University Press, Stanford, CA.
Held, D. (2002). Law of States, Law of Peoples. *Legal Theory*, 8(1), 1–44
Held, D. (2010a). 'Principles of Cosmopolitan Order', in Wallace Brown, G., and Held, D. (eds) *The Cosmopolitanism Reader.* Polity Press, pp. 229–247.
Held, D. (2010b). 'Reframing Global Governance: Apocalypse Soon or Reform', in Wallace Brown, G., and Held, D. (eds) *The Cosmopolitanism Reader.* Polity Press, pp. 293–311.
Held, D. (2010c). *Cosmopolitanism: Ideas and Realities.* Polity Press, Cambridge.
Held, D., and McGrew, A. (2000). *The Global Transformations Reader.* Polity Press, Cambridge.
Held, D., and McGrew, A. (2007). *Globalisation/AntiGlobalisation.* Polity Press, Cambridge.
Hettne, B. (1994). 'The New Regionalism: Implications for Development and Peace', in Hettne, B., and Inotai, A. (eds) *The New Regionalism. Implications for Global Development and International Security.* UNU/WIDER.
Hettne, B., Inotai, A., and Sunkel, O. (1999). *Globalism and the New Regionalism.* MacMillan Press.
Hirst, P., and Thompson, G. (1999a). *Globalisation in Question* (2nd ed.). Polity, Cambridge.

Hirst, P., and Thompson, G. (1999b). 'The Tyranny of Globalisation: Myth or Reality?', in Buelens, F. (ed.) *Globalisation and the Nation State*. Edward Elgar.

Hirst, P., Thompson, G., and Bromely, S. (2009). *Globalisation in Question: The International Economy and the Possibilities of Governance* (3rd ed.). Polity Press, Cambridge, UK.

Hoffmann, S. (1966). Obstinate or Obsolete? The Fate of the Nation State and the Case of Western Europe. *Daedalus*, 93 (Summer), 862–915.

Hoffmann, S. (1995). *The European Sisyphus. Essays on Europe, 1964–1994*. Boulder Westview Press.

Kaldor, M. (2010). 'Humanitarian Intervention: Towards a Cosmopolitan Approach', in Wallace Brown, G., and Held, D. (eds) *The Cosmopolitanism Reader*. Polity Press, pp. 334–350.

Keohane, R.O., and Nye, J.S. (1977). *Power and Interdependence*. Little Brown, Boston.

Leibfried, S., and Pierson, P. (eds) (1995). *European Social Policy: Between Fragmentation and Integration*. The Brookings Institution, Washington.

Lindberg, L.N., and Scheingold, S.A. (1970). *Europe's Would-be Polity: Patterns of Change in the European Community*. Prentice–Hall, Englewood Cliffs.

March, J.G., and Olsen, J.P. (1989). *Rediscovering Institutions: The Organisational Basis of Politics*. New York.

Marks, G., and McAdam, D. (1996). Social Movements and the Changing Structure of Political Opportunity in the European Union. *West European Politics*, 19, 249–278.

Marx, K. (1978). 'On the Jewish Question', in Tucker, R.C. (ed.) *The Marx-Engels Reader* (2nd ed.). W.W. Norton, London.

Milward, A.S. (2000). *The European Rescue of the Nation State*. Routledge, London.

Mittelman, J.H. (2000). *The Globalisation Syndrome: Transformation and Resistance*. Princeton University Press, Princeton.

Moravcsik, A. (1991). Negotiating the Single European Act: National Interests and Conventional Statecraft in the European Community. *International Organisation*, 45(1), 19–56.

Moravcsik, A. (1993a). Preferences and Power in the EC: A Liberal Intergovernmentalist Approach. *Journal of Common Market Studies*, 31(4), 473–524.

Moravcsik, A. (1993b). 'Integrating International and Domestic Theories of International Bargaining', in Evans, P.B., Jacobson, H.K., and Putnam, R.D. (eds) *Double-edged Diplomacy: International Bargaining and Domestic Policy*. University of California Press, Berkeley.

Moravcsik, A. (1998). *The Choice for Europe: Social Purpose and State Power from Messina to Maastricht*. UCL Press, London.

Moravcsik, A., and Schimmelfennig, F. (2009). 'Liberal Intergovernmentalism', in Wiener, A., and Diez, T. (eds) *European Integration Theory*. Oxford University Press, Oxford, pp. 67–87.

Niemann, A., and Schmitter, P. (2009). 'Neofunctionalism', in Wiener, A., and Diez, T. (eds) *European Integration Theory*. Oxford University Press, Oxford, pp. 45–66.

Nousios, P., Overbeek, H., and Tsolakis, A. (2012). *Globalisation and European Integration: Critical Approaches to Regional Order and International Relations*. Routledge, London.

Overbeek, H.W. (1995). 'Globalisation and the Restructuring of the European Labor Markets: The Role of Migration', in Simai, M. (ed.) *Global Employment. An International Investigation into the Future of Work*. Zed Books and United Nations University Press, London and Tokyo.

Overbeek, H. (1999). *The Budapest Process: Internationalisation of Migration Control*. Paper presented to the 40th Annual Conference of the International Studies Association, 16–20 February 1999, Washington D.C., mimeo.

Overbeek, H. (2000). 'Globalisation, Sovereignty and Transnational Regulation: Reshaping the Governance of International Migration', in Gosh, B. (ed.) *Managing Migration: Time for a New International Regime*. Oxford University Press, Oxford.

Pellerin, H., and Overbeek, H.W. (2001). 'Neoliberal Regionalism and the Management of People's Mobility', in Bieler, A., and Morton, A.D. (eds) *Social Forces in the Making of the 'New Europe'*. Palgrave.

Pollack, M.A. (1996). The New Institutionalism and EU Governance: The Promise and Limits of Institutionalist Analysis. *Governance*, 9(4), 429–458.

Pollack, M.A. (1997). Delegation, Agency and Agenda Setting in the European Community. *International Organisation*, 51(1), 99–134.

Pollack, M. (2010). 'Theorizing EU Policy-Making', in Wallace, H., Pollack, M., and Young, A.R. (eds) *Policy Making in the European Union*. Oxford University Press, Oxford, pp.15–42.

Risse-Kappen, T. (1995). *Bringing Transnational Relations Back in: Non State Actors, Domestic Structures and International Institutions*. Cambridge University Press, Cambridge.

Risse-Kappen, T. (1996). Exploring the Nature of the Beast: International Relation Theory and Comparative Policy Analysis Meet the European Union. *Journal of Common Market Studies*, 34(1), 53–80.

Risse, T. (2000). Let's Argue! Communicative Action in International Relations. *International Organisation*, 54(1), 1–39.

Risse, T. (2009). 'Social Constructivism and European Integration', in Wiener, A., and Diez, T. (eds) *European Integration Theory* (2nd ed.). Palgrave, Basingstoke, pp. 221–240.

Rosamond, B. (2000). *Theories of European Integration*. MacMillan, London.

Rosenau, J.N. (1990). *Turbulence in World Politics*. Harvester Wheatsheaf, Brighton.

Rosenau, J.N. (1997). *Along the Domestic-foreign Frontier*. CUP, Cambridge.

Ruggie, J. G. (1993). Territoriality and beyond: Problematizing Modernity in International Relations. *International Organisation*, 47(1), 139–174.

Rupert, M. (1995). *Producing Hegemony*. Cambridge University Press, Cambridge.

Sassen, S. (1981). *Exporting Capital and Importing Labor: The Role of Caribbean Migration to New York City*. NYU, New York.

Sassen, S. (1988). *The Mobility of Labour and Capital*. Cambridge University Press, Cambridge.

Sassen, S. (1991). *The Global City: New York, London, Tokyo*. Princeton University Press, Princeton, NJ.

Schmitter, P.C. (1970). A Revised Theory of Regional Integration. *International Organisation*, 24(4), 836–868.

Smith, H. (2002). 'The Politics of Regulated Capitalism: A Historical Materialist Approach to European Integration', in Rupert, M., and Smith, H. (eds) *Historical Materialism and Globalisation*. Routledge, London.

Soysal, Y. (1998). 'Towards a Post-national Model of Membership', in Shafir, G. (ed.) *The Citizenship Debates: A Reader*. University of Minnesota Press, Minneapolis, pp. 189–220.

Soysal, Y.N. (2000). Citizenship and Identity: Living in Diasporas in Post-war Europe? *Ethnic and Racial Studies*, 23(1), 1–15.

Strange, S. (1991). 'An Eclectic Approach', in Murphy, C.N., and Tooze, R. (eds) *The New International Political Economy*. Lynne Rienner, Boulder, p. 34.

Strange, S. (2002). 'States, Firms and Diplomacy, 1992', in Tooze, R., and May, C. (eds) *Authority and Markets, Susan Strange's Writings on International Political Economy*. Palgrave, London.

Talani, L.S. (2012). *Globalisation, Hegemony and the Future of the City of London*. Palgrave, London.

Talani, L.S. (2014). *European Political Economy: Theories and Issues*. Ashgate.

Taylor (eds), Frameworks for international Co-operation, London: Pinter.

Taylor, P. (1994). 'Functionalism: The Approach of David Mitrany', in Groom, A.J.R., and Taylor, P. (eds) *Frameworks for International Co-operation*. Pinter, London.

Tranholm-Mikkelsen, J. (1991). Neo-functionalism: Obstinate or Obsolete? A Reappraisal in the Light of the New Dynamism of the EC. *Millennium: Journal of International Studies*, 20(1), 6.361.

Van Apeldoorn, B., Overbeek, H., and Ryner, M. (2003). 'Theories of European Integration: A Critique', in Cafruny, A., and Ryner, A. (eds) *A Ruined Fortress? Neo-liberal Hegemony and the Transformation in Europe*. Rowman and Littlefield.

Van der Pijl, K. (1984). *The Making of an Atlantic Ruling Class*. Verso, London.

Van der Pijl, K. (1988). 'The Socialist International and the Internationalisation of Capital', *After the Crisis: Occasional Papers*. University of Amsterdam, Faculty of political and social science.

Van der Pijl, K. (1989). Ruling Classes, Hegemony and the State System. *International Journal of Political Economy*, Fall, 7–35.

Van der Pijl, K. (1998). *Transnational Classes and International Relations*. Routledge, London.

Van der Pijl, K. (2011). *Arab Revolts and Nation-State Crisis*, NLR 70, July–August 2011.

Waever, O. (1996). 'The Struggle for Europe: A Discourse Analysis of France; Germany and European Union', University of Southern California Center for International Studies, School of International Relations, 'Rethinking Security' Seminar Paper No.11.

Waever, O. (2009). 'Discursive Approaches', in Wiener, A., and Diez, T. (eds) *European Integration Theory* (2nd ed.). Palgrave, Basingstoke, pp. 163–180.

Wallace Brown, G., and Held, D. (eds) (2010). *The Cosmopolitanism Reader*. Polity Press, Cambridge, UK.

3
The Paradox of Marginalisation: Globalisation, Marginalisation and Civil Society in the MENA Area

Introduction

In this book a transnationalist conceptualisation of globalisation is adopted. With respect to this, there is one important point to underline; although in absolute terms the countries marginalised from globalisation may seem to have improved some of their economic or social indicators, what is relevant for the analysis is how they fare in relative terms. As further elaborated below and in subsequent chapters, the argument is not that the countries considered have not gathered *any* benefits from globalisation or have not been integrated at all, but rather that they have gathered fewer benefits than other countries and therefore, in relative terms, their position in the global political economy has worsened.

This is particularly relevant if we consider that the definition of globalisation adopted here implies that it is a dynamic process, a sort of virtuous circle that once activated produces more and more integration. Indeed, a conceptualisation of globalisation resting on the central role played by technological development entails the need for a constant updating and requalification of skills for societies to keep up with scientific progress (Mittelman 2000; Robinson 2004).

Societies failing to embark on this constant updating, although they in absolute terms may gain some skills, are doomed to be progressively more and more marginalised from globalisation and therefore be more and more worse off.

This poses the problem of the polarisation of wealth in both social and geographical terms. Those societies and societal strata who already have access to educational and vocational systems and have the economic possibility of remaining in education for longer, if not to stay in education forever (the so called concept of the 'knowledge society'), are in a much better position in the global political economy. On the contrary, the lower strata of society, as well as the weakest ones, like the elders or the women, and especially those living in marginalised countries, will be increasingly left aside by the fast moving world of the new skills necessary to keep up with globalisation. It follows that the social and geographical wealth gap is deemed to increase, leading to the paradox of 'marginalisation within globalisation'. Indeed, as Mittelman puts it:

> The further away populations are from the global economy, whether in rich or poor countries, the worse they fare in terms of well-being, wealth and social protection. These divisions exist not only between states but also within states. (Mittelman 2000: 122)

In light of this, the first section of this chapter is devoted to verifying the level of technological integration (or marginalisation) of the Arab world and the MENA countries and their capacity to catch up with the skills necessary to gather the full benefits of globalisation.

However, in the transnationalist perspective, the restructuring of production leading to flexible specialisation does not rely only on a change in the techno-economic structure of a specific territory, but also implies cultural transformations affecting civil society (Mittelman 2000: 122–123). Indeed, in the transnationalist conceptualisation, globalisation is a dialectical, dynamic process affecting civil society, transforming societal institutions and conducing to the establishment of the new social relations (Mittelman 2000). Thus, as Mittelman puts it:

> In so far as the flexible specialisation model as a productive system requires strong relations with civil society, socio-cultural institutions may represent either a constraining or a potentially enabling factor. (Mittelman 2000: 122–123)

It is therefore necessary to analyse also the evolution of civil society institutions and social capital in the MENA area to see how they have been modified by globalisation-induced economic restructuring. This is the subject of the second section of this chapter.

Technological marginalisation

Technological innovation is integral to globalisation, especially new information technologies, transportation and communication. Although these are becoming spread around the globe, this does not happen evenly among regions and nations and therefore the scope for broadening global inequalities increases, instead of decreasing (Mittelman 2000: 226). Furthermore, technological development has not been taking place completely by chance, but is itself a socially and institutionally embedded process which is much more likely to happen in those societies fostering it; it is therefore less likely to take place in countries that are already lagging behind (Dicken 2011: 76). This is a typical self-reinforcing dynamic which leaves the losers further and further away.

This is particularly true in the case of the Arab world where technological integration has been very weak in the last decades. For some scholars:

> The Arabs can be said to be suffering from technological anorexia; and they are disheartened because they are powerless. Arab analysts point to a state of paralysis on both the national and regional levels. (Shafik 1999: 212)

Also according to the conclusions of the second Arab Human Development Report, completely dedicated to building a knowledge society, the situation of Arab technological production and expertise was dire (AHDR 2003).

In order to substantiate these considerations this section will first look at the technological sources of globalisation and then assess to what extent they have been achieved in the Arab world and, more specifically, in the three countries analysed.

The qualitative definition of globalisation adopted in this book starts from the assumption that the current phase of capitalist development is defined by some technological achievements that make it different from any other stages in the development of the world economy. In particular, scholars refer to the current phase as the early stages of the fifth Kondratiev wave (K-wave); a digital, information and communication technology one (Dicken 2011: 77). Each K-wave is characterised by various dimensions: the main 'carrier' branches, the infrastructure, the solutions offered to previous problems by the new techno-economic paradigms, the organisation of firms and forms of cooperation and competition, and, most importantly for our purposes, the geographical focus, which clearly does not include the MENA area (Dicken 2011: 79). In Dicken's conceptualisation, in the current wave of technological innovations, the above dimensions are substantiated as in Figure 3.1.

This scheme allows us to recognise the technological innovations which are progressively more significant as sources of integration in the global political economy and to define the indicators used in the literature to identify the degree of integration of a country or region in it. There is a generalised consensus in the literature (Dicken 2011; Strange 1998) that the telecommunications revolution and the widespread use of internet and digital resources that facilitate not only generic communication, but also learning and production processes, are the most significant technological innovations of the current phase of capitalist development.

However, the spread in the use of ICT technologies is extremely uneven around the globe. Instead of producing a general shrinking of the time-space surface, technological innovations have exacerbated, in relative terms, the peripherisation of some parts of the world. The digital divide is therefore a reality increasingly privileging certain countries and

Main 'carrier' branches	**Infrastructure**	**Solutions offered to previous problems by the new techn-oeconomic paradigms**	**Organisation of firms and forms of cooperation and competition**	**Geographical focus**
Computers, Digital information technology, Internet, Software, Telecommunication, Optical fibres, Robotics, Ceramics, Biotechnology.	Digital networks, Satellites.	Flexible manufacturing systems, Networking, Economies of scope, Electronic control systems and components, Systematisation, Integration of design, production and marketing.	Networks of large and small firms based increasingly on computer networks and close cooperation Technology, Quality control, Training, Investment planning and production planning (justin–time).	Japan, USA, Germany, Sweden, Other Europe, Taiwan, Korea, Canada, Australia

Figure 3.1 Kondratiev fifth long wave: late 1990s onwards

Source: adapted from Dicken (2011: 79)

certain places over others, especially urban spaces and big cities in the developed world (Sassen 1991, Talani et al. 2013). Moreover, as access to communication technologies is, nowadays, fundamental to acquire vital information and knowledge, its increasingly uneven distribution around the globe poses increasingly serious developmental problems (Dicken 2011: 95).

The figures released by ITU (2013) confirm the existence of a clear technological divide between developing and developed countries.[1]

Within the developing world, Asia is the region of the world improving the most in terms of access to ICT technologies, accounting for more than half of all mobile phone/device subscriptions in 2013. As far as the internet is concerned, ITU estimated that 2.7 billion people, which is 39 per cent of the world's population, would be using the internet by the end of 2013. Access to the internet would however remain limited in the developing world with no more than 31 per cent of the population forecast to be able to be online at the end of 2013, compared with 77 per cent in the developed world. Europe would remain the most connected region in the world with 75 per cent internet penetration, while Asia and the Pacific would have 32 per cent rate of penetration and Africa only 16 per cent (ITU 2013).

Also, household internet penetration, which is often considered the most important measure of internet access, was forecast to be growing, with 41 per cent of the world's households connected to the internet by the end of 2013. However, notwithstanding the generally positive outlook, 90 per cent of the 1.1 billion households around the world that are still unconnected are in the developing world.

In 2013 two thirds of the world's population, around 4.5 billion people were still offline and they were overwhelmingly in the developing world, especially Africa (ITU 2013).

Moreover, although the cost of fixed broadband services dropped enormously between 2008 and 2013, decreasing by 82 per cent if measured as a share of GNI per capita, in developing countries residential fixed broadband services remained very expensive, accounting for over 30 per cent of average monthly GNI per capita compared to just 1.7 per cent of average national income in wealthy countries. In some developing countries, that figure rises to well over 50 per cent (ITU 2013).

Also, differences in high-speed broadband internet access persist. The best performers in terms of access speeds were in Asia: the Republic of Korea, Hong Kong (China) and Japan. In Africa, on the contrary, fewer than 10 per cent of fixed broadband subscriptions offered speeds of at least 2Mbit/s (ITU 2013).

Finally, in developing countries the gender divide was still very significant with 16 per cent fewer women than men using the internet, compared with only 2 per cent fewer women than men in the developed world (ITU 2013).

Hence, the analysis of indicators relating to the usage of telecommunications and internet or digital resources (so-called Information and Communication Technology, ICT indicators) can help in establishing whether or not a country and/or a region is catching up with the globalisation process.

The UN (2008) identifies 41 core ICT indicators, divided into four groups:

1. ICT infrastructure and access (12 indicators, see Annex 1).
2. Access to, and use of, ICT by households and individuals (13 indicators, see Annex 2).
3. Use of ICT by businesses (12 indicators, see Annex 3).
4. The ICT sector and trade in ICT goods (4 indicators, see Annex 4).

Reference is made below to some such indicators in the Arab world in general and in Egypt, Libya and Tunisia in particular. It is worth noting, however, that the author does not consider these indicators the only relevant ones to assess marginalisation, as symptoms of lack of integration via ICT indicators do not appear totally reliable. Indeed, if we look at indicators of access to technology for countries such as China, these are still relatively low (although they have been improving at a faster rate than anywhere else), but this cannot and does not mean that the country is not being increasingly integrated in the global economy. Therefore, Chapter 4 elaborates more on economic indicators of marginalisation.

Given these considerations, the Arab region[2] and the countries considered in this study are, without doubt, lagging behind in terms of access to the new technologies.

With respect to the first category of indicators, ICT infrastructure and access, for example, the position of Egypt, Libya and Tunisia is very negative, with Tunisia and Egypt not reaching even 5 internet subscriptions per 100 inhabitants in 2011 (Figure 3.2).

Even worse is the situation of the number of fixed broadband subscriptions per 100 inhabitants in the three countries considered, with Egypt recording less than 2 in 2010, Libya around 1, and Tunisia not reaching 5 (Figure 3.3).

In terms of access to, and use of, ICT by households and individuals, the latest data do not portray a particularly positive picture. The proportion of households with a computer in Egypt in 2011 was around

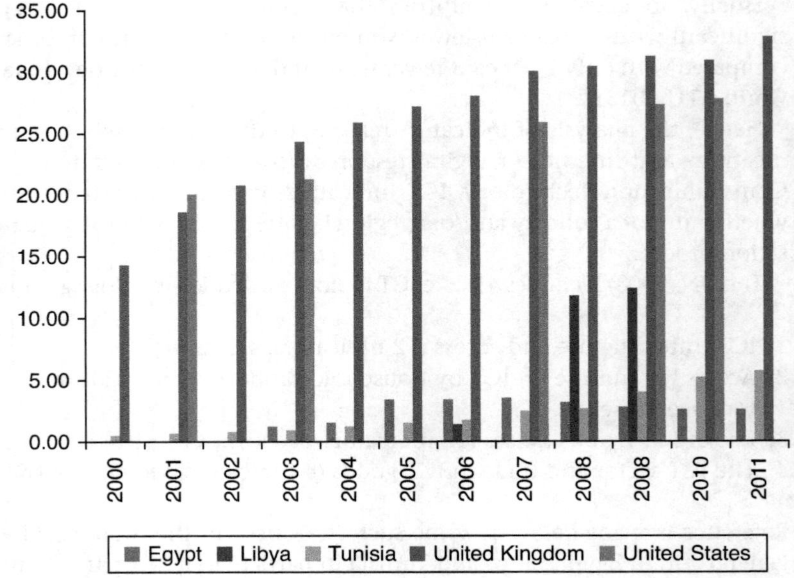

Figure 3.2 Fixed (wired) internet subscriptions per 100 inhabitants (A4)

Source: ITU statistics

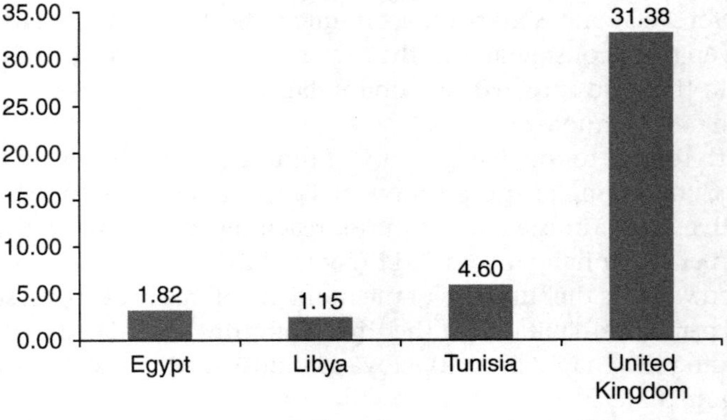

Figure 3.3 Fixed (wired) broadband subscriptions per 100 inhabitants, 2010 (A5)

Source: ITU statistics

36 per cent and the number of individuals who used a computer was only 32 per cent. Only 30 per cent of the Egyptian population had access to the internet at home as opposed, for example, to 85 per cent of the British population. In Tunisia the situation was even worse, with only 19 per cent of households with a computer and only 11 per cent of the population with access to the internet at home. In 2011 the proportion of individuals who used a computer in Tunisia was only 24 per cent and even less, 17 per cent, used the internet, whereas in the UK this figure was 87 per cent. In Libya, the percentage of estimated internet users in 2010 was 14 per cent (ITU 2013).

Concerning the use of ICT by businesses, data on regions outside Europe and excluding OECD member countries are fairly scattered. Until 2003, hardly any developing economy was collecting ICT usage statistics from businesses. In the last few years, more and more developing and transition economies started producing these statistics, yet they are mainly located in the Latin American and Caribbean regions.

The data provided by UNCTAD and Eurostat show a very similar picture for the use of ICT by businesses as that found with households; widespread use of computers and internet is present only in developed economies. Moreover, in developing and transition economies the

Table 3.1 Core indicators on access to, and use of, ICT by households and individuals, 2010–2011

		Proportion of households with:		Proportion of individuals who used ICTs in the last 12 months	
	Year of latest data	(HH4) computer	(HH6) internet access at home	(HH5) computer	(HH7) internet
Egypt	2011	36.4	30.5	32.4	–
Libya	–	–	–	–	–
Tunisia	2010	19.1	11.4	24.9*	17.1*
United Kingdom	2011	84.5	85.1	–	86.8**
United States	2010	75.5	71.1	–	71.7***

* Population age 10+
** Population age 16–74
*** Population age 3+
– Data not available

Source: ITU World Telecommunication/ICT Indicators Database

proportion of employees using a computer or internet is much lower than the proportion of businesses using a computer or internet. This means that within businesses with ICT, not many employees regularly use it (UN 2008: 55).

In the MENA region, some country statistics are available only for Egypt. In Egypt, the proportion of businesses having internet was 53 per cent at the end of 2007, as opposed to 93 per cent in the EU 25 (UN2008). The proportion of employees using computers was 18 per cent and only 10 per cent were using the internet, whereas for the EU 25 these figures were 49 per cent and 37 per cent respectively (UN 2008).

In terms of core indicators for the ICT sector and trade in ICT goods, there is no data available for the region and for the countries considered. However, World Bank indicators for Science and Technology can help understanding the situation of these countries with respect to the technological content of their economies.[3]

Indeed, the percentage of high technology exports, that is, products with high R&D intensity, such as aerospace, computers, pharmaceuticals, scientific instruments, and electrical machinery, is very low in the MENA developing countries, recorded at only 3.2 per cent. In Egypt it is almost non-existent with 0.9 per cent of manufacturing export while in Tunisia it is around 5 per cent. For the sake of comparison, China's high technology exports are 27.5 per cent of its total, Britain's around 21 per cent and the US 19 per cent (Figure 3.4).

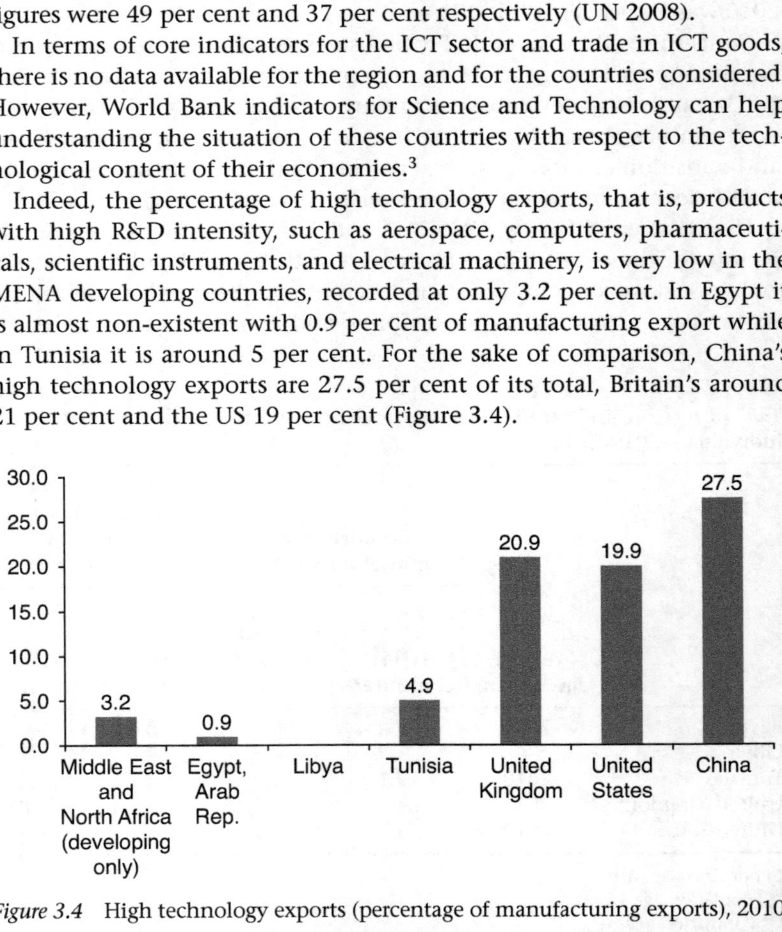

Figure 3.4 High technology exports (percentage of manufacturing exports), 2010

Source: Elaboration by the author on data from the World Bank website http://web.worldbank.org/WBSITE/EXTERNAL/DATASTATISTICS/0,,menuPK:232599~pagePK:64133170~piPK:64133498~theSitePK:239419,00.html as accessed on 15 March 2013

Even more relevant to ascertain the level of technological starvation of the MENA countries are figures relating to the number of patents per million inhabitants. As the graph in Figure 3.5 shows, Egypt, Libya and Tunisia are basically producing no new patents at all and are therefore not contributing to technological progress in any significant way.

If knowledge and information are key to keeping up with the process of globalisation and avoiding further marginalisation, it is worth looking also at basic education indicators as well as indicators of the use of ICT in education. In the words of the Arab Human Development Report:

> A knowledge-based society is one where knowledge diffusion, production and application become the organising principle in all aspects of human activity: culture, society, the economy, politics, and private life. (AHDR 2003: 2)

In Arab countries, key knowledge dissemination processes, such as education and socialisation, are profoundly constrained by social, economic, institutional and political impediments (AHDR 2003: 2). In particular, dwindling economic resources limit the possibility for individuals,

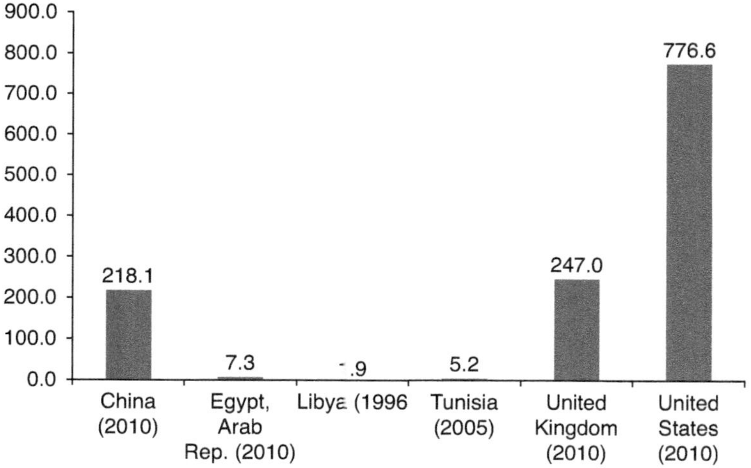

Figure 3.5 Number of patents by residents per million inhabitants – last available data

Source: Elaboration by the author on data from the World Bank website http://web.worldbank.org/WBSITE/EXTERNAL/DATASTATISTICS/0,,menuPK:232599~pagePK:64133170~piPK:64133498~theSitePK:239419,00.html as accessed on 15 March 2013

families and institutions to acquire the epistemological and societal skills necessary for knowledge production.

Despite some gains in the quantitative expansion of education in Arab countries in the last decades, these are still modest in comparison with other developing countries and do not allow the countries to meet the requirements of a knowledge society (AHDR 2003: 3).

For example, in 2010, the Arab World and the MENA area still had lower literacy levels in the total adult population than the developing countries' average (Figure 3.6).

Many children still did not have access to basic education and public spending on education had actually declined in the MENA area from around 22 per cent of government expenditure in 2002 to 16 per cent in 2008.[4]

Looking at some indicators of the use of ICT in education, the situation of MENA countries is not particularly positive. In Tunisia, for example, in 2008 only 40 per cent of schools had a telephone and around the same percentage had access to the internet. Data for Egypt and Libya are not available (UNCTAD 2008).

In all cases, nevertheless, the most important challenge facing Arab education is its deteriorating quality (AHDR 2002: 47–51; AHDR 2003: 51–56). In Egypt, for example a wide field survey revealed that mastery of the basic skills of reading and writing, and mathematics, which should be obtained in primary school, was exceptionally low, recorded at about 40 per cent and 30 per cent respectively (AHDR 2003: 55).

In 2010/2011, all of the Arab countries which took part in the Trends in Mathematics and Science Study (TIMSS), a competition in mathematics and science for year 5 pupils, ended up at the bottom of the table. In mathematics, Tunisia was ranked fourth from the last with 359 points. As a point of comparison, Singapore was first with 606 points, followed by Korea with 605, Hong Kong with 602 and Chinese Taipei with 591.[5]

Overall the data confirm that the region and the countries analysed here are lagging behind in terms of the technological and educational requirements to catch up with the process of globalisation.

As the development of civil society is often in the literature associated with the level of education and the use of modern technologies (AHDR 2003: 38; Mittelman 2000) this might point to a certain underdevelopment of civil society and social capital in these countries. However this conclusion is far too superficial and closer attention to all the factors influencing the evolution and characteristics of civil society is needed. To this we turn our attention in the next section.

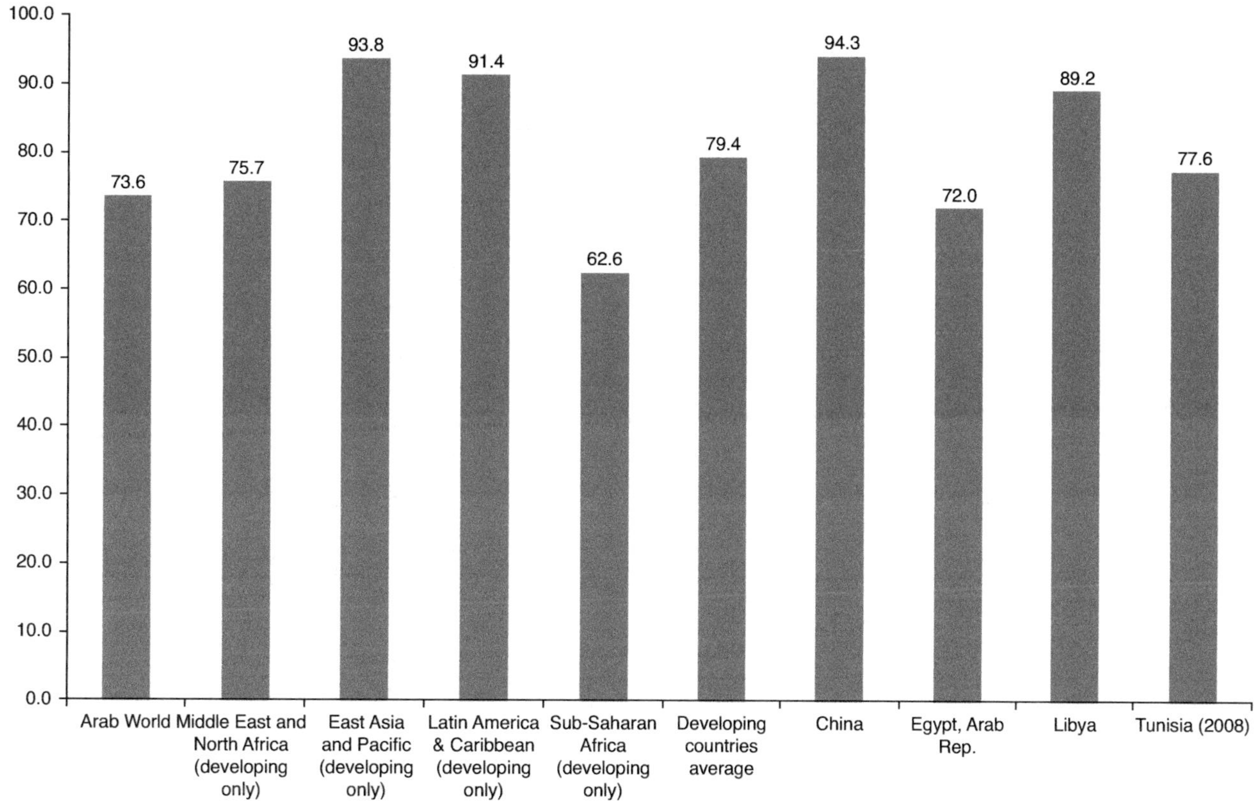

Figure 3.6 Adult literacy year 2010 (percentage, age 15 and above)

Source: Elaboration by the author on data from the World Bank website http://web.worldbank.org/WBSITE/EXTERNAL/DATASTATISTICS/0,,menuPK:232599~pagePK:64133170~piPK:64133498~theSitePK:239419,00.html as accessed on 15 March 2013

Civil society, social capital and marginalisation

As already elaborated in the previous chapter, the notion of civil society adopted by transnationalists is mainly a Gramscian one. Gramsci conceptualised civil society as the primary political realm, where socio-economic groups acquire consciousness of their interests and expectations, ideologies are produced and spread, and alliances formed (Gramsci 1975, 1999).

It is in the context of civil society that the battle for the conquest of true hegemonic power takes place, thanks also to the fundamental role played by organic intellectuals. This means that any socio-economic group aspiring to take the lead of the state needs to gain consensus in the context of civil society by both taking care of the economic needs of the other socio-economic strata and convincing them through ideological means that the interests of the dominant socio-economic historic bloc coincide with the interests of society as a whole (Gramsci 1975, 1999).

On the other hand, the idea of civil society has been associated also with the notion of social capital as developed nearly one century ago, in 1916, with the work of L. Judson Hanifan (Putnam 2000: 19). In the tradition influenced by the work of Bourdieu, social capital is defined as resources embedded in civil society and accessed and used by actors for action (Bourdieu 1980: 2–3). The broadly used conception of social capital from Coleman emphasises its impact at the level of community (Coleman 1988).· This conception has acquired a substantial heuristic value thanks to the contribution of Robert Putnam (2002: 3). The core idea of social capital is that a person's social assets, family, friends and associates are not irrelevant in a person's life. On the contrary, they are crucial to solve situations of crisis or to obtain economic or other advantages. This is not only true for individuals but for communities too, to the extent that the density of social capital in a given community can bring about material advantages and avoid or limit the impact of crises. In few words, civil society matters, or, in Putnam's words:

> civil society affects the health of our democracies, our communities and ourselves. (Putnam 2002: 6)

The link between social policy and social capital lies in the amount and quality of mutual welfare delivered informally by friends, mutual support groups and community (neighbourhood or identity/religious-based) associations, which adds to and reinforces the social service nets provided by law. Social capital represents communal assets produced and reproduced by inter-personal relations based on trust and reciprocity and sustained by solidarity norms and values, including religious ones, as well as (in some contexts such as family and friendship networks) by emotional investment. Social capital relations are by their nature inclusive rather than exclusive.

Three interrelated and cumulative dimensions of social capital are important. These are: bonding social capital (relationships at the basic level of the family, built on identity and sense of belonging), bridging social capital (relationships that tie together different families and neighbourhoods into a larger civic community able to pursue common goods and outcomes) and linking social capital (relationships that connect the civic community and political/policy-making institutions).

Importantly, the amount of social capital in a community is not a given; it varies across time and space which makes it imperative to study this notion in different societies and different historical periods.

How do social networks and relations matter? They matter first of all for the people who belong to them, providing for psychological and social comfort, but also for plain economic returns. This is what the economists would call 'the internal value' of social capital and it defines social capital as a private good. One classic example is the case of employment opportunities created by the intervention of friends or relatives or, more generally, 'social connections'.

However there is also an external value of social capital, as its existence provides benefits also for those who do not belong to the social networks in question. In the economists' jargon, there are some positive externalities from social capital. For example a neighbourhood watch programme against local crime produces a safer environment also for those who do not take part in it. From this point of view, social capital represents also a public good. Even more importantly, it helps to solve collective action problems as it produces trustworthy relations. In other words, the existence of a social interaction based on trust can help people to act for the collective good without coercion or immediate reciprocation.

In operative terms, scholars distinguish between a narrow and a wider definition of social capital (Worms 2002: 138). In a narrow sense, social capital refers only to the networks and groups joined voluntarily by individuals and involving regular face-to-face meetings. This could be cultural associations, religious groups or even sport clubs. In a broader sense, individuals can belong to social groups also by chance, or birth, or constraint, as in the case of a family or a social class or a neighbourhood. Finally, in the widest meaning social capital refers to situations where meetings are irregular and casual, like groups of commuters, or participants in a public demonstration.

Consequently, the social cohesion of civil society can be measured at various levels:

1. Within groups and communities.
2. Between different groups and communities.

This distinction, as well as the distinction between the narrow and the wider definition of social capital, is especially relevant when dealing with social capital in Muslim-majority countries. Indeed, as further elaborated below, the most relevant form of social capital in these countries is narrow social capital, especially religious social capital (RSC). Moreover the recent evolution of civil society and social capital in MENA countries, especially resource-poor ones, substantiates the hypothesis that new forms of social cohesion have been created both horizontally, that is within social classes, and vertically, that is between social classes.

Finally what is most relevant is whether social capital is created through public intervention or is a completely private venture. Indeed, the relations between state and civil society are very complex. The state is shaped by society, but society is also shaped by the state and its political institutions and legislation, as becomes very clear when studying MENA countries' civil societies. The state can also hinder the formation of social capital through repressive policies, as in the case of Tunisia.

To address questions relating to the existence of social capital both in general and particularly in Muslim societies, it is important to understand how to measure it. There is indeed an ongoing debate in the social sciences about whether the level of participation in voluntary associations and, in a related way, the density of associations can be considered a good measure of social capital and whether an increased number of associations necessarily allows for the increase of trust in hosting communities.

In a number of empirical studies, trust has been considered as a good measure of social capital. This, in turn, has been positively associated with economic growth, and more efficient provision of public goods (Knack and Keefer 1997). Trust is considered as an element that can cope with market imperfections and moral hazard in an uncertain environment, especially in economies where contracts are not sufficiently reinforced by formal institutions, as, for example, in the countries considered in this book. Very often in the literature membership of voluntary associations, such as the Muslim Brotherhood, has been systematically linked to the notion of social capital as the basis of trust (Glaeser et al. 2002). For instance trusting attitudes may be determined by social relations in associations and clubs recognised as important vectors of interactions. Moreover, voluntary organisations are considered as contributing to building people's capacities to participate in political life. Finally, participation in a voluntary organisation can mean an adherence to some values and social norms (Glaeser et al. 2002).

However, some authors (Knack and Keefer 1997) question the existence of a relationship between social capital and membership of groups and voluntary associations, and emphasise the fact that promoting of associations and participation in groups can be counterproductive and even reduce the level of trust in the community. As a consequence, the discussion is open as to whether membership of religious associations, most notably Islamic Social Institutions, constitutes social capital at all.

Religious organisations are generally considered in the literature about social capital as just another form of voluntary association (Putnam 2000). Evidence shows, however, that Religious Social Capital (RSC), as represented for example by faith-based organisations active in civil society, plays a distinctive role not only in building social capital but also with respect to its wider implications, including political ones (Harrigan and El-Said 2009: 13). In addition, as we will see below, the Arab world is peculiar in the extent to which social capital is generated mainly through religious institutions, also due in part to the distinctive characteristics of Islam.

Following Gramsci (1975, 1999), it is conceivable to hypothesise that the impact of globalisation on the Arab States considered, especially its impact in terms of crisis of the nation state, produced the conditions for the emergence of a new socio-economic historic bloc striving to become hegemonic. This was based on alternative ideologies such as Islam and underpinned by different socio-economic alliances, namely a new alliance between the 'discontented' middle class(es) and the 'dispossessed' lower one (Roccu 2012), what Harvey (2008) calls the discontented and the dispossessed.[6] According to the relevant literature (Ayubi 2008: 343; Clark 2004; Roccu 2012), in the Middle East the bulk of the middle class would be represented by civil servants, who are, by definition, discontented by the retreat of statist regimes (Said 2007: 6). This is compounded by professionals and a very limited group of small and medium entrepreneurs, sometimes explicitly Islamic business (Schlumberger 2008). Indeed, most of the very small entrepreneurs would belong to the category of the 'dispossessed' lower classes. With respect to the business component of the middle class, both in Egypt and in Tunisia, state capital tended to ally more with international capital than with local small and medium capital, which was generally weak, according to Ayubi's conceptualisation (Ayubi 2008: 180–181).

As noticed by Ayubi:

> The private business bourgeoisie, insofar as it was allowed to exist, became subservient to the State and to the requirements of state capitalism. (Ayubi 2008: 181)

Even the heavy liberalisation policies adopted in both countries as a consequence of globalisation-induced economic restructuring seem to have failed to incorporate into the system local private small and medium entrepreneurs not connected to the regimes (Roccu 2012; Ayubi 2008: 329–357).

On the other hand, the dispossessed are the poor, that is, those who do not have possessions and therefore are unable to access the market place to meet their basic needs (Clark 2004: 11; 'Morti di Fame', Ayubi 2008: 179).

Both strata have been increasingly marginalised by the statist regimes in the Middle East, from the political sphere as well as also from the socio-economic and cultural ones (Roccu 2012; Ayubi 2008: 181). Indeed, the latest batch of economic restructuring measures mainly affected the lower and middle classes (Ayubi 2008: 352; Heydemann 2004; Roccu 2012). In the words of Ayubi (2008: 181):

> Marginalisation is an important phenomenon in many Third World countries, not only because of the large size of the lumpenproletariat but also because of the dangerous phenomenon of the unemployment (or underemployment) of the educated.

Such marginalisation is a very important breeder of protest movements, such as 'Political Islam' (Ayubi 2008: 181–182).

What is hypothesised here is that, in the Arab world, especially in the Middle East, Islam progressively became the point of reference for those strata of civil society marginalised by the existing regimes: the discontented middle classes and the lower classes. This means that in practical terms, Islam increasingly came to represent their main ideology, as well as the basis of their identity and, wherever possible, of their social relations and networks. In other words, it became the source of their social capital. This might have been favoured by the ideological weakness of the existing power bloc, which limited its capacity to gain hegemony in civil society (Ayubi 2008: 399). Thus, in this context, the impact of globalisation on civil society would be the creation of a new socio-economic alliance between the marginalised strata of civil society cemented by a common ideology, Islam. How this took place is the subject of the next section.

Islam and civil society

The purpose of this section is to found out whether the crisis of the nation state as a consequence of globalisation and the lack of a regional integration project in the MENA area has been accompanied by a progressive re-Islamisation of civil society, particularly the middle and lower classes, and whether this is reflected in the emergence of a distinct Islamic social capital within those socio-economic groups (similarly Clark 2004; Harrigan and El-Said 2009). The idea is to ascertain to what extent Islamic Social Capital and Islamic Social Institutions favoured the decline of previously well-established political solutions, or whether they have been constrained by repressive policy-making (Jamal 2007).

Already before the outburst of the Arab Spring, commentators and experts on Arab politics had noticed how from the 1990s Arab societies had undergone fundamental changes (Ayubi 2008; Clark 2004; Rutherford 2008:2; Harrigan and El-Said 2009). In Egypt, for example, economic crises, economic restructuring and globalisation had progressively undermined the statist order created during the Nasserist rule. In line with our transnationalist perspective, these changes brought about a weakening of state control over the economy and society, especially the withdrawal of the public sector and the progressive demise of the subsidy system (Ayubi 2008). Rutherford (2008: 2) notes how these transformations also eroded the already weak political ideology legitimating the regime, whose liberal conception of law within the judiciary was increasingly challenged by the Islamic conception of governance proposed by the Muslim brotherhood and political Islam. In a word, the declining statism of the regime, which was no longer sustainable given the constraints imposed on the state by globalisation, was increasingly challenged by an alternative political ideology based on Islam (Rutherford 2008: 2). It is outside the scope of this very short section to discuss the economic ideology of Islam or rather the complex and contradictory relationship between Islam and neo-liberalism, which has been addressed exhaustively elsewhere (Tripp 2006; Rodinson 2007).

On the other hand, the role of Islam in society and politics is a highly debated question, not only between scholars, but also within Islam itself (Ramadan 2012). With respect to its basic principles, Islam can be considered a unified whole (Ramadan 2012: 72). However, countless interpretations exist relating to secondary prescriptions as well as to the objectives of the Islamic texts, to the extent that experts of Muslim-majority societies generally speak about 'Islams' in the plural to underline the diversity of Islamic social and cultural contexts (Ramadan 2012: 72). As Ramadan puts it:

> What is meant by the concept of 'Islamic Civilisation' is precisely this: One single Islam, a diversity of interpretations and a plurality of cultures. (Ramadan 2012: 74)

Political Islam does not come in a single, unified version either, although its origins have to be traced back to the late 19th century reformers who were both pan-Islamic and anti-colonial and had a great impact on 20th century Islamic thought (Ramadan 2012: 75; similarly Clark 2004: 13–14; Ayubi 1991). According to them, Muslims had to go back to their religious teachings, acquire consciousness of their subordination and free themselves from the chains of colonialism. From this perspective, Islam as a religion was invoked and played a fundamental role in the liberation from colonialism as well as in the future political, economic and cultural organisation of Muslim-majority states. It was however only with the creation of the Muslim Brotherhood by Hassan al-Banna (1906–1949) that what is known now as 'political Islam' or 'Islamism' acquired a much clearer definition. Relying heavily on the thoughts of the first generation of reformers, al-Banna proposed early on a program of re-Islamisation of Egypt (Ramadan 2012: 75).

Currently, Islamist movements are divided mainly on the following issues: (1) the definition of who is a Muslim and what are their prerogatives; (2) the use of violence; (3) the application of the sharia as a closed legal system or open to foreign references such as democracy; (4) whether it is acceptable to create an Islamist political party or it is preferable to retain the status of a religious and social organisation; (5) the role of women in Muslim-majority societies; (6) the relationship with people of other religions or no religion in society; (7) the relationship with the West (Ramadan 2012: 79; Snider 2007).

To understand the capacity of Islamism to conquer the realm of civil society, it is extremely important to underline that not only did it originate as a legalistic, societal movement, but it also never lost its original strategy of reforming society from the bottom up, by educating the masses in order to change society as a whole and restructure the state into the Islamic State (Tripp 2006; Clark 2004: 11–12).

Indeed, the relationship between religion and sovereignty has always been a contested one in the Arab State. Even in the most advanced Islamic constitutions, such as the Tunisian one, moving away from the sharia to a legal system devoid of theological influence proved extremely difficult; the legislature stipulated that Islam is the religion of the state. Consequently, citizens were not free to choose their beliefs, or lack thereof (Meddeb 2003: 74).

In Egypt, the re-Islamisation of society and the American alliance went hand in hand, constituting another paradox, which is known in the literature as the Egyptian paradox (Meddeb 2003: 107). The explanation might be found in the need of the regime to protect itself from the violent sections of the Muslim Brotherhood which attempted to assassinate Nasser in 1954, successfully managed to eliminate Sadat in 1981[7], almost killed Mubarak in 1995, and were increasingly gaining consensus in civil society (Rutherford 2008: 20). Indeed, although politically the Islamists had not yet won power, they were increasingly taking control of the social body. As Meddeb puts it:

> In the war of words, the state thought it had to take away from the fundamentalists the argument denouncing the non-conformity of their society to Islamic norms. To defuse this criticism, the state decided to entrust to Al-Azhar the governance of souls, provided it would minimise the reach of political Islam. After such a tacit agreement, society found itself metamorphosed. (Meddeb 2003: 110)

What remains to be ascertained now is how Islamism was successful in its endeavour to gain cultural hegemony in Muslim-majority countries, to what extent and why.[8]

A prominent source for identifying the role of Islamists in civil society, their level of penetration and their capacity to substitute the state in the provision of public goods is represented by the Arab Human Development Reports (AHDR), prepared by a team of prominent Arab intellectuals under the auspices of the United Nations Development Program (UNDP) between 2002 and 2009. These reports argued that throughout the Middle East Islamist groups had increasingly obtained broad popular support, had provided effective service networks and developed a formidable capacity to mobilise followers.

As underlined in the AHDR of 2002 the Arab world has a very established tradition of religious civil society organisations based on the 'waqf' system.[9] Since the end of the 19th century this led to the creation of Islamic cultural associations and charities which, in line with the programme of political Islam, were heavily involved in education, provision of health care and other social and religious matters. These organisations, whose activities within civil society were limited if not prohibited by the state in the past, witnessed a strong revival later on, especially in more recent decades as a consequence of the increasing difficulty of the state to provide similar services, or, in the words of the report:

> more or less encouraged by public authorities needing their assistance in times of difficulty. (AHDR 2002: 109)

On the contrary, non-religious civil society organisations encountered several external constraints in playing their role effectively, such as for example the imposition of bureaucratic constraints in the form of control of civic associations by public authorities (AHDR 2009: 71). Moreover, non-religious civic associations were considered by the AHDR to be dysfunctional in various ways. They lacked internal democracy, as demonstrated by the weak participation of women and youth and the concentration of power in the hands of a single individual, usually, the founder of the organisation (AHDR 2002: 110). This usually led to conflicts and often splits. Moreover, they were seen as lacking transparency in their decision-making processes and incapable of settling disputes peacefully through debates. In administrative terms they were considered unable to respect clear-cut rules of management and accountability. All these shortcomings contributed to non-religious NGOs encountering many problems in financing their activities. On the contrary, civil associations with a religious background were much more successful at maintaining financial independence. This was the case because they enjoyed credibility and legitimacy in society as their actions accorded with traditional Arab and Muslim norms of civic action, associating such activities with welfare and charity work. Moreover, their missions were clear and their social impact immediate as they satisfied pressing and sensitive needs of the population (AHDR 2002: 110). Finally they could rely on donations from the private sector under the form of Zakat[10] as well as providing certain services for a fee.

As underlined by the reports, this was clearly not the case with other, more advocacy-oriented kinds of civil society organisations which provided for functions or services alien to, or at least not appreciated by, the society at large. They provoked distrust amongst private donors, entering into antagonistic relations both with civil society and with the authorities and having to rely heavily on finances coming from international donors (AHDR 2009: 71). This, in turn, deepened public hostility towards their activities and increased their incapacity to communicate with domestic societal actors who did not contribute to their activities either through voluntary work or through financial help (AHDR 2002: 110).

Thus, throughout the Middle East, it is almost exclusively Islamist charities and social welfare organisations that have played a major role in addressing the socio-economic needs of Muslim societies.

In some resource-poor Muslim-majority societies, this role has been increasing with the crisis of the nation state and has not only affected the poorer strata of society (Clark 2004: 11–12). In fact, Clark (2004) demonstrates through the case studies of Islamic medical clinics in Egypt, the Islamic Center Charity Society in Jordan, and the Islam Women's Charitable Society in Yemen that they were run by and served also the interests of the middle classes (Clark 2004; similarly Rutherford 2008).[11] Hence, Islamic social institutions (ISIs) were not only a means to conquer the lower classes, as often underlined in the literature (Harrigan and El-said 2009: 2; Zubaida 1992: 9; Roussillon 1991: 45; Al Sayyid 1993: 45), but have clearly been playing an increasingly essential role in providing social networks that strengthened the ties of solidarity amongst the different components of the middle class, as well as between this and the lower class.

As clearly underlined by Clark:

> Then, as now, the middle class established nongovernmental organisations in reaction to state weakness. (Clark 2004: 5)

This also allowed for the diffusion of Islamic ideas amongst these classes, which produced as its outcome new social and political movements based on Islam as opposed to other, more secular, ideologies:

> ISIs are more than just a challenge to the State's ability to do its job; they are a challenge to the secular state itself. They represent an alternative organisation of state and society – a potentially revolutionary one – based on Islam. (Clark 2004: 5–6)

In the case of Egypt, the Muslim Brotherhood represented by far the most important religious civil society organisation and no doubt also the most successful one (Clark 2004).

The creation of the Muslim Brotherhood happened in1928, just a few years after the demise of the spiritual caliphate exercised by the Ottoman Empire. The objectives of the Brotherhood were quite specific from the beginning and included a return to Islam which had to be obtained through a bottom-up strategy based on programmes of mass education, social and economic reform and progressive implementation of Islamic legislation. The final aim was to set up an 'Islamic State' (Ramadan 2012: 75). To achieve this new moral, social and legal order, the program conceived by al-Banna required a complete transformation of the educational system, asking, for example, for primary schools be attached to mosques. The formation of political parties was forbidden and civil servants were required to have religious training (Meddeb 2003: 98). It seems clear that, from its establishment, political Islam, especially as embodied by the Muslim Brotherhood, had a clear agenda of conquering civil society before establishing an Islamic State. It defined itself not as a political party, but as a solidarity-based social and educational organisation alternative to the state (Rutherford 2008: 78; Lia 1998: 37; Mitchell 1993: 214–216). Eventually, al-Banna's ideas transcended national boundaries and gained millions of supporters all over the Arab world (Ramadan 2012: 75).

Thus, the Muslim Brotherhood was from its origins a civil society organisation building religious social capital especially amongst the strata of society who did not have full access to the public goods provided by the state. A more violent component came to the forefront in Egypt in the early 1960s as a reaction to the consolidation into power of Colonel Gamal Abdel Nasser (1918–1970). The Brotherhood then started to include different trends, ranging from its mainly societal and legalistic origins to more radicalised and violent elements following Nasser's repression in the 1950s and 1960s (Ramadan 2012: 78). With the retreat of the state and the progressive reduction of its services to the middle classes, the reach of the Muslim Brotherhood as a social solidarity system has substantially increased (Clark 2004: 11–12). This societal dimension, therefore, has become all the more important. If the strategy of the Muslim Brotherhood during the regimes of Nasser and Sadat was divided between violent opposition to the regime and a grassroots programme of conquest of civil society by focusing especially on education, during the course of Mubarak's regime, especially from the early 1990s, its reach became more capillary (Jamal 2007). By 1992 the MB led all of the major professional associations, apart from that of journalists, and all of the university students' unions. The more that the regime faced difficulties in maintaining control of the economy and guaranteeing even the most basic services in some deprived areas, the more the MB intervened and substituted the state by establishing Islamic schools, health clinics based on Islamic rules and values and credit unions (Clark 2004: 14–18, 42–81; Rutherford 2008; Zahid 2010). Moreover, this alternative network of schools, hospitals and social services was heavily supported by the so-called 'Islamic business sector' (Ayubi 2008: 408). It is outside the scope of this discussion to identify foreign sources of financing of Islamic Social Institutions (Ramadan 2012).

It might be true that the Islamists and the MB abstained from taking the lead of the events of Midan Tahrir between 25 and 28 January 2011. However, as rightly explained by Hamid (2011a: 29):

> For the members of Egypt's Muslim Brotherhood... Arab Spring may not have been entirely of their making, but it surely was the answer to their prayers.

Indeed, the leaders of the MB were careful to instruct their militants not to shout explicit Islamist slogans in Tahrir square, to avoid the US or other Western countries intervening to crack down on the Islamist threat. However, the Brotherhood made its presence during the revolts of vital importance, providing medical services to the protesters, protecting them from violent repression and keeping order (Hamid 2011a: 29).

Contrary to Egypt, in Tunisia the retrenchment of the state in terms of welfare provisions was not so marked and, because of the control of the regime on civil society and its repressive policies, civic groups, including Islamic groups, did not manage to be active on social issues (Harrigan and El-Said 2009: 2–4; Hibou 2011).

In Tunisia, the Islamic political opposition, Al Nahda, was a direct product of the regime. In response to the growing relevance of secular civil society organisations, such as labour unions, student movements and other secular political groupings in the early 1970s, Bourguiba allowed the formation of a religious association for the Preservation of the Koran (Alexander 2000; Harrigan and El-Said 2009). This organisation later became the Jamma Islamiyya and initially limited its activities to questions of faith and morality. However, with the economic crisis of the late 1970s, the Islamists started to propose a more socio-economic project, opening themselves to unions and workers (Alexander 2000). Political concerns followed suit in the 1980s with the establishment of the Islamic Tendency Movement (MTI), an Islamist political movement which was refused recognition from the government and heavily repressed (Harrigan and El-Said 2009: 169). The change of regime in 1987, with Ben Ali freeing thousands of Islamists, including the leader Rachid Ghanoushi, brought the MTI to change its name to Hizb' Al Nahda (the Reinassance Party) looking for a government recognition that never arrived. Instead, after the Islamists independent list won 14 per cent of the vote as opposed to 5 per cent of all other opposition groups combined, Al Nahda was brutally repressed by the regime of Ben Ali, and any other form of independent civil society activity was frozen (Hibou 2011).

Therefore, given the incredibly repressive nature of the Tunisian regime in more recent years, the Islamist movements could not be actively involved in social and charity activities on the ground as it had been the case for the MB in Egypt. Despite this, the re-Islamisation of Tunisian society was a reality for at least a decade before the uprising of 2011 (Harrigan and El-Said 2009: 171). As the human rights activist Ilhem Abdelkifi pointed out:

> Tunisians are religious. [Al-Nahda] will attract those who do not know where to go. (Hamid 2011b: 114)

Furthermore, interviews with Islamist leaders indicated globalisation and economic restructuring as relevant factors in producing a return to Islam. In particular, Rachid Ghanoushi explicitly condemned economic restructuring brought about by globalisation for:

> marginalising the most vulnerable and favouring the most powerful. (Harrigan and El-Said 2009: 173)

Thus, even in the case of Tunisia, where ruthless repression made it impossible for Islamist movements to take control of civil society and build religious social capital, economic reforms and globalisation are generally recognised as the sources of the re-Islamisation of society in recent times (Harrigan and El-Said 2009: 174; Ayubi 2008: 420; Halliday 2002; Henry and Springborg 2001).

As noticed by Noueihed:

> Arab leaders demonstrated a knack for 'upgrading authoritarianism' to survive the challenges posed not only by globalisation ... One of several tactics they employed was to curtail, co-opt, compete with and therefore undermine efforts to build a strong civil society through the creation of non-governmental organisations. (Noueihed 2012: 15)

This was certainly the case in Libya, where Ghadhafi soon after taking power started a policy of complete eradication of any sort of civil society structure (Kawczynski 2011). Granted, this was somehow easier in this country than anywhere else. The literature is indeed consensual on tracing back the origins of the fragmentation of Libyan civil society in the legacy of the Italian colonisation (Kawcinsky 2011; Simons 2003: ch. 1; Vanderwalle 2006: 40; Marshall 2011). The Italians were ruthless in their colonisation efforts and tore Libyan society apart leaving little in exchange (Marshall 2011). Given the way in which the Italian colonisation process was carried on and concluded, Libyan society did not benefit from the establishment of solid political institutions, an effective legal system or an education infrastructure (Vandewalle 2006: 33). However, if some elements of civil society are to be identified in the Libyan case, these are related to the spread of Islam. Already under King Idris, immediately after independence, the Muslim Brotherhood managed to penetrate Libya from neighbouring Egypt. Despite the heavy repression of its members carried on by Ghadhafi, the Muslim Brotherhood remained active into the 1980s and 1990s. Although clearly a small group of mainly educated people and intellectuals, it did represent one of the few instances of civil society organisations in the country. When Ghadhafi finally decided to crush it completely, at the end of the 1990s, the Brotherhood's presence in Libya was much reduced, but the consequence was, as in other countries, the radicalisation of Islam and its deeper penetration in the minds of Libyan people as the only possibility of resistance to the Dictator (Kawczynski 2011).[12] This happened, however, after Libya had been politically and economically isolated by the West, a political economy isolation which brought about economic marginalisation as we will see in Chapter 7 (Simons 2003; Marshall 2011). No doubt these dynamics will play a role in the post-Ghadhafi Libyan political and social order, although the situation is much complicated by other elements such as tribal rivalries and, above all, the question of the control of oil (Marshall 2011).

Concluding, globalisation-induced economic restructuring, by either restricting the ability of the state to protect the poor and the middle classes or by causing a profound identity crisis in civil society through state repression, strengthened the hand of political Islam and undermined the legitimacy of the regimes in the resource-poor countries of the MENA area, including Egypt and Tunisia (Harrigan and El-Said 2009: 1–2; Clark 2004: 11–12; Hakimian and Moshaver 2000).

Such a process did not occur suddenly on the eve of the Arab Spring. In Egypt this was clearly the consequence of a capillary penetration of Islam in civil society thanks to its capacity to foster social capital and develop well-established solidarity networks both between lower and middle classes as well as within them (binding and bridging social capital, in the classification of the relevant literature) (similarly Richards and Waterbury 1998: 348–350).

Thus, in Egypt, as well as in other resource-poor MENA countries such as Jordan (Knowles 2005) and Yemen, the Islamic Social Institutions (ISIs), which were adding to the creation of social capital, also created horizontal and vertical social networks of solidarity among the discontented middle classes and the dispossessed poor ones. However, these prevailing forms of social capital were based on an Islamic view of society and the state; they were therefore alternative to both the status quo and to more secular social movements. In these cases, civil society was indeed empowered by globalisation, as proposed by transnationalists. However, this occurred by favouring the creation of a distinct Islamic social capital, binding both the middle classes and the poorer strata of society more closely in the name of a vision of the state and society alternative to both the existing regimes and a more secular project (Zahid 2010). Islamism, as an ideology, permeated the middle and poor strata of society cementing a new socio-economic alliance, or, as Gramsci would put it, a new socio-economic historic bloc.[13]

Similarly, in Tunisia Islamism came to penetrate deeply into civil society and to represent a strong factor of cohesion between the middle and lower classes. Given the repressive nature of the state, which tightly controlled civil society as well as the welfare state, this could not happen through faith-based welfare provisions and religious social capital. However, by negating an evolution of civil society towards a model already prevailing in other Arab states, it enlarged the sources of discontent, especially amongst the marginalised strata of society, thus creating a vacuum which Islam increasingly filled. In a way, the evolutions of the Egyptian and Tunisian civil society (or lack of it) are the two sides of the same coin: by adopting *de facto* opposite attitudes towards the development of Islamic Social Institutions and social capital, the two regimes obtained exactly the same result, the empowerment of the Islamic ideology in opposition to both the status quo and any other alternative ideological/political projects.

Thus, as the corrupted nationalistic regimes in Egypt and Tunisia failed to guarantee prosperity to their societies, so these same societies turned to Islamism as the only alternative to the status quo. These new approaches to constitutional order based on political Islam progressively grew into meaningful alternatives to the declining statism of the regimes (Rutherford 2008: 2).

To a certain extent, this analysis about the radicalisation and penetration of Islam in society can be applied also to the case of Libya. However, the case of Libya, as an oil-producing country, requires a more detailed analysis of the political economy of oil to which we turn in Chapter 7.

Annex 1 Core indicators on ICT infrastructure and access

Basic Core Indicators	
A1	Fixed telephone lines per 100 inhabitants
A2	Mobile cellular telephone per 100 inhabitants
A3	Computers per 100 inhabitants
A4	Internet subscribers per 100 inhabitants
A5	Broadband internet subscribers per 100 inhabitants
A6	International internet bandwidth per inhabitant (bits)
A7	Percentage of population covered by mobile cellular telephony
A8	Internet access tariffs (20 hours per month), in US$ (A8a) and as a percentage of per capita income (A8b)
A9	Mobile cellular tariffs (100 minutes of use per month), in US$ (A9a) and as a percentage of per capita income (A9b)
A10	Percentage of localities with public internet access centres (PIACs) by number of inhabitants (rural/urban)
Extended Core Indicators	
A11	Radio sets per 100 inhabitants
A12	Television sets per 100 inhabitants

Annex 2 Core indicators on access to, and use of, ICT by households and individuals

Basic Core Indicators	
HH1	Proportion of households with a radio
HH2	Proportion of households with a TV
HH3	Proportion of households with a fixed line telephone
HH4	Proportion of households with a mobile cellular telephone
HH5	Proportion of households with a computer
HH6	Proportion of individuals who used a computer (from any location) in the last 12 months
HH7	Proportion of households with internet access at home
HH8	Proportion of households who used internet (from any location) in the last 12 months

Continued

Annex 2 Continued

Basic Core Indicator	
HH9	Location of individual use of the internet in the last 12 months: At home At work Place of education At another person's home Community internet access facility Commercial internet access facility Others
HH10	Internet activities undertaken by the individual in the last 12 months: Getting information: About goods or services Related to health or health services From government organisations/public authorities via web or email Other information or general web-browsing Communicating Purchasing or ordering goods or services Internet banking Education or learning activities Dealing (interacting) with government organisations/public authorities Leisure activities: Playing/downloading videos or computer games Downloading movies, music or software Reading/downloading electronic books, newspapers or magazines Other leisure activities
Extended Core Indicators	
HH11	Proportion of individuals with use of a mobile phone
HH12	Proportion of households with access to internet by type of access: Narrowband access Broadband access (See Annex 3 for detailed categories)
HH13	Frequency of individual access to the internet in the last 12 months (by any location): At least once a day At least once a week but not every day At least once a month but not every week Less than once a month
HH14	Proportion of households with electricity

Annex 3 Use of ICT by businesses

Basic Core Indicators	
B1	Proportion of businesses using computers
B2	Proportion of employees using computers
B3	Proportion of businesses using internet
B4	Proportion of employees using internet
B5	Proportion of businesses with a web presence
B6	Proportion of businesses with an intranet
B7	Proportion of businesses receiving orders over the internet
B8	Proportion of businesses placing orders over the internet
Extended Core Indicators	
B9	Proportion of businesses using the internet by type of access: Narrowband Broadband
B10	Proportion of businesses with a local area network (LAN)
B11	Proportion of businesses with an extranet
B12	Proportion of businesses using internet by type of activity: Sending or receiving email Getting information about goods or services Getting information from government organisations/public authorities via websites or email Performing internet banking or accessing other financial services Interacting with government organisations/public authorities Providing customer services Delivering products online Other information services or research activities

Annex 4 The ICT sector and trade in ICT goods

ICT1	Proportion of business sector workforce involved in the ICT sector (usually expressed as a percentage)
ICT2	Value added in the ICT sector (as a percentage of total business sector value added)
ICT3	ICT goods imports as a percentage of total imports
ICT4	ICT goods exports as a percentage of total exports

Notes

1. The list of the countries belonging to each region as well as to the developing/developed world is based on the UN classification and is available at the ITU website: http://www.itu.int/ITU-D/ict/definitions/regions/index.htm, accessed on 7 March 2013.

2. According to the ITU classification Egypt, Libya and Tunisia belong to the Arab world. See http://www.itu.int/ITU-D/ict/definitions/regions/index.htm, as accessed on 7 March 2013.
3. World Bank Statistics, web-site http://data.worldbank.org/indicator/SE.XPD.TOTL.GB.ZS?page=1 as accessed on 22 March 2013.
4. World Bank Statistics, web-site http://data.worldbank.org/indicator/SE.XPD.TOTL.GB.ZS?page=1 as accessed on 22 March 2013.
5. Seehttp://www.educationcounts.govt.nz/__data/assets/pdf_file/0011/114995/Key-Findings-NZ-Participation-in-TIMSS-and-PIRLS-2010–2011.pdf, p. 11.
6. For a very good account of the definition of middle class in the Middle East see Luciani (2007: 163): '[t]he middle class per se has no other distinguishing feature except that it finds itself between a top class, comprising the elite, and a lower class, comprising the masses'. See also Roccu (2012); Clark (2004); Ayubi (2008).
7. Sadat was killed in 1981 by a member of the Jihad, a militant Islamic group that had split from the MB in the early 1970s (Rutherford 2008: 83).
8. A different issue is the discussion of the role of civil society in promoting democracy in general and in the Middle East. For this see Blair (1997); Finkel (2004); Hearn (2000); Henry and Springborg (2001); Hoogh and Stolle (2003); Huntington (1991); Ibrahim (1993); Krishna (2002); Letki (2004); Newton (2001); Norton (1993); and Ottaway and Carothers (2000).
9. This is a system of donations to Islamic charitable trusts.
10. Charity
11. For a thorough analysis of the middle classes in the Middle East see Clark (2004); Ayubi (2008); and Roccu (2012).
12. Ghadhafi was successful in quashing the two most prominent Islamist factions in the country, the Libyan Islamic Group (the Libyan branch of the Muslim Brotherhood) and the Libyan Islamic Fighting Group (LIFG). The latter was formed in the early 1990s by Libyan jihadists who had fought in Afghanistan against the Soviet Union. In the mid-1990s, the regime launched ground and air attacks against LIFG bases and arrested suspected sympathisers, quickly disrupting the group's cohesiveness and capabilities. In 1996, in Abu Salim, Tripoli's main political prison, guards killed 1,270 prisoners, many of them Islamists. This incident, more than any other during Ghadhafi's rule, would become one of the main rallying cries for the opposition movement that would eventually bring down the regime. See Al-Turk (2011).
13. For a convincing account of the role played by the Islamists in the events of 25 January 2011 in Egypt see Hamid (2011a).

References

Arab Human Development Report (2002). *Creating Opportunities for Future Generations*, AHDR available at http://www.arab-hdr.org/contents/index.aspx?rid=1 as accessed on 5 April 2013.

Arab Human Development Report (2003). *Building a Knowledge Society*, AHDR, available at http://www.arab-hdr.org/contents/index.aspx?rid=2 as accessed on 5 April 2013.

Al Sayyid, M. (1993). A Civil Society in Egypt? *Middle East Journal*, 47(2).

Alexander, C. (2000). Back from the Democratic Brink: Authoritarianism and Civil Society in Tunisia. *Middle East Report*, October–December 1997.

Al-Turk, A. (2011). 'Libya from Revolt to State-Building', in Pollack, K.M. (ed.) *The Arab Awakening*. The Brookings Institution, Washington, pp. 111–117.

Ayubi, N. (1991). *Political Islam: Religion and Politics in the Arab World*. Routledge, London.

Ayubi, N. (2008). *Over-stating the Arab State: Politics and Society in the Middle East*. I.B. Tauris, London.

Blair, H. (1997). 'Donors, Democratisation, and Civil Society: Relating Theory to Practice', in Hulme, D., and Edwards, M. (eds) *Too Close for Comfort? NGOs, States and. Donors*. Macmillan, Basingstoke and St Martin's Press, New York.

Bourdieu, P. (1980). Le Capital Social: Notes Provisoires. *Actes de la Recherche in Sciences Sociales*, 31, 2–3.

Clark, J. (2004). *Islam, Charity and Activism*. Indiana University Press.

Clement Moore, H., and Springborg, R. (2010). *Globalization and the Politics of Development in the Middle East*. Cambridge University Press.

Coleman J. (1988). Social Capital in the Creation of Human Capital. *American Journal of Sociology*, 94, 95–120.

Dicken, P. (2011). *Global Shift: Mapping the Changing Contours of the World Economy* (6th ed.). Guilford.

Finkel, S.E. (2004). Can Democracy Be Taught? *Journal of Democracy*, 14(4), October 2003, 137–151.

Glaeser E. L., Laibson, D., and Sacerdote, B. (2002). An Economic Approach to Social Capital. *Economic Journal*, 112(483), 437–458.

Gramsci, A. (1975). *Quaderni dal carcere*. Einaudi, Torino.

Gramsci, A. (1999). *Selections from the Prison Notebooks of Antonio Gramsci*. Elecbook electronic books, London.

Hakimian, H., and Moshaver, Z. (eds) (2000). *The State and Global Change: The Political Economy of Transition in the Middle East and North Africa*. Curzon, London.

Halliday, F. (2002). 'The Middle East and the Politics of Differential Integration', in Dodge, T., and Higgot, R. (eds) *Globalisation and the Middle East: Islam, Economy, Society and Politics*. Royal Institute of International Affairs, London, pp. 42–45.

Hamid, S. (2011a). 'Islamists and the Brotherhood: Political Islam and the Arab Spring', in Pollack, K.M. (ed.) *The Arab Awakening*. The Brookings Institution, Washington, pp. 29–39.

Hamid, S. (2011b). 'Tunisia', in Pollack, K.M. (ed.) *The Arab Awakening*. The Brookings Institution, Washington, pp. 111–117.

Harrigan, J., and El-Said H. (2009). *Economic Liberalisation, Social Capital and Islamic Welfare Provision*. Palgrave, London.

Harvey, D. (2008). 'The Right to the City', *New Left Review*, 53, September–October 2008.

Hearn, J. (2000). Aiding Democracy? Donors and Civil Society in South Africa. *Third World Quarterly*, 21(5), October 2000, 815–830.

Henry, C., and Springborg, R. (eds) (2001). *Globalisation and the Politics of Development in the Middle East*. Cambridge University Press, Cambridge.

Heydemann, S. (ed.) (2004). *Networks of Privilege in the Middle East: The Politics of Economic Reforms Revisited*. Palgrave Macmillan, Basingstoke.

Hibou, B. (2011). *The Force of Obedience: The Political Economy of Repression in Tunisia*. Polity Press, Cambridge.

Hoogh, M., and Stolle, D. (2003). *Generating Social Capital*. Palgrave, London.

Huntington, S. (1991). *The Third Wave: Democratisation in the Late Twentieth Century*. University of Oklahoma Press, Norman, OK.

Ibrahim, S.E. (1993). Crises, Elites, and Democratisation in the Arab World. *Middle East Journal*, 47(2), Spring 1993, 292–305.

ITU (2013). ICT Facts and Figures, website http://www.itu.int/ITU-D/ict/facts/material/ICTFactsFigures2013.pdf as accessed on 7 March 2013.

Jamal, A. (2007). *Barriers to Democracy: The Other Side of Social Capital in Palestine and the Arab World*. Princeton University Press, Princeton, NJ.

Kawczynski, D. (2011). *Seeking Gaddafi: Libya, the West and the Arab Spring*. Biteback Publishing Ltd.

Knack, S., and Keefer, P. (1997). Does Social Capital Have an Economic Payout? A Cross-Country Investigation. *The Quarterly Journal of Economics*, 112(4), 1251–1288.

Knowles, W. (2005). *Jordan since 1989: A Study in Political Economy*. I.B. Tauris, London.

Krishna, A. (2002). Enhancing Political Participation in Democracies: What is the Role of Social Capital? *Comparative Political Studies*, 35(4), May 2002, 437–460.

Letki, N. (2004). Socialisation for Participation? *Political Research Quarterly*, 57(4).

Lia, B. (1998). *The Society of the Muslim Brothers in Egypt: The Rise of an Islamic Mass Movement 1928–1942*. Ithaca Press, Reading.

Luciani, G. (2007). 'Linking Economic and Political Reform in the Middle East: The Role of the Bourgeoisie', in Schlumberger, O. (ed.) *Debating Arab Authoritarianism: Dynamics and Durability in Nondemocratic Regimes*. Stanford University Press, Stanford, CA, pp. 161–176.

Marshall, J.K. (2011). *Libya: A Look into History*. Thomas R. Mann, Editor. Kindle edition.

Meddeb, A. (2003). The malady of Islam, Basic Books.

Mitchell, R. (1993). *The Society of the Muslim Brothers*. OUP, Oxford.

Mittelman, J.H. (2000). The Globalisation Syndrome: Transformation and Resistance. Princeton University Press, Princeton.

Newton, K. (2001). Trust, Social Capital, Civil Society and Democracy. *International Political Science Review*, April 2001, 22(2), 201–214.

Norton, A.R. (1993). The Future of Civil Society in the Middle East. *Middle East Journal*, 47(2), Spring1993, 205–216.

Noueihed, L. (2012). *The Battle for the Arab Spring*. Yale University Press.

Ottaway, M., and Carothers, T. (2000). *Funding Virtue*. Carnegie Endowment for Intl Peace.

Putnam, R. (2000). *Bowling Alone: The Collapse and Revival of American Community*. Simon and Schuster, New York.

Putnam, R. (2002). *Democracies in Flux*. Oxford Scholarship online, www.oxfordscholarship.com as accessed on 19 February 2007, p. 3.

Ramadan, T. (2012). *The Arab Awakening: Islam and the New Middle East*. Penguin.

Richards, A., and Waterbury, J. (1998). *A Political Economy of the Middle East*. Westview Press.

Robinson, W. (2004). *A Theory of Global Capitalism: Transnational Production, Transnational Capitalists, and the Transnational State.* Johns Hopkins University Press, Baltimore, MD.
Roccu, R. (2012). 'Of Middle Classes, Economic Reforms and Popular Revolts', in Panebianco, S., and Rossi, R. (eds) *Winds of Democratic Change in the Mediterranean?* Rubbettino, Palermo, pp. 61–82.
Rodinson, M. (2007 [1987]). *Islam and Capitalism.* Saqi, London.
Roussillon, A. (1991). *'Entre Al Jihad et al Rayyan', Modernisation et nouvelles forms de mobilisation sociale.* Dossiers du centre d'etudes et documentation economiques, Cairo.
Rutherford, B. (2008). *Egypt After Mubarak: Liberalism, Islam, and Democracy in the Arab World,* Princeton University Press.
Said, M. (2007). 'The Fall and Rise in Wage Inequality in Egypt: New Evidence from the ELMPS, 2006', *ERF Working Paper Series,* WP 0708, Economic Research Forum, Cairo.
Sassen, S. (1991). *The Global City: New York, London, Tokyo.* Princeton University Press, Princeton NJ.
Schlumberger, O. (2008). Economic Reform, Economic Order, and Development: Patrimonial Capitalism. *Review of International Political Economy,* 15(4), 622–649.
Simons, G. (2003). *Libya and the West.* Centre for Libyan Studies.
Shafik, N. (1999). 'Technology: A Disintegrative Factor in the Arab World', in Hudson, C.M. (ed.) *The Middle East Dilemma.* Tauris, London.
Snider, L. (2007). 'The Clash of Mental Models in the Middle East: Neoliberal vs. Islamic Ideas', in Roy, R., Denzau, K., and Willett, T. (eds) *Neoliberalism: National and Regional Experiments with Global Ideas.* Routledge, London, pp. 206–228.
Strange, S. (1998). *Mad Money.* Manchester: Manchester University Press.
Talani L.S., Clarkson, A., and Pacheco-Pardo, R. (eds) (2013). *Dirty Cities: Towards a Political Economy of the Underground in Global Cities.* Palgrave Macmillan, Basingstoke.
Tripp, C. (2006). *Islam and the Moral Economy: The Challenge of Capitalism.* Cambridge University Press, Cambridge.
UN [United Nations] (2008). *The Global Information Society: A Statistical View.* Partnership on Measuring ICT for Development, April 2008, LC/W.190. At: http://www.itu.int/ITU-D/ict/material/LCW190_En.pdf as accessed on 7 March 2013.
Vanderwalle, D. (2006). *A History of Modern Libya.* Cambridge University Press.
Worms, J. (2002). 'France: Old and New Civic and Social Ties in France', in Putnam, R.D. (ed.) *Democracies in Flux: The Evolution of Social Capital in Contemporary Society.* Oxford University Press, New York, pp.137–188.
Zahid, M. (2010). *The Muslim Brotherhood and Egypt's Succession Crisis.* I.B.Tauris, London.
Zubaida, S. (1992). Islam, The State and Democracy. *Middle East Report,* 179, 9.

4

The Economic Marginalisation and Lack of Regionalisation of the MENA Area

Introduction

The theoretical analysis discussed so far identified in the economic marginalisation of the MENA area and in its lack of political and economic integration a relevant political economy factor of the recent wave of political turmoil and change. From the theoretical point of view, the following issues appear particularly relevant:

1. The paradox of the lack of regionalisation of the MENA area within globalisation.
2. The paradox of marginalisation of the MENA area within globalisation.
3. The paradox of the empowerment of civil society amid the crisis of the state.

The MENA area is therefore at the crossroads of some of the most significant structural developments of the new global political economy.

The paradox of regionalisation within globalisation is one of the pillars of the qualitative, transnationalist approach to the impact of globalisation on local political dynamics. This entails that those regions experiencing a high degree of integration into the global economy tend to increase also their level of economic and, to a certain extent, political regional integration (Mittelman 2000; ch. 2). The Middle East and Northern Africa region is a clear example of the opposite dynamic.[1]

The MENA area is considered here as a paradigmatic case of marginalisation within globalisation, and as a clear example of lack of regionalisation, in line with the relevant literature. Indeed, despite a number of attempts to create an integrated economic and even political region, the literature unanimously portrays such attempts as a failure (see, e.g. Dodge and Higgot 2002; also Hakimian and Moshaver 2001; Hudson 1999).

This chapter assesses the state of regional integration in the MENA area and in the Arab world. For the sake of this analysis, it is important to clarify the geographical definition of the area considered. Following the International Monetary Fund (IMF), the MENA region comprises a group of countries bound together by their geographical location, close historical and cultural ties, and common economic challenges. In the classification of the IMF, the MENA region comprises 20 countries: Algeria, Bahrain, Djibouti, Egypt, Iran, Iraq, Jordan, Kuwait, Lebanon, Libya, Mauritania, Morocco, Oman, Qatar, Saudi Arabia, Sudan, Syria, Tunisia, United Arab Emirates, and Yemen.[2] Moreover, to account for fundamental differences in economic structure, countries within the region are divided into oil-exporting countries and other MENA countries, which are traditionally referred to as non-oil or resource-poor MENA countries (Egypt, Jordan, Lebanon, Morocco, Syria, Tunisia and Yemen). The oil-exporting MENA countries are further divided into the members of the Gulf Cooperation Council (GCC) (Bahrain, Kuwait, Oman, Qatar, Saudi Arabia and United Arab Emirates) and other MENA oil-exporters (Algeria, Iran and Libya). Following the World Economic Outlook convention (IMF 2003), a country is classified as an oil exporter if its oil export earnings during the period 1994–1998 constituted more than 50 per cent of total export earnings. Since this convention the only change has been that Sudan, which remains in the Middle East and North Africa region, is now classified as a country with non-fuel primary products as the main source of export earnings.[3]

The first section of this chapter addresses the institutional and political dimension of Arab economic 'integration' (or, better, 'disintegration' – Hudson 1999).

The analysis will then move to the economic dimension of integration with the discussion of the three main indicators of integration into the global political economy, namely the degree of trade integration, the level of foreign direct investment and the degree of trade openness. The aim is to determine to what extent the MENA area in general, and the three countries studied here in particular, are integrated into the global economy and enjoy a healthy degree of regional economic integration or not.

In the last section, the level of intra-regional solidarity will be assessed with reference to the dynamics of aid-capital flows.

The institutional dimension of economic (dis)integration in the MENA region

Since the creation of the Arab League in 1945, there have been various plans aimed at creating regional institutions that could integrate the Arab economies (Owen 1999). Starting already in 1953, the Arab League tried to promote multilateral trading agreements within the MENA region. Amongst them, it is worth mentioning provisions to exempt Arab agricultural commodities from tariff barriers and to reduce tariffs on some industrial goods. For example, as further elaborated below, in 1957, Egypt, Iraq, Jordan, Kuwait and Syria signed an agreement aimed at achieving full economic union, going under the name of the Arab Economic Unity Agreement. This led to the creation in 1958 of the Council of Arab Economic Union, based in Cairo and whose main role was to foster the process of Arab economic integration. In 1964 the same countries apart from Kuwait established the Arab Common Market with the aim to abolish all tariff and non-tariff barriers in the following ten years. The literature is however unanimous in considering this and numerous other attempts at integrating institutionally the economies of the region as a clear failure (Owen 1999; Owen and Pamuk 1999; Dodge and Higgot 2002; El-Agraa 1997).

Experts of Arab (dis)integration refer to various phases of Arab attempts to establish a multilateral institutional framework to further regional economic integration (Diab 1963: chs 1 and 2; Musrey 1969: chs 5 and 6, quoted in Owen 1999). In the first phase, going back to as far as the Treaty for Joint Defence and Economic Cooperation by the ministers of Egypt, Jordan, Lebanon, Iraq, Syria, Saudi Arabia and (North) Yemen in 1950,[4] the focus was on reducing tariff barriers and facilitating free movement of people and capital through the establishment of free trade areas. Following this rationale, in 1953 the members of the Arab League signed the Convention for Facilitating Trade and Regulating Transit which provided for an agreement to abolish tariffs on agricultural products and minerals.[5] However, given the protectionist attitude of states like Iraq, as well as the insistence of countries such as Saudi Arabia and Yemen on imposing duties on imported goods, similar efforts at eliminating trade barriers were unsuccessful (Owen and Pamuk 1999).

By the end of the 1950s, Arab countries tried to establish a European-style common market. During the crisis of the Suez Canal, Arab countries had found a new cohesion and this helped the Arab League's Economic Council achieving an agreement in principle for the establishment of an

Arab Common Market in 1958. This was followed on 6 June 1962 by a joint commitment of Egypt, Jordan, Iraq, Syria and Kuwait to engage in a process of unification of both economic policies and economic legislation. As already mentioned, this led to the signature on 13 August 1964 by the five States of a resolution to establish the Arab Common Market, due to start on 1 January 1965.[6]

In accordance with the provisions of the Agreement for Economic Unity among Arab League States, the Council of Arab Economic Union established the Arab Common Market with the aim of achieving, by January 1974:

1. freedom of movement of persons and capital;
2. freedom of exchange of national and foreign commodities;
3. freedom of residence, work, employment and the undertaking of economic activities; and
4. freedom of transport and transit as well as the use of means of transport, seaports and civil airports.[7]

To achieve these objectives, the treaty provided for the progressive abolition of all duties and quantitative restrictions. As mentioned, Kuwait eventually failed to ratify the Treaty, whilst the other states experienced great difficulty in respecting their pledge to reduce tariffs and restrictions. Exemption of products from tariff reduction became the norm and the abolition of quantitative restrictions was not implemented successfully. Finally, the countries in question failed to agree on a common external tariff, and by 1971 the idea of creating an Arab Common Market was substituted by a much lighter putative free trade area (Sayigh 1999: ch. 11).

Diab (1963) proposed an insightful analysis of the impact on intra-regional trade of both multilateral and bilateral agreements between the Arab states in the period from 1951 to 1960. The conclusions reached by this scholar were not positive (Diab 1963: ch. 4, as quoted in Owen 1999). More recently, Yusif Sayigh (1983: 147–155) calculated that inter-Arab trade during the 1950s and 1960s never became more than a tenth of the Arab total. Remarkably, this is the same figure as nowadays (see next section). The reasons why this happened have been classified by the literature into two categories (Owen and Pamuk 1999): one is the lack of political will, the other is the lack of economic differentiation amongst the integrating countries, which limited the possibilities to trade. Indeed, apart from Kuwait, which however failed to ratify the agreement establishing the Arab Common Market, the other members had very similar economic structures and tended to produce the same range of agricultural and manufactured goods.

According to Owen, (1999), this explanation requires some qualifications. First of all, the Arab regimes of that period tended to adopt an economic model of development which was very similar to that of Soviet Import-Substituting Industrialisation (ISI). Such a model implied the substitution of previously imported manufactured goods with local ones to be sold in a protected local market. According to the author, this decision is at the roots of both the lack of economic growth in these countries and the lack of intra-regional trade. In fact, when an economic structure is not fostering exports, foreign exchange is very scarce and mainly utilised to import raw materials and capital goods. Moreover, these countries tended to be prone to periodic balance-of-payments crises which led to reduced convertibility for local currencies and increased capital controls. Under these conditions, foreign reserves almost disappeared, rendering manufacturing production almost impossible, even for only local consumption and much more so for the regional market. Equally serious was the lack of skills in newly nationalised industries, which made it difficult for the countries concerned to market their goods abroad. In such circumstances it is no surprise that regional economic integration could not thrive. This was especially the case in Egypt under the Nasserite regime. On the other end of the spectrum were countries like Lebanon, with its small, more export-oriented economy, and the oil-exporting Gulf countries which had followed an opposite, more successful development model (Owen and Pamuk 1999).

In the Maghreb and the Mashreq any attempts to create common markets during the 1960s also collapsed. At the roots of these failures were, again, political reasons related to the lack of political will of the countries involved to cede control over their economic policies or to allow access to their domestic markets. Various attempts were made to create a Maghreb Union, starting with the setting up of the Permanent Consultative Council in Tunis in 1966 with the task of promoting greater regional integration. However, the project of establishing a North African market never materialised (Zartman 1999). The reason is, again, according to Owen (1999), the adoption of an import substitution-led model of growth. This was aggravated in Algeria by the existence of state trading organisations with monopolies over the import of many strategic foreign products (Owen 1999).

Another reason proposed in the literature to explain the failure of economic integration projects in the MENA region is the mismatch between economic reality and commercial treaties. To put it bluntly, the whole idea of increasing intra-regional trade by establishing institutional mechanisms such as free trade areas and common markets was simply a way to conceal the grim reality of trade flows (Owen 1999). Even the oil price increases in the 1970s did not have any positive impact on trade, despite substantially improving both capital and labour flows. However, even the latter outcomes were not due to the proactive role of centralised Arab institutions. Indeed, as far as migration is concerned, apart from some facilities provided by Egypt for its emigrants in Iraq at the beginning of the 1980s, intra-Arab migration was mainly uncontrolled and unregulated. Also the movement and direction of capital flows did not follow any plan, but was mainly unpredictable and related to the political objectives of the different countries (Sayigh 1978, 1983, 1999).

It is true that, after the oil booms of the 1970s, Arab integration projects witnessed a revival. However, in Owen's opinion (1999; also Owen and Pamuk 1999), the main reason for such a renaissance was their redistributive nature. This related to the will of oil-exporting Arab countries to transfer some of the wealth accumulated through oil exports to resource-poor MENA countries. The creation of the Abu Dhabi Fund for Arab Economic Development in 1971,[8] along the same lines as the Kuwait one (1961),[9] is to be inserted within this context. In 1974 Saudi Arabia[10] and Iraq[11] also decided to establish similar national funds (Van den Boogaerde 1991). Furthermore, between 1968 and 1976, various regional institutions were established with the objective of financing local and regional development projects or allowing for the provision of balance of payments support. Among them there were the Arab Fund for Economic and Social Development, created in 1968; the Arab Bank for Economic Development in Africa and the Islamic Development Bank, founded in 1973; the Arab–African Technical Assistance Fund, the Arab–African Oil Assistance Fund, the Special Fund for Arab Non-oil-exporting Countries, all of them established in 1974 (Sayigh 1978); and the Arab Monetary Fund created in 1976. The relevant literature tends to consider this phase more as one of regional transfers from oil-rich countries to resource-poor ones than as a genuine phase of multilateral economic integration in the MENA area (Van den Boogaerde 1991: Introduction; Owen 1999; Sayigh 1978, 1983, 1999).

The extent to which Arab economic institutional arrangements were ineffective is evidenced also by the experience of smaller sub-regional groupings such as the Gulf Cooperation Council (GCC),[12] the Maghreb Union (Zartman 1999), and the short-lived Arab Cooperation Council which was created in the late 1980s among Egypt, Iraq, Jordan and Yemen. Among these bodies, the only one which could survive through the 1980s was the GCC. This provided for a genuine common market, with a common external tariff and common internal laws and regulations. But it should be noticed that the Gulf countries were also the only ones which were actually genuinely trading with each other, although in the literature some doubts are cast relating to the effective level of integration of even the GCC (Abdulla 1999). The rest of the area did not experience any similar successes (Sayigh 1999; Owen 1999).

During the 1980s, the proportion of intra-Arab to total Arab trade, was still very limited, with only 5.2 per cent of total Arab exports in 1980 and 6.6 per cent in 1984 sent to another Arab country. Moreover, due to the fall of oil prices, the absolute values involved were declining from $12 billion-worth of inter-Arab exports in 1980 to $8.4 billion in 1984.[13] Besides, as pointed out above, much of the (already limited) amount of intra-Arab trade was taking place among the Gulf oil-producers themselves (Owen 1999).

The lack of economic regionalisation of the Arab economies in the 1980s can be explained by making reference to a number of factors. Among these a prominent role was played by the debt crisis that hit a number of Arab countries as a result of falling oil prices. Resource-poor MENA countries, especially Egypt and Jordan, suffered more from the crisis as their economies relied on remittances from migrants in the Gulf, and on Arab aid. The ensuing economic stabilisation programmes further shrunk those economies, which hindered intra-regional trade, while the first Iraq war reduced the level of communication in the area, increasing political divisions in particular among the Gulf States and their western Arab neighbours, as well as among the GCC states themselves. As a result, attempts at Arab economic cooperation were nullified and economic interactions in the zone diminished dramatically (Owen 1999; Sayigh 1999).

Overall, Arab economic integration in the 1980s fared even worse than in the 1970s, mainly because of dwindling oil revenues (Sayigh 1999). In the 1970s the oil-induced affluence enjoyed by oil-rich countries had prompted them to take on a more proactive role in financing the economies of poorer Arab countries. It had also multiplied their demand for Arab workers, fostering inter-Arab migration. In this context, institutional economic integration was viewed more sympathetically. However, with the decrease of oil revenues in the 1980s, the idea of economic integration suffered and regional integration projects were basically abandoned (Owen and Pamuk 1999).

The 1990s were instead characterised by a new impetus to institutionalise economic integration in the MENA Area. This, however, was not coming from within, but from without the area, more specifically, from the European Union. The background for these initiatives was the Euro-Mediterranean partnership (EMP) launched in Barcelona in November 1995 and evolving into the Union for the Mediterranean in 2008.[14]

The Barcelona Process inaugurated a new approach to the relationship between the European Union and the countries of the MENA region. It provided the framework for managing both bilateral and regional relations. The Barcelona Process can be described as made up of economic, security and cultural baskets. In particular, the economic basket was aimed at creating a deep Euro-Mediterranean Free Trade Area, removing barriers to trade and investment not only between the EU and Southern Mediterranean countries but also between the Southern Mediterranean countries themselves.[15] Signatories included the members of the EU, as well as 14 southern Mediterranean countries. Another important element of the Barcelona Process was a substantial increase in financial assistance from the EU to the southern Mediterranean countries compared to previous agreements. More than 5 bn Euros were made available to countries in the MENA area from 1996 until 2006 by two sequential MEDA programmes.[16]

Although never without contradictions, the Barcelona Process seemed to have activated a crucial dialogue between the southern shores of the Mediterranean and the European economic, political and cultural sphere. The process also achieved sizeable results, particularly in terms of economic integration and political cooperation, and increased the hopes for further achievements to be obtained in the future with respect to the more complex cultural and political dimensions (Unver Noi 2011).[17]

However, a first blow to the process came with the terrorist attacks of 11 September 2001, which marked a watershed in the relations between the Muslim and the non-Muslim worlds. The most controversial and long-lasting consequence of these events on the Euro-Mediterranean process was securitisation, especially of migration issues. Securitisation is a process by which migration and refugee policies are more and more treated as security issues, with all that this means in terms of adoption of security-related tools to deal with them (see Huysmans 2000; also Junemann 2004c). There is a huge debate in the literature on whether the terrorist threat from Muslim fundamentalism has reshaped the EU attitude towards Muslim migrants and citizens in a much more clearly security-oriented fashion (Kostakopoulou 2000; Ugur 1995; Miles and Thränhardt 1995; Huysmans 2000).

In terms of foreign policy, such a development had universally appreciated consequences in terms of moving the political discourse from low politics to high politics and, especially, making socio-economic cooperation dependent on the adoption of measures designed to curb security threats. There have even been scholars explaining the restrictive attitude of some Arab regimes towards democratisation as a consequence of the new security climate engendered by September the 11th. The argument runs as follows: domestic governments could justify and legitimise their stepping back from the respect of basic democratic principles or even human rights as a fight against a deadly threat. This connection was made in the case of Mubarak's decision to isolate human rights organisations in Egypt (Grunert 2004). Other scholars underlined how the focus on security seriously undermined previous efforts to reinforce the dialogue between civilisations and the cultural cooperation fostered by the third basket of the EMP (Gillespie 2004). Finally, the development of the European Security and Defence Policy was perceived, after September the 11th, as a potential threat for Muslim countries, although some political elites welcomed it as a positive alternative to American military primacy (Junemann 2004b).

To be sure, a main obstacle to the Euro-Mediterranean partnership was, and still is, also the Palestinian question (Stetter 2004; also Asseburg 2004) as was clearly demonstrated by the events of December 2008.[18] This poses broader questions about the role of Israel in the EMP and in the subsequent developments, or non-developments, of the Euro-Mediterranean process (Tovias 2004).

With the enlargement of the EU in 2004, Brussels promoted a new policy towards its neighbouring countries. This took the name of the European Neighbourhood Policy (ENP) and was aimed at creating commercial and strategic alliances with the countries that share borders with the EU. With respect to its southern partners the ENP builds on EMP by offering bilateral incentives to increase connections with Europe.[19] As a result, after the onset of the ENP, the EMP maintained only its regional, multilateral dimension, losing its bilateral one. In terms of financial assistance the ENP discontinued the MEDA programmes and has replaced them since 2007 with a single instrument, the European Neighbourhood and Partnership Instrument (ENPI).[20] This covers the needs of all neighbouring countries, not only those in the MENA area (Aliboni 2005; Tassinari 2005; Balfour and Missiroli 2007).

If this was a set-back in the process of cross-Mediterranean integration, an even stronger blow came from the substitution of the Barcelona Process with the Union for the Mediterranean, created by the 43 Euro-Mediterranean Heads of State and Government in Paris on July 2008 (Bicchi 2007; Attina and Stavridis 2001; Del Sarto 2006; Adler et al. 2006; Peterson and Sjursen 1998; Dannreuther 2004).

While the ENP is chiefly a bilateral policy between the EU and each partner country, the Union for the Mediterranean (UfM) is a regional and multilateral cooperation agreement which has found many difficulties in taking off, if it ever did. This happened especially because of the very tense relationships between Israel and the other members of the partnership after the Gaza war of 2008–2009, but also because of the institutional and financial characteristics of the UfM which make it very different from the Barcelona Process (Bicchi 2006, 2011; Diana 2011; Bicchi and Gillespie 2011; Montanari 2007).

In terms of south–south integration, the Agadir agreement, signed on 25 February 2004 to establish a free trade area between Jordan, Morocco, Egypt and Tunisia, entered into force in 2007.[21] The intention was, again, to build an Arab Common Market.[22] Yet in the light of recent political events and economic difficulties, it is debatable whether this project will be more successful than the one inaugurated in the 1960s.

Overall, the MENA region, far from benefiting from the general trend towards regionalisation, appears unable to pursue a successful regional integration exercise, not even from an economic viewpoint (Chorou 2004). Even in the globalisation era, the road ahead for the institutionalisation of economic integration of the MENA area seems impervious and full of uncertainties.

In the next section we will analyse in more depth the effective economic integration of the MENA region and the integration of the area into the global political economy.

The lack of economic integration in the MENA region

Investment and trade flows

Integration into the global political economy is generally assessed through the use of some main economic indicators (Mittelman 2000, Overbeek 2000; Hirst and Thompson 2009). These are: Foreign Direct Investment stock and inflows, the level of Mergers and Acquisitions, and production for exports. Below reference is made to such indicators to verify the degree of integration of the MENA region into the global political economy.[23]

The paradox of regionalisation (or lack thereof) and the paradox of marginalisation within globalisation emerge clearly already looking at the patterns of world stock FDIs.

Despite the dramatic increase of world FDI stock since 1980, it is worth noting that the biggest share of them is still held by developed nations (which have actually increased their share since 1980) (Figure 4.1).

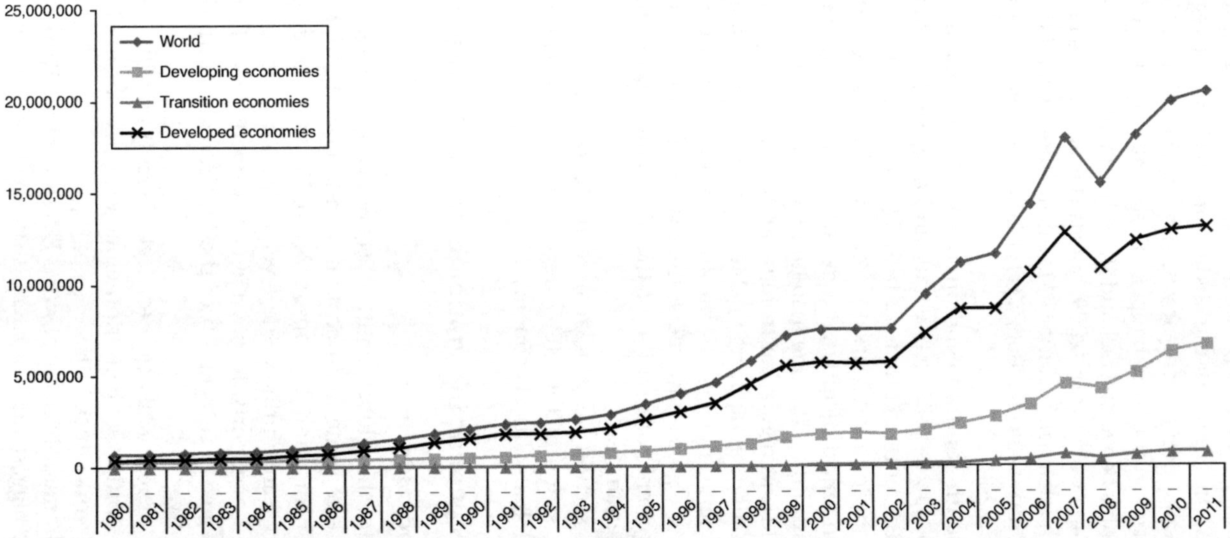

Figure 4.1 Stock of FDI: developed and developing economies (US$ Millions at current prices)

Source: UNCTAD, elaboration by the author

As far as developing countries are concerned, Asia is the region with the highest stock of FDI (Figure 4.2).

The Americas (Caribbean, Central and Southern America) record the second biggest share of FDI stock with 10 per cent in 2011, much higher than the 6.5 per cent of 1981. Instead, the MENA region is clearly lagging behind, with Northern African countries totalling only 1 per cent, of world FDI stock, a figure which has fallen even lower than the already pretty low level of 1.5 per cent of 1981 (Figure 4.3).

It is interesting to note that the three countries considered in this book all experienced a decrease in the percentage share of total FDI stock between 1981 and 2011, a clear indicator of their marginalisation from the global economy (Figure 4.4). In particular, in Egypt the share of global FDI stock moved from 0.4 per cent to 0.36 per cent, in Libya from 0.15 per cent to basically 0, and in Tunisia from 0.45 per cent to less than 0.15 per cent.

The degree of economic marginalisation of the three countries appears even more clearly from the dynamics of FDI inflows. Before the Arab

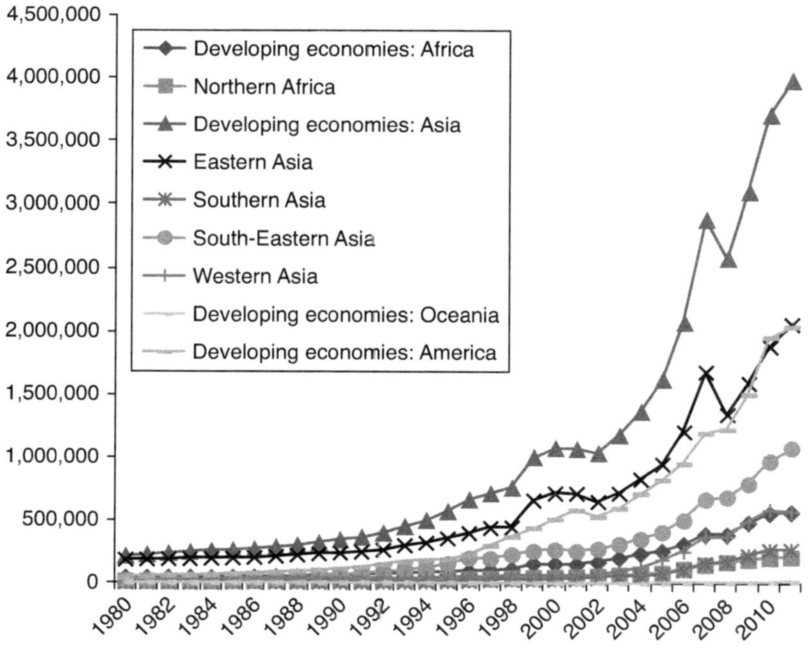

Figure 4.2 Stock of FDI: developing economies (US$ millions at current prices)
Source: UNCTAD, elaboration by the author

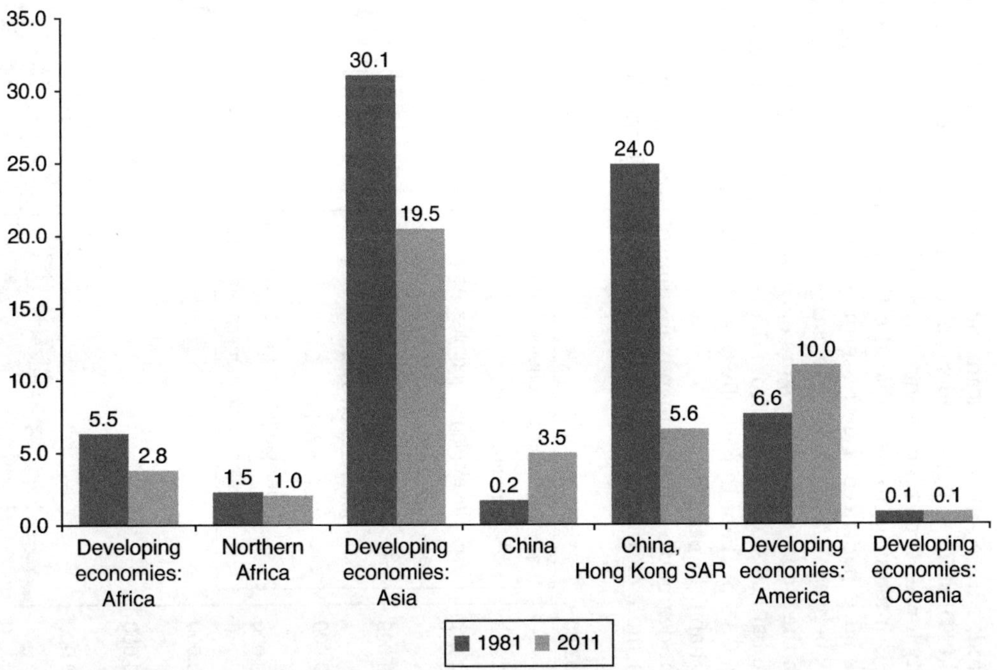

Figure 4.3 Percentage share of total FDI stock, 1981 and 2011

Source: UNCTAD, elaboration by the author

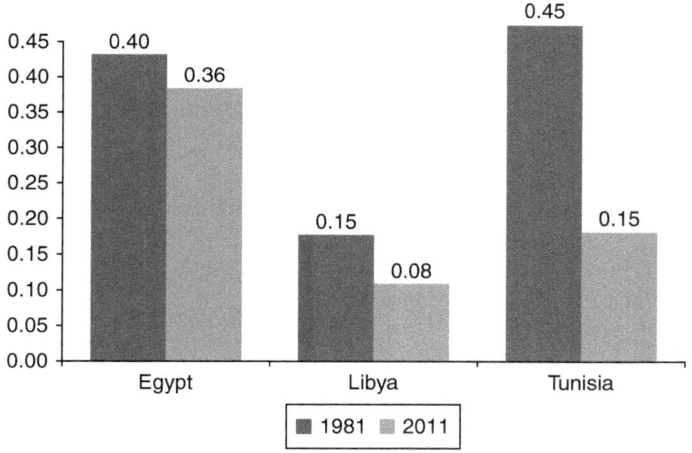

Figure 4.4 Egypt–Tunisia–Libya: per cent share of world total FDI stock, 1981 and 2011

Source: UNCTAD, elaboration by the author

Spring, in 2010, Egypt and Tunisia already presented a declining share of total world FDI inflows (Figure 4.5), which was exacerbated in all countries by the events of 2011.

An indicator often used in the literature to assess the degree of involvement of a region/country in the global political economy is the value of Mergers and Acquisitions. The biggest share of Mergers and Acquisitions is by far taking place between developed economies (78 per cent in 2011), especially in Europe (38 per cent). As far as developing countries are concerned, Asia is the region with the largest share of merger and acquisition sales, with 10.5 per cent in 2011, of which the majority took place in South-East, and East Asia (6.2 per cent). The MENA area, on the contrary, is clearly lagging behind with North Africa reporting a share of 1.37 per cent of total sales in 2011 and West Asia a similar figure of 1.85 per cent. In particular, before the uprisings the percentage share of sales over world total was already negligible in Egypt (0.06 per cent in 2010) and in Libya (0.03 per cent in 2010) and non-existent in Tunisia (0 per cent in 2010) (Table 4.1).

Finally, from the 1980s the share of exports from the MENA area fell substantially. This index is usually regarded as a measure of

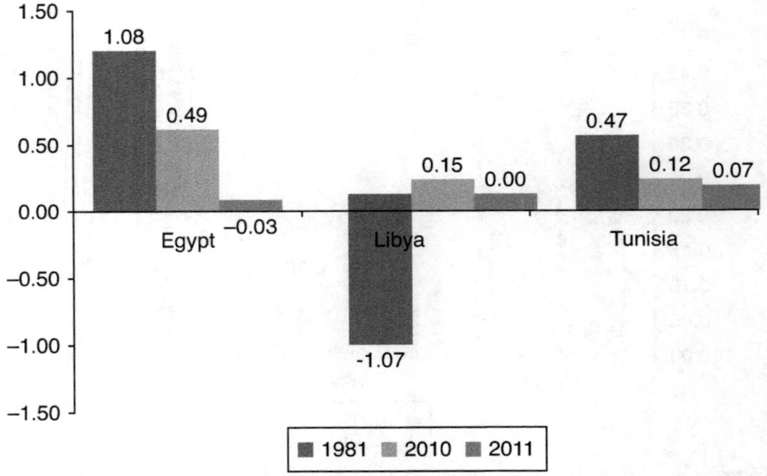

Figure 4.5 Egypt–Tunisia–Libya: per cent share of world total FDI flows 1981, 2010, 2011

Source: UNCTAD

Table 4.1 Mergers and acquisitions (sales) by country and region, 2010–2011

Region/economy	2011 Millions of $	2011 Share	2010 Millions of $	2010 Share
World	525,881		344,029	
Developed economies	409,691	77.91	257,152	74.75
Europe	200,363	38.1	124,973	36.33
European Union	172,257	32.76	115,974	33.71
Developing economies	83,220	15.82	82,378	23.95
Africa	7,205	1.37	8,072	2.35
North Africa	1,353	0.36	1,142	0.33
Algeria	–	0.00	–	0.00
Egypt	609	0.12	195	0.06
Libya	20	0.00	91	0.03
Morocco	274	0.05	846	0.25
Sudan	450	0.09	–	0.00
Tunisia	–	0.00	9	0.00
Asia	55,302	10.52	36,873	10.72
East and South-East Asia	32,715	6.22	26,417	7.68
East Asia	12,575	2.39	16,972	4.93
China	11,176	2.13	6,306	1.83
South-East Asia	20,139	3.83	9,445	2.75
South Asia	12,875	2.45	5,569	1.62

Continued

Table 4.1 Continued

	2011	2011	2010	2010
Region/economy	**Millions of $**	**Share**	**Millions of $**	**Share**
Bahrain	30	0.01	452	0.13
Iraq	717	0.14	–	0.00
Jordan	391	0.07	–103	–0.03
Kuwait	16	0.00	463	0.13
Lebanon	–	0.00	642	0.19
Oman	–	0.00	386	0.11
Qatar	28	0.01	13	0.00
Syrian Arab Republic	–	0.00	41	0.01
Turkey	7,348	1.40	2,053	0.60
United Arab Emirates	554	0.11	756	0.22
Yemen	–	0.00	20	0.01
Latin America and the Caribbean	20,689	3.93	28,414	8.26
Oceania	23	0.00	9,019	2.62
Transition economies	32,970	6.27	4,499	1.31
Least Developed countries(LDCs)	504	0.10	2,201	0.64

Note: Cross-border M&A sales are calculated on a net basis as follows: sales of companies in the host economy to foreign TNCs minus sales of foreign affiliates in the host economy. The data cover only those deals that involved an acquisition of an equity stake of more than 10%. Data refer to the net sales by the region/economy of the immediate acquired company

Source: UNCTAD cross-border M&A database(www.unctad.org/fdistatistics)

integration in the global political economy. In West Asia it went from the 9.5 per cent of 1981 to the 7 per cent of 2012, while in Northern Africa it moved from 1.9 per cent in 1981 to 1.1 per cent in 2012 (Figure 4.6).

Figure 4.7 below shows that the share of exports from Egypt and Tunisia remained basically stable (when it did not decline) and pretty low (always below 0.2 per cent) in the last 30 years.

In terms of intra-regional trade integration, as detailed in the previous section, there have been various attempts to promote trade integration in the MENA region, ranging from free trade areas, customs unions and even plans to establish common markets. Notwithstanding this, or perhaps as a result of the impossibility of identifying a successful regional economic arrangement, it is striking how limited the level of intra-regional trade still is. To start with, the total imports and exports of the MENA area with the rest of the world in 2011 were very limited (Figure 4.8).

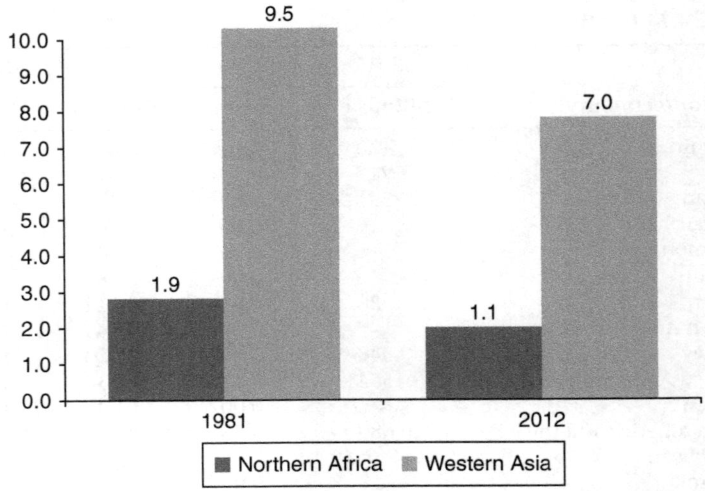

Figure 4.6 Share of exports to rest of the world from North Africa and West Asia, 1981 and 2012

Source: UNCTAD database, elaboration by the author

More specifically, the percentage share of intraregional exports in the MENA area is only a fraction of the percentages of regional trade with other parts of the world. IMF figures relating to the period from 2003 to 2011 show that the region exports mostly to advanced economies, while the share of intra-regional trade is just one tenth of the total (see Figure 4.9). Additionally, although the share of exports to emerging and developing countries has increased, the intra-regional share of total exports within the MENA area has hardly changed from the 1960s, remaining around 10 per cent.

What is noticeable from the data above is the increase of imports to the MENA area from other emerging and developing countries, whose share has increased by 18 per cent. The increase of imports from emerging and developing countries may have crowded out the potential for intra-regional integration by providing cheap goods produced by less developed countries in the region.

Data on the percentage share of exports to the Arab world (members of the Arab Monetary Fund) over total exports provide a similar picture. Indeed, total exports to Arab countries were always well below 10 per cent in the decade between 1997 and 2007 (Table 4.3).

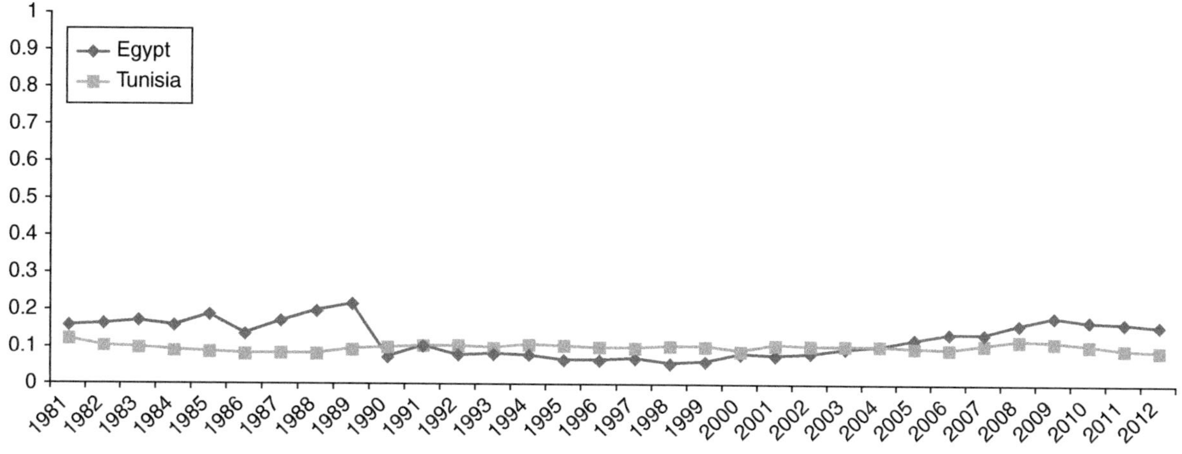

Figure 4.7 Share of exports to rest of the world from Egypt and Tunisia, 1981–2012

Source: UNCTAD database, elaboration by the author

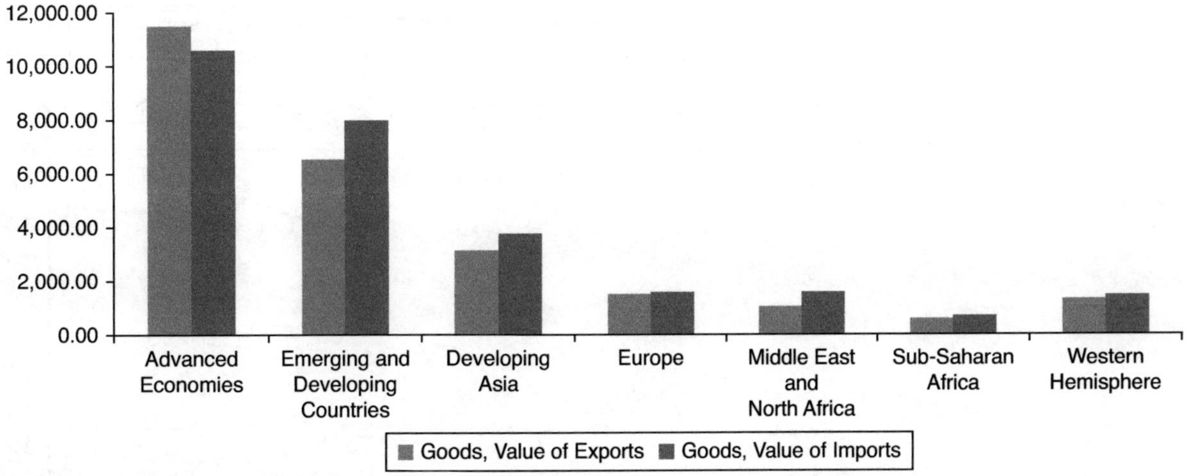

Figure 4.8 World exports and imports for 2011 (US$ millions)

Source: IMF database DOTS www.imf.org as accessed in July (2013)

Table 4.2 MENA exports and imports to partner regions as a share of world exports and imports, 2003–2011

	Exports									Imports								
	2003	2004	2005	2006	2007	2008	2009	2010	2011	2003	2004	2005	2006	2007	2008	2009	2010	2011
Advanced economies	67	64	64	61	58	58	53	51	51	61	58	58	56	55	51	53	49	45
Developing Asia	12	13	14	18	20	21	23	25	26	13	15	17	19	20	21	22	24	26
Emerging and developing countries	29	28	32	35	36	39	42	42	36	41	41	43	44	47	47	50	54	9
Middle East and North Africa	10	10	10	9	9	9	11	11	11	12	14	15	16	15	15	14	17	18
	2	2	2	2	2	2	2	2	2	1	1	1	1	1	1	1	1	1

Source: IMF DOTS, elaboration by the author

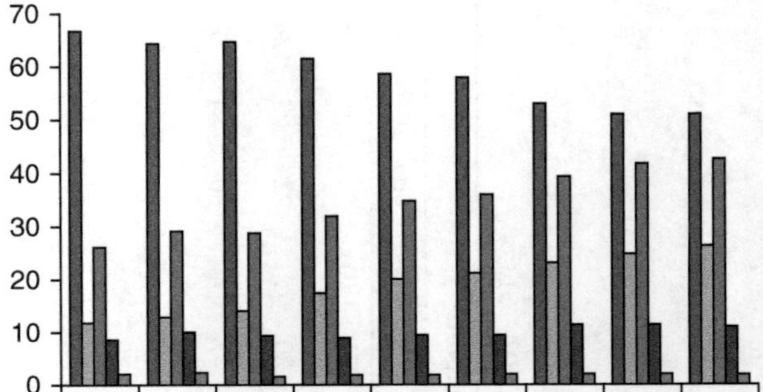

	2003	2004	2005	2006	2007	2008	2009	2010	2011
Advanced Economies	67	64	64	61	58	58	53	51	51
Developing Asia	12	13	14	18	20	21	23	25	26
Emerging and Developing Countries	26	29	28	32	35	36	39	42	42
Middle East and North Africa	9	10	10	9	9	9	11	11	11
Sub-Saharan Africa	2	2	2	2	2	2	2	2	2

Figure 4.9 Share of exports from the MENA region to other areas, 2003–2011
Source: IMF DOTS (2013)

Table 4.3 Percentage share of exports to other Arab countries over total exports, 1997–2007

	1997	1998	1999	2000	2001	2002	2003	2004	2005	2006	2007
Jordan	49.6	43.0	38.5	40.0	50.4	47.6	41.3	41.0	42.6	42.6	42.9
Emirates	4.8	6.3	5.3	4.5	5.4	6.1	6.4	6.5	4.6	5.9	5.4
Bahrain	12.7	16.8	13.3	8.0	10.9	11.0	12.0	11.0	11.1	11.5	12.6
Tunisia	7.6	7.2	6.9	7.4	8.4	9.2	7.7	6.8	8.8	9.3	9.1
Algeria	1.7	1.4	2.1	1.4	1.8	2.5	2.5	2.6	2.1	2.1	2.3
Saudi Arabia	10.9	12.9	10.0	7.8	9.2	9.4	10.9	11.7	11.9	12.7	12.5
Sudan	34.2	41.1	32.7	13.5	11.6	16.4	11.9	11.4	8.0	8.8	4.8
Syria	6.3	5.8	21.0	16.2	15.4	22.1	20.9	29.9	16.2	37.4	39.2
Somalia	83.5	85.5	94.7	92.2	73.4	62.9	79.3	80.0	84.0	86.9	87.2
Iraq	24.3	10.4	3.9	3.3	4.8	7.0	3.9	6.6	2.6	3.1	3.5
Oman	12.8	20.1	14.8	11.1	11.1	13.4	11.3	11.9	11.0	12.4	11.3
Qatar	8.6	6.1	8.2	5.4	3.5	8.0	4.4	5.3	5.6	5.9	4.5
Kuwait	2.8	4.2	3.4	2.3	3.0	3.3	3.0	5.5	2.8	2.7	2.8
Lebanon	48.6	44.8	43.5	45.8	44.5	48.6	41.8	53.0	53.5	43.8	47.0
Libya	6.0	7.0	6.5	4.1	3.3	5.1	4.1	3.6	3.0	2.4	3.2
Egypt	9.0	12.8	9.1	8.6	9.2	10.9	13.3	11.3	11.9	10.4	9.8
Morocco	4.2	4.0	4.0	3.5	4.1	3.7	3.4	3.3	3.4	3.5	3.5
Mauritania	0.9	0.8	0.0	1.1	2.6	1.2	2.6	3.7	0.8	1.8	3.4
Yemen	4.3	11.7	6.9	5.7	5.4	12.0	12.5	8.3	10.3	11.8	12.6
Total	8.2	9.5	8.0	6.1	7.1	8.5	8.2	8.7	7.7	8.5	8.3

Source: Elaboration by the author on data from the AMF

Overall, the ratio of inter-Arab trade to total external trade for all Arab countries members of the AMF between 1997 and 2007 was rarely above 10 per cent (Table 4.4 below).

In terms of trade openness of Middle Eastern economies, the World Bank calculates trade restrictiveness indexes annually. The Overall Trade Restrictiveness Index (OTRI) summarises the trade policy stance of a country by calculating the uniform tariff that will keep its overall imports at the current level when the country in fact has different tariffs for different goods. Other related indices are the Trade Restrictiveness Index (TRI) and the Market Access Overall Trade Restrictiveness Index (MAOTRI) and the Ad Valorem Equivalent of Non-tariff Barriers (Kee et al. 2008, 2009, forthcoming).[24]

From the figures in Table 4.5 it is particularly clear how resource-poor countries in the MENA area, especially Egypt, Libya and Tunisia, score very poorly in terms of trade openness.

Trade integration in the MENA area is rarely a subject of research in economics (a review is presented in Fazio 2009). Economists, however, point to the existence of a mismatch between the outcomes that economic theory would predict and the present level of trade integration in the MENA area, even within the existing trade blocs (such as the Gulf

Table 4.4 Ratio of total inter-Arab trade to total external trade

Country	1997	1998	1999	2000	2001	2002	2003	2004	2005	2006	2007
Jordan	13.12	13.95	13.99	18.71	24.35	30.03	33.42	36.71	51.51	61.68	66.86
Emirates	2.71	3.33	4.13	4.03	4.86	5.50	5.69	5.99	6.27	5.91	6.96
Bahrain	6.82	8.26	8.57	8.24	8.71	19.55	18.33	21.94	39.75	25.97	30.22
Tunisia	4.82	4.51	4.31	4.91	6.42	7.13	7.95	8.21	8.58	9.80	11.03
Algeria	1.39	1.97	1.34	1.27	1.53	2.06	2.83	2.73	2.69	2.53	2.60
Saudi Arabia	6.05	8.52	7.13	6.11	7.96	8.09	7.88	8.72	8.94	11.17	12.47
Sudan	6.74	8.28	15.95	12.98	14.64	14.48	29.75	27.95	21.95	27.44	22.70
Syria	7.98	10.66	2.33	10.67	11.53	11.57	21.85	21.81	22.19	18.71	18.98
Somalia	22.71	31.22	34.87	50.06	45.80	52.84	71.59	73.87	79.23	79.75	95.40
Iraq	2.22	3.47	1.90	2.43	4.48	7.00	7.52	8.67	12.77	25.32	26.54
Oman	10.98	17.15	17.63	14.82	17.41	18.89	21.23	17.88	19.07	18.58	17.83
Qatar	4.16	4.98	6.04	6.64	7.89	6.13	9.56	6.67	7.55	10.08	8.30
Kuwait	4.61	5.84	5.88	4.70	5.97	6.83	6.11	5.82	6.62	5.57	5.95
Lebanon	12.67	10.00	9.26	10.82	14.92	16.05	15.55	19.59	25.39	23.88	23.47
Libya	4.14	6.88	6.86	5.05	5.40	5.66	6.43	5.17	3.47	3.77	3.86
Egypt	2.61	3.74	5.45	6.67	9.64	7.80	6.88	6.89	9.80	12.18	15.05
Morocco	3.85	4.26	4.01	5.51	8.90	8.66	8.27	7.64	8.81	13.39	13.99
Mauritania	2.34	3.88	3.28	2.69	4.41	6.15	9.05	9.42	36.75	10.82	13.05
Yemen	7.69	10.36	13.07	12.85	16.58	20.97	28.72	33.42	24.58	30.46	40.85
Total	4.82	6.18	5.96	5.94	7.71	8.50	8.97	8.95	9.76	10.79	11.65

Source: Arab Monetary Fund

Table 4.5 Trade restrictiveness indices of selected MENA countries, 2009

	Indices based on applied tariffs												Indices based on MFN tariffs					
	OTRI			OTRI_T			MAOTRI			MAOTRI_T			OTRI			OTRI_T		
	ALL	AG	MF	ALL	AG	MF	ALL	AG	MF	ALL	AG	MF	ALL	AG	MF	ALL	AG	MF
United Arab Emirates	3.0%	3.8%	3.0%	3.0%	3.8%	3.0%	5.1%	14.3%	4.7%	3.3%	4.6%	3.2%	3.2%	4.2%	3.2%	3.2%	4.2%	3.2%
Bahrain	4.3%	6.8%	4.2%	4.3%	6.8%	4.2%	3.1%	9.1%	3.0%	1.0%	1.1%	1.0%	4.9%	7.9%	4.7%	4.9%	7.9%	4.7%
Egypt Arab Rep.	**33.4%**	**44.0%**	**31.6%**	**8.8%**	**14.1%**	**7.9%**	**12.1%**	**25.0%**	**10.3%**	**2.1%**	**5.4%**	**1.7%**	**34.4%**	**45.1%**	**32.6%**	**9.8%**	**15.3%**	**8.9%**
Iraq						0.4%	24.0%	30.0%	40.0%	22.3%	30.0%							
Jordan	22.3%	21.1%	22.6%	5.2%	7.2%	4.9%	11.1%	16.1%	10.7%	2.3%	10.0%	1.7%	25.6%	25.7%	25.6%	8.5%	11.8%	7.9%
Kuwait	3.8%	1.4%	4.1%	3.8%	1.4%	4.1%	8.2%	10.0%	9.0%	6.2%	0.0%	6.7%	4.3%	2.0%	4.7%	4.3%	2.0%	4.7%
Lebanon							5.0%	9.3%	4.3%	1.0%	1.1%	90.0%						
Libya							**1.1%**	**44.2%**	**0.4%**	**90.0%**	**43.4%**	**20.0%**						
Morocco	15.5%	60.2%	9.8%	7.7%	20.9%	6.0%	18.3%	35.9%	12.1%	2.4%	3.4%	2.0%	23.0%	65.8%	17.7%	15.2%	26.4%	13.8%
Mauritania							16.5%	61.5%	10.0%	70.0%	2.6%	0.0%						
Oman	6.3%	38.7%	3.2%	2.6%	2.6%	2.6%	3.0%	5.7%	2.9%	1.1%	1.3%	1.0%	7.9%	40.2%	4.9%	4.3%	4.1%	4.3%
Qatar	3.9%	1.9%	4.0%	3.9%	1.9%	4.0%	4.5%	1.6%	4.5%	1.4%	40.0%	1.4%	4.7%	2.6%	4.8%	4.7%	2.6%	4.8%
Saudi Arabia	1.4%	1.8%	1.4%	80.0%	70.0%	80.0%	2.4%	7.3%	2.3%	1.1%	1.8%	1.1%	1.6%	2.0%	1.5%	90.0%	80.0%	1.0%
Sudan	44.1%	44.3%	44.1%	17.5%	15.0%	17.8%	2.1%	28.4%	20.0%	1.0%	12.6%	0.2%	47.0%	50.4%	46.5%	20.3%	21.1%	20.2%
Somalia							4.1%	4.3%	1.8%	1.9%	2.0%	1.5%						
Syrian Arab Republic	6.7%	7.7%	6.4%	6.7%	7.7%	6.4%	7.0%	18.1%	4.6%	1.1%	3.0%	0.7%	7.9%	9.4%	7.5%	7.9%	9.4%	7.5%
Tunisia							**12.0%**	**35.9%**	**9.9%**	**1.6%**	**10.8%**	**0.8%**						
Yemen	4.6%	4.8%	4.5%	4.6%	4.8%	4.5%	1.7%	14.6%	0.6%	0.6%	2.8%	0.4%	6.1%	6.7%	5.8%	6.1%	6.7%	5.8%

Source: World Bank

Cooperation Council) (Al-Atreash and Yousef 1999). Some authors have explored the possibility of an increase in trade and monetary integration in Africa as a consequence of the introduction of the euro (Honohan and Lane 2000; Masson 2007; Subramanian and Tamirisa 2003). They all seem to be very negative about the prospects for further intra-regional trade integration in Africa and in the Middle East.

Fazio (2009), using a gravity model specification to identify the emergence of trade blocs along different geographical directions, concludes that, within the Euro-Mediterranean Partnership, EU trade nevertheless remains clearly dominant. Moreover, North European trade still dominates trade within the EU. Southern Mediterranean trade is still below average, and the integration between the EU and the Southern Mediterranean, despite the introduction of the euro, is still very limited.

In conclusion, far from catching up with the rest of the world, the MENA area seems to be increasingly marginalised from the global political economy. Indeed, the analysis of all usual indicators of integration, such as the level and share of global FDIs, the number and values of mergers and acquisitions, and the performance of exports and trade openness, indicates a growing peripherisation of the area. Moreover, intra-regional trade integration has been, at best, stable for the last 30 years.

Below, the degree of inter-Arab solidarity is assessed with reference to aid capital flows.

Inter-Arab aid capital flows

The analysis of official development assistance (ODA) does not seem to confirm the existence of a pattern of integration in the MENA region. In fact, far from showing intra-Arab solidarity, aid flows seem to be highly influenced by external factors, such as the increase of oil prices in the 1970s, their decrease in the 1980s, and geopolitical interests of both intra- and extra-regional actors in the 1990s and 2000s (Zahlan 1999). It is worth noting that, together with remittances, intra-regional assistance transfers represent the bulk of intraregional capital flows (Zahlan 1999).

To start with, the level of intra-regional assistance in the Arab world has been highly variable over the course of the years. OECD data show that while in the early 1970s total aid flows to Arab countries were limited, they peaked in 1977 at almost $16 billion (Harrigan et al. 2005: 247–270). As already noticed in the previous section, however, similar transfers were principally a way for oil-rich countries to redistribute part of their wealth to resource-poor ones. On the contrary, after the oil price

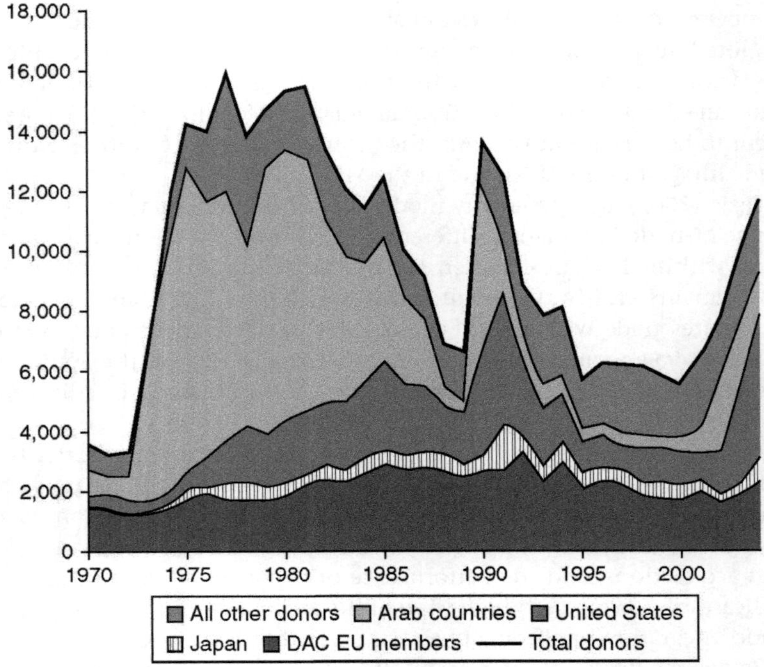

Figure 4.10 Real flows of net ODA to the Arab region, 1970–2004 (US$ millions)
Source: OECD, as quoted by UN-ESCWA (2007)

collapse of 1986, these amounts were substantially reduced to the level of $6.7 billion in 1989 (World Bank 2010: xiii).

ODA in the region increased again over the course of the Gulf War, during 1990 and 1991, but in this occasion it was because of the financial intervention of Western countries, especially the USA. The main country to benefit from these additional funds was Egypt. When the first Iraq War ended, foreign assistance declined, reaching a low of $5.7 billion in 1995. Money first returned to flow in the region in the autumn of 2000, when the second intifada started, and again with the outbreak of the second Iraq War in March 2003. As a result, by 2004 Arab countries were receiving aid money for an amount of almost $12 billion, a substantial amount which nevertheless does not compare to the sums transferred in the late 1970s and early 1980s (UN Economic and Social Commission for Western Asia 2007: 7).

As far as intra-regional aid is concerned, Saudi Arabia has traditionally been the main donor Arab country in the region. Table 4.6 below

Table 4.6 Nominal aid flows from Arab sources, 1970–2010 (US$ millions)

	1970–74	1975–79	1980–84	1985–89	1990–94	1995–99	2000–04	2005	2006	2007	2008	2009	2010	1970–2010	Percentage change 2009–10	Countries share in total 1970–2010
Total Arab countries	7.696	31,870	32.741	15.515	13.429	6.811	15,170	1.878	3.263	3.508	6.363	4,550	4,360	147.154	–4.2	100.0
GCC countries	6.611	29,130	30,450	14.831	13,190	6.811	15,170	1.878	3.263	3.508	6.363	4,550	4,360	140,115	–4.2	95.2
United Arab Emirates	923	4,857	2,768	272	1,957	482	804	137	231	464	114	46	47	13,102	2.2	8.9
Saudi Arabia*	4,013	18,515	21,503	12,253	8,698	4,359	12,339	1,101	2,187	2,181	5,663	4,004	3,702	100,517	–7.5	68.3
Oman	...	...	6	198	189	77	118	36	17	3	25	22	32	723	45.5	0.5
Qatar	279	1,076	692	28	44	187	408	138	515	426	225	178	309	4,505	73.6	3.1
Kuwait **	1,396	4,682	5,481	2,080	2,302	1,706	1,501	466	314	434	336	300	270	21,268	–9.8	14.4
Other Arab countries	1,085	2,740	2,291	684	239	...	...	...	...	...	...	...	...	7,039	...	4.8
Algeria	73	449	354	262	45	...	...	...	...	...	...	...	...	1,183	...	0.8
Iraq	453	1,577	1,091	–76	76	...	...	...	...	...	...	...	...	3,121	...	2.1
Libya	559	714	846	498	118	...	...	...	...	...	...	...	...	2,735	...	1.9

* Data for the years 1990–2010 are from the Saudi Ministry of finance; they represent total development aid

** Data for 2010 is estimated

... Unavailable

Sources: National data; Joint Arab Economic Report (2011), various issues; OECD, Development Co-operation Report, various issues

shows that Saudi Arabia provided for more than 68 per cent of total Arab donations in the period between 1970 and 2010. In particular, in the period between 2000 and 2004 Saudi Arabia provided 78 per cent of total official aid assistance, according to the United Nations Economic and Social Commission for Western Asia (ESCWA) (UN-ESCWA 2007: 7). Total net ODA given by Saudi Arabia in 2004 was estimated to be $1,734 million, which corresponds to 47 per cent of total non-DAC donors (where DAC countries are the members of the Development Assistance Committee) (UN-ESCWA 2007: 7). Saudi Arabia does not provide intra-regional aid through multilateral organisations but rather on a bilateral basis, through the government or the Saudi Fund for Development (Saudi Fund) extending soft loans directly to the governments of recipient states. The UN has estimated that between 1975 and 2005, the Saudi Fund provided assistance to 71 countries for a total of $6.83 billion (UN-ESCWA 2007: 8). Around 50 per cent of this money was allocated to infrastructure and energy projects; 21 per cent to social projects, including health and education; and the rest went to help productive activities, mainly agriculture and industry. In 2005 the Fund was committed for an amount of $214 million, which was mainly allocated to Algeria, Ivory Coast, Ethiopia, Lebanon, Morocco and Turkey. According to the Arab Monetary Fund the Saudi Fund extended $7,636.9 million in loans from its establishment until 2004 (see Table 4.7).

Kuwait and the United Arab Emirates are the two other main Arab donors in the area. They have accounted for around 14.4 per cent and 9 per cent of total Arab aid respectively between 1970 and 2010 (see Table 4.6). In 2004 Kuwait provided $209 million ODA (UN-ESCWA 2007: 8). The Kuwait Fund for Arab Economic Development (Kuwait Fund) was managing this money which was extended through both bilateral and multilateral donations. Overall, it is estimated that during the period from its establishment until 2004 the Kuwait Fund provided loans totalling $13,014.4 million (see Table 4.7). The majority of these transfers were directed to other Arab countries and were used to finance mainly transport, communication and energy infrastructure projects. In addition, the Fund also financed projects in agriculture and industry, technical assistance and financial studies (UN-ESCWA 2007: 8). In 2004, the loan commitments of the Kuwait Fund amounted to $372 million, and they were allocated to Afghanistan, Bahrain, Bangladesh, China, Egypt, Mauritania and Palestine (UN-ESCWA 2007: 8).

Table 4.7 Arab-based national, regional and multilateral ODA, 2004 (US$ millions)

	Total aid extended since creation	**To Arab region**	**To Africa**	**To Asia**	**To Latin America**	**To other countries**	**Share of each institution**
Regional Arab institutions							
Arab fund (AFESD)	15923.4	15923.4	0	0	0	0	21.98
Arab Monetary Fund	4293	4293	0	0	0	0	5.93
Sub-total	20216.4	20216.4	0	0	0	0	27.91
National institutions for ODA							
Abu Dhabi fund	3316.8	2595.6	147	567	0	7.2	4.58
Saudi fund	7636.9	3674.7	1440.6	2367.8	59.9	93.9	10.54
Kuwait fund	13014.4	6965.1	2280.5	3196	302.5	270.3	17.97
Sub-total	23968.1	13235.4	3868.1	6130.8	362.4	371.4	33.09
Share of each beneficiary region	100	55.22	16.14	25.58	1.51	1.55	
Non-exclusively Arab institutions							
Islamic bank	20528.3	10049.2	2014.6	8422.7	17.5	24.3	28.34
Arab Bank for the Development of Africa	2348	9.6	2338.4	0	0	0	3.24
OPEC fund	5371	955.3	2173.7	1547.4	641	53.6	7.42
Sub-total	28247.3	11014.1	6526.7	9970.1	658.5	77.9	39.00
Share of each beneficiary region	100	38.99	23.11	35.3	2.33	0.28	
Total Arab and associated funds	72431.8	44465.9	10394.8	16101	1020.9	449.3	100.00
Total share of each beneficiary region	100	61.39	14.35	22.23	1.41	0.62	

Source: UN (2007), from data of the Arab Unified Economic Report (AUER) 2005

Between 2004 and 2008, ODA flows from Arab sources increased. In Saudi Arabia, petroleum export prices swelled from $36 per barrel in 2004 to an average of $93 per barrel in 2008. As a result, official reserves moved from $84 billion in 2004 to a peak of $424 billion in 2008, providing ample possibilities for financing ODA outflows. Kuwait and UAE experienced a similar trend. Arab ODA is estimated to have almost doubled in 2008 from the previous year reaching over $6 billion. The bulk of this amount came from Saudi Arabia. In 2009, the fall of oil revenues contributed to a reduction of foreign exchange reserves in the three countries and this was reflected in lower ODA transfers (World Bank 2010: 5–10). In 2010, Arab development assistance was estimated at $4.36 billion, averaging 0.4 per cent of their combined gross national income (GNI). In the period 1970–2010, total development assistance by Arab donors reached $147.15 billion of which 68.3 per cent was provided by Saudi Arabia, 14.4 per cent by Kuwait, 8.9 per cent by UAE and 3.1 per cent by Qatar (AMF, (2011): Annex tables 11/1, 11/2 and figure 11.1).

While in the 1970s and 1980s the Gulf countries which were members of the GCC, aside from Saudi Arabia, contributed to total Arab donations considerably, more recently their role has been negligible (Figure 4.11).

It is, however, important to note that while the total sum disbursed by Arab countries to the Arab region is certainly relevant, still most of ODA to the region comes from non-Arab sources (see Table 4.8). Indeed,

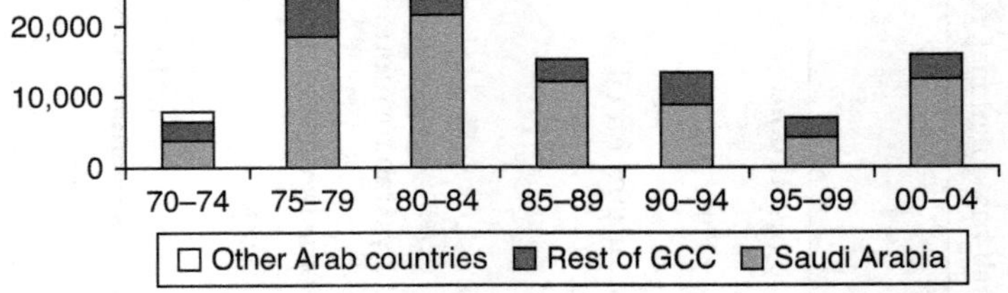

Figure 4.11 Amount of Arab aid donations, annual averages, 1970–2004 (US$ millions)

Note: Data include donations to non-Arab countries
Source: UN-ESCWA (2007)

Table 4.8 Top five donors of gross ODA, 2003–2004, averages (US$ millions)

Algeria		Bahrain		Comoros		Djibouti	
France	165	Arab Countries	95.6	France	13.9	France	25
EC	72	France	0.93	IDA	5.9	IDA	20
Spain	26	Japan	0.23	EC	4	Japan	8
Italy	25	UNTA	0.17	UNTA	1.8	EC	7
Germany	11	Germany	0.06	UNICEF	0.7	United States	5
Egypt		**Iraq**		**Jordan**		**Lebanon**	
United States	767	United States	2286	United States	666	EC	61
EC	160	Japan	333	UNRWA	89	France	55
France	149	United Kingdom	228	Japan	72	UNRWA	54
Germany	134	Netherlands	107	Germany	71	United States	29
Arab Countries	104	EC	99	EC	59	Japan	14
Libyan Arab Jamahiriya		**Mauritania**		**Morocco**		**Oman**	
France	2.6	Japan	54	France	302	Arab countries	62.2
Germany	2.58	EC	51	EC	184	Belgium	6.3
Italy	1.73	IDA	49	Japan	89	Japan	4
Turkey	0.77	France	48	Arab countries	82	France	0.8
UNHCR	0.7	United States	19	Germany	75	UNTA	0.8
Palestine		**Somalia**		**Sudan**		**Syrian Arab Republic**	
UNRWA	268	EC	38	United States	277	EC	70
United States	234	Norway	37	EC	158	Arab countries	48
EC	184	United States	33	United Kingdom	75	Japan	31
Norway	54	Netherlands	15	Norway	45	UNRWA	28
Sweden	37	Italy	12	Germany	32	France	23
Tunisia		**Yemen**					
France	167	IDA	91				
Japan	110	Germany	34				
EC	104	United States	33				
Germany	46	Japan	30				
Italy	41	Netherlands	29				

Source: UN (2007), from OECD data

only in Syria, Egypt and Morocco are Arab countries among the top five donors as data relating to gross ODA for the year 2003–2004 by main donors per country shows. Whereas in the period between 1970 and 2004, Syria received 84 per cent of its total aid from Arab countries (see Table 4.9), Morocco and the other Maghreb countries were mainly financed by the EU, and Egypt and Iraq received most of their funds from the US (38 and 48 per cent of total ODA respectively during 1970–2004) (see Table 4.9). Finally, countries in conflict were aided mostly by multilateral organisations (under the label 'Other donors' in Table 4.9). Palestine, for example, received 50 per cent of total aid from this source.

The figure below shows the share of Arab assistance and extra-regional assistance to Arab countries for the period 1970–2008. In cumulative terms it is only in Bahrain, Oman and Syria that Arab ODA accounts for the bulk (over 70 per cent) of total ODA from all sources. However, in Syria, for example, the share of the total ODA that came from Arab sources declined tremendously between the 1970s, when it was 90 per cent, and the last decade when it was less than 20 per cent. In countries such as Morocco, Lebanon, Yemen and Jordan, Arab ODA represents between 20 and 40 per cent of total ODA. However, in Jordan and Yemen, Arab ODA was significant only prior to the Gulf War of 1990 and 1991, while in Lebanon the share of Arab ODA is still important but has dropped over time. Finally, in places such as the West Bank and Gaza, Somalia, Sudan, Turkey, Egypt, Mauritania and Djibouti, over the last 40 years the level of cumulative Arab ODA accounted for only 10–20 per cent of the total. Moreover, in Somalia, Sudan and Turkey the share of Arab ODA dropped since 1990 while in Egypt it has been declining since the 1970s (World Bank 2010: 14).

Concluding, it is worth underlining the following. First, intra-regional aid in the MENA area is heavily influenced by geopolitical considerations. Second, notwithstanding the revival of Arab official assistance to the region in the wake of the second Iraq War, currently aid flows from Arab sources are less relevant than in the late 1970s and early 1980s. However, even during this period they were mainly redistributive in nature. Finally, countries relying heavily on external aid, such as Egypt, have been receiving it mainly from countries outside the region (such as the US in the case of Egypt). Thus, as far as the redistribution of aid capital flows is concerned, the MENA region does not appear particularly integrated.

Table 4.9 Cumulative net ODA to selected Arab recipients by major donors, 1970–2004

	United States		DAC members of the EU		Japan		Arab donors		Other donors		All donors
	(Millions of $)	(%)	(Millions of $)	(%)	(Millions of $)	(%)	(Millions of $)	(%)	(Millions of $)	(%)	(Millions of $)
Algeria	19	0	8,123	71	114	1	829	7	2,353	21	11,401
Bahrain	0	0	47	1	19	0	3,944	97	64	2	1,074
Comoros	12	1	1,067	51	60	3	241	11	732	35	2,112
Djibouti	98	2	2,328	59	169	4	687	17	689	17	3,971
Egypt	38489	38	17,606	17	4,957	5	30,128	30	9,802	10	100,982
Iraq	5308	48	2,255	20	1,186	11	296	3	2,048	18	11,092
Jordan	5248	17	3,185	10	1,868	6	17,842	56	3,605	11	31,748
Lebanon	703	8	1,727	21	55	1	3,508	42	2,296	28	8,289
Libyan Arab Jamahiriya	0	0	355	53	6	1	3	0	304	46	668
Mauritania	462	5	2,729	27	441	4	2,661	26	3,889	38	10,182
Morocco	1,820	6	11,375	40	1,193	4	9,356	33	4,753	17	28,497
Oman	247	6	88	2	130	3	3,657	87	104	2	4,227
Palestine	1,135	12	1,926	21	254	3	1,576	17	4,471	48	9,362
Somalia	2,647	17	4,694	30	181	1	2,556	17	5,324	35	15,402
Sudan	3,400	13	7,013	26	811	3	6,389	24	9,368	35	26,981
Syrian Arab Republic	547	2	1,584	5	1,157	3	27,968	84	2,050	6	33,307
Tunisia	677	5	7,406	55	793	6	1,323	10	3,340	25	13,539
Yemen	971	5	3,339	18	839	4	9,028	48	4,663	25	18,840

Notes: Percentages in the table represent the share of various donors to total aid for each of the respective recipient countries. Kuwait, Qatar, Saudi Arabia and United Arab Emirates are major Arab donors and were therefore excluded from the table. 'Other donors' includes multilateral organisations.

Source: UN 2007, from OECD data

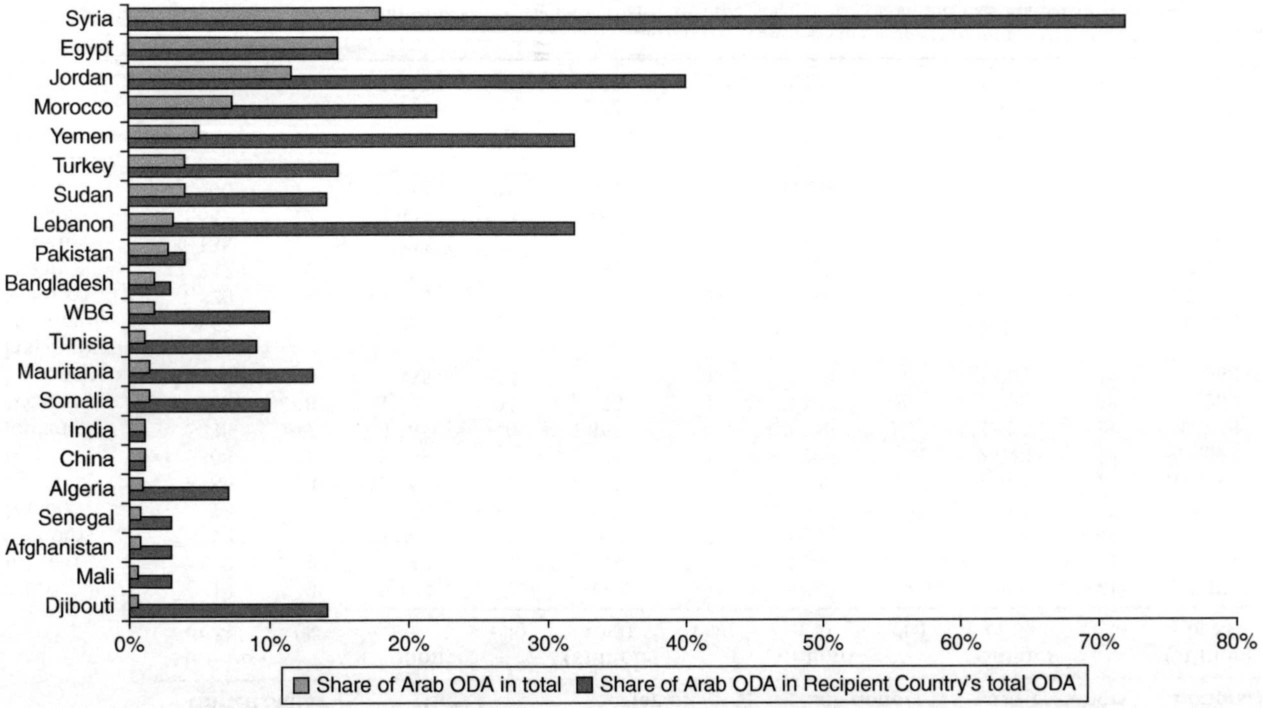

Figure 4.12 Share of Arab assistance over total assistance to Arab countries, 1970–2008 (%)

Source: World Bank (2010)

Conclusion

The analysis presented in this chapter points to the conclusion that to talk of integration in the MENA region is an oxymoron. It would be more appropriate, following the relevant literature, to refer to the process of MENA regional (dis)integration.

Indeed, contrary to the dynamics experienced by other regions of the globe the Arab region is still fundamentally and increasingly divided and lacks both *de jure* and *de facto* integration. This is most notably so in comparison with the three regions identified in the literature as the 'triad', namely Europe, the Americas and South Eastern Asia, which have achieved high and increasing levels of economic and institutional integration.

On the basis of the analysis of intra-regional aid flows, it seems inappropriate even to exaggerate the role of solidarity among the Muslim 'Umma' as a stable path to integration. Indeed, ODAs within the region seem to have been primarily determined by geopolitical considerations. In addition, financial support has not been provided exclusively, or even predominantly, by Arab countries.

With such considerations in mind, it seems possible to conclude that the MENA region is notably lacking in economic and political integration in the wake of the globalisation era. The MENA region is thus a clear example of the paradox of a lack of regionalisation within globalisation and of economic marginalisation from the global political economy.

The next three chapters will assess the level of integration into the global political economy of the three countries under analysis starting with the case of Tunisia.

Notes

1. For an analysis of the reasons underlying the lack of integration of the ME area, see Kubursi (1999).
2. See IMF world economic outlook on-line, website: http://www.imf.org/external/pubs/ft/weo/2012/02/weodata/weoselagr.aspx#a406 as accessed on 8 April 2013
3. See IMF website: http://www.imf.org/external/pubs/ft/weo/data/assump.htm as accessed on 8 April 2013
4. For the full text of the treaty see http://avalon.law.yale.edu/20th_century/arabjoin.asp as accessed on 10 April 2013
5. For the full text of the convention see http://www.wto.org/gatt_docs/English/SULPDF/90760427.pdf as accessed on 10 April 2013
6. For the original text of the Agreement see http://www.wto.org/gatt_docs/English/SULPDF/90780034.pdf as accessed on 8 April 2013.

7. For the original text of the Agreement see http://www.wto.org/gatt_docs/English/SULPDF/90780034.pdf as accessed on 8 April 2013.
8. See http://www.adfd.ae/pages/default.aspx as accessed on 10 April 2013.
9. See www.kuwait-fund.org as accessed on 10 April 2013.
10. See www.saudinf.com as accessed on 10 April 2013.
11. The Iraq Fund ceased to distribute funds in 1982 (Van den Boogaerde 1991).
12. See www.gcc-sg.org/eng as accessed on 10 April 2013.
13. All figures in $ refer to United States dollars unless otherwise stated.
14. For the full text of the Barcelona declaration see http://trade.ec.europa.eu/doclib/docs/2005/july/tradoc_124236.pdf
15. See http://ec.europa.eu/trade/creating-opportunities/bilateral-relations/regions/euromed/
16. See http://www.eeas.europa.eu/euromed/index_En.htm
17. Unver Noi (2011)
18. The Gaza War, known in Israel as Operation Cast Lead and in Gaza and by Hamas as the Gaza Massacre or the Battle of al-Furqan [the criterion] was a three-week armed conflict in the Gaza Strip between Israel and Palestinian militants during the winter of 2008–2009. It began on 27 December 2008 and ended on 18 January 2009 with each side declaring a unilateral ceasefire.
19. For more information see website: http://ec.europa.eu/world/enp/faq_En.htm#1.6 as accessed on 9 April 2013.
20. http://ec.europa.eu/europeaid/where/neighbourhood/overview/how-does-enpi-work_En.htm
21. For the full text of the agreement see website: http://www.agadiragreement.org/CMS/UploadedFiles/10ac3206–5a49–4dd8–833e-0783d2ea4190.pdf as accessed on 9 April 2013.
22. See Jordan Ministry of Industry and trade website: http://www.mit.gov.jo/Default.aspx?tabid=733 as accessed on 9 April 2013.
23. Others prefer to use absolute numbers which are not provided here for the theoretical reasons so far discussed. See Clement Moore and Springborg (2010).
24. Definitions:Overall Trade Restrictiveness Index (OTRI): The OTRI captures the trade policy distortions that each country imposes on its import bundle. It measures the uniform tariff equivalent of the country tariff and non-tariff barriers (NTB) that would generate the same level of import value for the country in a given year. Tariffs can be based on the MFN tariffs which applied to all trading partners, or the Applied tariffs, which takes into account the bilateral trade preferences. The Ad Valorem Equivalents of NTB were estimated by Kee et al. (, 2009).Tariff-only Overall Trade Restrictiveness Index (OTRI_T): The OTRI_T is the OTRI that only focuses on tariffs of each country. No NTBs are considered in the calculation of OTRI_T. Similar to OTRI, tariffs can be based on both MFN and Applied tariffs.Market Access Overall Trade Restrictiveness Index (MAOTRI): The MAOTRI captures the trade policy distortions imposed by the trading partners of each country on its export bundle. It measures the uniform tariff equivalent of the partner country tariff and non-tariff barriers (NTB) that would generate the same level of export value for the country in a given year. Tariffs can be based on the MFN tariffs which applied to all trading partners, or the Applied tariffs, which takes into

account the bilateral trade preferences. The Ad Valorem Equivalents of NTB were estimated by Kee et al. (2009).Tariff-only Market Access Overall Trade Restrictiveness Index (MAOTRI_T): The MAOTRI_T is the MAOTRI that only focuses on the tariffs of the trading partners of each country. No NTBs are considered in the calculation of MAOTRI_T. Similar to MAOTRI, tariffs can be based on both MFN and Applied tariffs.

References

Abdulla, A.K. (1999). 'The Gulf Cooperation Council: Nature, Origin and Process', in Hudson, M.C. (ed.) *Middle East Dilemma: The Politics and Economics of Arab Integration*. Columbia University Press, New York, ch. 7.

Adler, E., Crawford, B., Bicchi, F., and Del Sarto, R.A. (eds) (2006). *The Convergence of Civilisations: Constructing a Mediterranean Region*. University of Toronto Press.

Al-Atreash, H.M., and Yousef, T. (1999). *Intra-Arab Trade – Is it too little?* IMF Working Paper, WP/00/10.

Aliboni, R. (2005). The Geopolitical Implications of the European Neighbourhood Policy. *European Foreign Affairs Review*, 10(1), 1–16.

Arab Monetary Fund (2011). Joint Arab Economic Report, At: http://www.amf.org.ae/content/joint-arab-economic-report accessed on 22 July 2013

Asseburg, M. (2004). 'The EU and the Middle East Conflict: Tackling the Main Obstacle to Euro-Mediterranean Partnership', in Junemann, A. (ed.) *Euro-Mediterranean Relations after September the 11th: International, Regional and Domestic Dynamics*. Frank-Cass, London, pp. 174–194.

Attina, F., and Stavridis, S. (eds) (2001). *The Barcelona Process and Euro-Mediterranean Issues from Stuttgart to Marseille*. Giuffre, Milan.

Balfour, R. and Missiroli, A. (2007). *Reassessing the European Neighbourhood Policy*. EPC Issue Paper No.54. June 2007.

Bicchi, F. (2006). 'Our Size Fits All': Normative Power Europe and the Mediterranean. *Journal of European Public Policy*, 13(2), 286–303.

Bicchi, F. (2007). *European Foreign Policy Making Toward the Mediterranean. Europe in Transition: NYU EU Studies*. Palgrave Macmillan, New York.

Bicchi, F. (2011). The Union for the Mediterranean, or the Changing Context of Euro-Mediterranean Relations. *Mediterranean Politics*, 16(1).

Bicchi, F., and Gillespie, R. (2011). 'The Union for the Mediterranean: Continuity or Change in Euro-Mediterranean Relations?' – special issue, edited by Bicchi, F. and Gillespie, R. *Mediterranean Politics*, 16 (1), ISSN 1362–9395.

Clement Moore, H., and Springborg, R. (2010). *Globalization and the Politics of Development in the Middle East*. Cambridge University Press.

Chorou, B. (2004). 'Arab Regional Integration as a Prerequisite for a Successful Euro-Mediterranean Partnership', in Junemann, A. (ed.) *Euro-Mediterranean Relations after September the 11th: International, Regional and Domestic Dynamics*. Frank-Cass, London, pp. 194–214.

Dannreuther, R. (ed.) (2004). *European Union Foreign and Security Policy*. Routledge, London and New York.

Del Sarto, R. (2006). *Contested State Identities and Regional Security in the Euro-Mediterranean Area*. Palgrave Macmillan, New York and Basingstoke.

Diab, M.A. (1963). *Inter-Arab Cooperation 1951–1960*. Economic Research Institute, American University of Beirut, Beirut.

Diana, H. (2011). The UfM and Development Prospects in the Mediterranean: Making a Real Difference? *Mediterranean Politics*, 16(1), 171–192.

Dodge, T., and Higgot, R. (2002). *Globalisation and the Middle East*. The Royal Institute of International Affairs, London.

El-Agraa, A.M. (1997). *Economic Integration Worldwide*. St. Martin's Press, New York.

Fazio, G. (2009). 'EMU and the Euro-Mediterranean Dialogue: Trade Interdependence between Mediterranean and Euro-area Countries', in Talani, L.S. (ed.) *The Future of EMU*. Palgrave.

Gillespie, R. (2004). 'Reshaping the Agenda? The Internal Politics of the Barcelona Process after September 11', in Junemann, A. (ed.) *Euro-Mediterranean Relations after September the 11th: International, Regional and Domestic Dynamics*. Frank-Cass, London, pp. 21–37.

Grunert, A. (2004). 'Loss of Guiding Values and Support: September 11 and the Isolation of Human Rights Organisations in Egypt', in Junemann, A. (ed.) *Euro-Mediterranean Relations after September the 11th: International, Regional and Domestic Dynamics*. Frank-Cass, London, pp. 133–153.

Hakimian, H., and Moshaver, Z. (2001). *The State and Global Change: The Political Economy of Transition in the Middle East and North Africa*. Curzon Press, Richmond.

Harrigan, J., Wang, C., and Said, H. (2005). The Economic and Political Determinants of IMF and World Bank Lending in the Middle East and North Africa. *World Development*, 34(2), 247–270.

Hirst, P., and Thompson, G. (1999). *Globalisation in Question*. Polity Press, Cambridge.

Honohan, P., and Lane, P.R. (2000). *Will the Euro Trigger More Monetary Unions in Africa?* World Bank Policy Research Working Paper, no. 2393.

Hudson, M.C. (ed.) (1999). *Middle East Dilemma: The Politics and Economics of Arab Integration*. Columbia University Press, New York.

Huysmans, J. (2000). The European Union and the Securitisation of Migration. *JCMS*, 38(5), 751–777.

IMF [International Monetary Fund] (2003). *World Economic and Financial Surveys, World Economic Outlook Public Debt in Emerging Markets, September 2003*. At: http://www.imf.org/external/pubs/ft/weo/2003/02/index.htm, accessed on 20 November 2005.

Junemann, A. (ed.) (2004a). *Euro-Mediterranean Relations after September the 11th: International, Regional and Domestic Dynamics*. Frank-Cass, London.

Junemann, A. (2004b). 'Repercussions of the Emerging European Security and Defence Policy on the Civil Character of the Euro-Mediterranean Partnership', in Junemann, A. (ed.) *Euro-Mediterranean Relations after September the 11th: International, Regional and Domestic Dynamics*. Frank-Cass, London, pp. 37–54.

Junemann, A. (2004c). 'Security Building in the Mediterranean after September the 11th', in Junemann, A. (ed.) *Euro-Mediterranean Relations after September the 11th: International, Regional and Domestic Dynamics*. Frank-Cass, London, pp. 1–21.

Kee, H.L., Nicita, A., and Olarreaga, M. (2008). Import Demand Elasticities and Trade Distortions. *Review of Economics and Statistics*, 90(4), 666–682.

Kee, H.L., Nicita, A., and Olarreaga, M. (2009). Estimating Trade Restrictiveness Indices. *Economic Journal*, 119, 172–199.

Kee, H.L., Neagu, C., and Nicita, A. (forthcoming). Is Protectionism on the Rise? Assessing National Trade Policies During the Crisis of 2008. *Review of Economics and Statistics*.

Kostakopoulou, T. (2000). The'Protective Union': Change and Continuity in Migration Law and Policy in Post-Amsterdam Europe. *Journal of Common Market Studies*, 3, 497–518.

Kubursi, A.A. (1999). 'Prospects for Arab Economic Integration After Oslo', in Hudson, M.C. (ed.) *Middle East Dilemma: The Politics and Economics of Arab Integration*. Columbia University Press, New York, ch. 14.

Masson, P. (2007). Currency Unions in Africa: Is the Trade Effect Substantial Enough to Justify Their Formation? *The World Economy*, doi: 10.1111/j.1467–9701.01028.x, 1–15.

Miles, R., and Thränhardt, D. (eds) (1995). *Migration and European Integration, the Dynamics of Inclusion and Exclusion*. Pinter Publishers, London.

Mittleman, J.H. (2000). *The Globalisation Syndrome: Transformation and Resistance*. Princeton University Press, Princeton.

Montanari, M. (2007). The Barcelona Process and the Political Economy of Euro-Mediterranean Trade Integration. *Journal of Common Market Studies*, 45(5), 1011–1040.

Musrey, A.G. (1969). *An Arab Common Market: A Study in Inter-Arab Trade Flows*. Frederick J. Praeger. New York, Washington, London.

Owen, R. (1999). 'Inter-Arab Economic Relations During the 20th Century: World Market vs Regional Market?', in Hudson, M.C. (ed.) *Middle East Dilemma: The Politics and Economics of Arab Integration*. Columbia University Press, New York, ch. 10.

Owen, R., and Pamuk, S. (1999). *A History of Middle East Economies in the 20th Century*. Harvard University Press, Cambridge, MA.

Overbeek, H., (2000), 'Globalisation, Sovereignty and Transnational Regulation: Reshaping the Governance of International Migration', in Gosh, B. (ed.) *Managing Migration: Time for a New International Regime*. Oxford University Press, Oxford.

Peterson, J., and Sjursen, H. (1998). *A Common Foreign Policy for Europe?: Competing Visions of the CFSP*. Routledge, London.

Sayigh, Y. (1978). *The Economies of the Arab World*. Biddles, London.

Sayigh, Y.A. (1983). 'A New Framework for Complementarity among the Arab Economies', in Ibrahim, I. (ed.) *Arab Resources: The Transformation of a Society*. Center for Contemporary Arab Studies, Washington DC and London, Croom Helm, Washington DC and London, pp. 147–155.

Sayigh, Y.A. (1999). 'Arab Economic Integration: The Poor Harvest of the 1980s', in Hudson, M.C. (ed.) *Middle East Dilemma: The Politics and Economics of Arab Integration*. Columbia University Press, New York, ch. 11.

Stetter, S. (2004). 'Democratisation without Democracy? The Assistance of the European Union for Democratisation Processes in Palestine', in Junemann, A. (ed.) *Euro-Mediterranean Relations after September the 11th: International, Regional and Domestic Dynamics*. Frank-Cass, London, pp. 153–174.

Subramanian, A., and Tamirisa, N.T. (2003). Is Africa Integrated in the Global Economy? *IMF Staff Papers*, 50, 352–372.

Tassinari, F. (2005). The European Sea. *Journal of Baltic Studies*, 36(4).
Tovias, A. (2004). 'Israeli Policy Perspectives on the Euro-Mediterranean Partnership in the Context of EU Enlargement', in Junemann, A. (ed.) *Euro-Mediterranean Relations after September the 11th: International, Regional and Domestic Dynamics*. Frank-Cass, London, pp. 214–233.
Ugur, M. (1995). Freedom of Movement vs. Exclusion: A Reinterpretation of the 'Insider' – 'Outsider' Divide in the European Union. *International Migration Review*, 29(4), 964–999.
UN Economic and Social Commission for Western Asia [ESCWA] (2007). *Economic Trends and Impacts: Foreign Aid and Development in the Arab Region*, 4, United Nations E/Escwa/Ead/2007/1, 4 January.
UNCTAD [United Nations Conference on Trade and Development] (2008). At: http://www.unctad.org, accessed on [date 2008].
Unver Noi, A. (2011). *The Euro-Mediterranean Partnership and Broader Middle East and North Africa Initiative: Competing or Complementary Projects*. University Press of America (14 November 2011).
Van den Boogaerde, P. (1991). *Financial Assistance from Arab Countries and Arab Regional Institutions*. International Monetary Fund Occasional Papers No. 87.
World Bank (2010). *Arab Development Assistance: Four decades of Co-operation*, June 2010, World Bank.
Zahlan, A.B. (1999). 'Labor Migration and Economic Integration in the Middle East', in Hudson, M.C. (ed.) *Middle East Dilemma: The Politics and Economics of Arab Integration*. Columbia University Press, New York, ch. 13.
Zartman, W.I. (1999). 'The Ups and Downs of Maghrib Unity', in Hudson, M.C. (ed.) *Middle East Dilemma: The Politics and Economics of Arab Integration*. Columbia University Press, New York, ch. 8.

5
Tunisia: At the Roots of the Arab Spring: Economic Restructuring without Integration

Introduction: it's the economy, stupid!

Commentators like to point out the extent to which Tunisia was an unlikely candidate to spark the revolution (Hamid 2011). Politically it seemed to be stable, although stability was a function of repression (Hibou 2011), and economically it had been praised by international organisations as an example. The country was indeed considered until very recently as one of the success stories of the region (Pollack 2011).

President Zine al-Abidine Ben Ali had succeeded Habib Bourguiba in 1987 in a bloodless coup known as the 'Jasmine Revolution'. Whereas his predecessor had adopted the statist approach typical of the post-independence rulers of the region, Ben Ali could not rely on a strong societal base and soon reverted to oppression as the means to maintain power (Perkins 2004). The mechanisms of repression varied in degrees and modalities but seemed to target everyone who was outside a very restricted circle of mainly family members, especially opposition groups. These included political Islam, after having helped its establishment as already discussed in Chapter 3 (Hibou 2011).

In economic terms Tunisia was praised as the success story of the MENA area, in particular as far as its economic restructuring was concerned. It is not by chance, indeed, that in 2008 the then managing director of the International Monetary Fund, Dominique Strauss-Kahn, called the Tunisian economy an 'example for emerging countries', while the World Bank named it a 'top reformer' as far as regulatory reform was concerned (Hamid 2011: 111).

Despite this, Tunisia was the first country to experience protests in the Arab Spring leading to regime change as a consequence of the riots.

With the benefit of hindsight, and especially within the context of the theoretical framework set out in this book, it seems clear that much of the economic restructuring which had been going on in the course of the last decades in Tunisia had failed to integrate the country within the global political economy. This created the conditions not only for the desperate gesture of Bouazizi sparking the revolts, but also for the more long-standing popularity of political Islam.

As this chapter will show, although it seemed not to be the problem, in the end it was the economy which undermined Ben Ali's political stronghold. To this aim, the chapter will first look at the evolution of the economic restructuring of the Tunisian economy. It will then assess to what extent these measures were successful in integrating Tunisia in the global political economy. It will finally introduce a discussion of further indicators of marginalisation, especially extra-regional migratory flows.

The restructuring of the Tunisian economy

Tunisia was the first country of the MENA area to inaugurate a policy of economic liberalisation in the period between 1970 and 1980 thanks to the appointment of a business-oriented Prime Minister, Hadi Nuwaira (Owen 2004: 116; Ayubi 2008: 356).

Not dissimilarly from the rest of the region, Tunisia had followed an import substitution approach to development in the decade of the 1960s (Owen 2004: 116). However, already in the early 1970s the country pioneered a new approach based on the opening up of its economy, later on made famous by Sadat's *Infitah* policy (Richards and Waterbury 1998: 233; Owen 2004: 117). As in the case of Egypt, the idea was to cement an alliance between foreign and state capital by attracting foreign investment (Ayubi 2008: 353). But, exactly as in the case of Egypt, these early attempts to increase FDI did not succeed (Richards and Waterbury 1998: 233).

Moreover, throughout the 1970s the state continued to dominate the Tunisian economy to the extent that in 1981 state-owned enterprises still accounted for around 60 per cent of manufacturing production value (Richards and Waterbury 1998: 233). In the agricultural sector the share of public investment even increased from 13 per cent in the period between 1971 and 1980 to 17 per cent in the period between 1981 and 1986 (Ayubi 2008: 353).

By the 1980s, most resource-poor MENA countries (starting with Turkey in 1979, followed by Morocco, Tunisia, Egypt and Algeria) experienced severe debt crises which exacerbated further the pressure to change their economic structure in a more neo-liberal fashion (Fawcett and Sayigh 1999). All of these countries were eventually obliged to implement the structural reform programmes dictated by the IMF as part of its conditionality to credit extension (Clement Moore and Springborg 2010). This pushed also Tunisia to change its reform strategy accordingly.

Before the intervention of the IMF in 1986 the Tunisian approach to economic reform was mainly that of liberalising by limiting state-led growth, according to which the state was at the head of productive activity providing the private sector with the intermediate goods necessary for production (Richards and Waterbury 1998).

As Tunisian debt to GDP continued to increase in the first half of the 1980s, from 48 per cent of GDP in 1980 to 63 per cent in 1986, this strategy proved more and more unsustainable. Moreover, the ratio of deficit to GDP reached quota, 5.2 per cent, in the five years before 1986. Finally, the looming debt crisis was accompanied by a current account one, with the current account deficit widening from 5 per cent of GDP in 1980 to 11 per cent in 1985–1986 (Richards and Waterbury 1998).

To counter the impending crisis, the then government led by Muhammed Mzali tried to implement a more substantial set of reforms. These included the curbing of consumer subsidy programs, a move that led to massive demonstrations and riots in 1984. As a result of the protests, the government withdrew its reforms, but this exacerbated Tunisia's debt problems to the extent that by the spring of 1986 the country could no longer afford to pay for its imports (Owen 2004: 117; Owen and Pamuk 1999). At this point, the government had only one choice: to turn to the IMF and accept the stand-by agreements which it had managed to avoid until then. As a result, from August 1986, Tunisia embarked in a new round of economic reform (Richards and Waterbury 1998).

The structural adjustment programme imposed on Tunisia by the IMF included the usual elements of devaluation of the currency, export promotion, reduction of import protection, liberalisations, privatisations and budgetary austerity.

At the moment of the IMF intervention, despite some growth in the size of the private sector as a consequence of the first liberalisation programmes, the role of the state in the economy was still dominant (Ayubi 2008: 354). In 1983, public expenditure accounted for 40.6 per cent of GDP, spending on public administration was around

12–13 per cent of GDP and salaries to civil servants made up for 28.3 per cent of all public expenditure (Ayubi 2008: 354). A structural adjustment programme was, however, attached to the IMF's opening up of a stand-by credit facility. This required a substantial curtailing of public expenditure, including expenditure related to the maintenance of public sector jobs and services. The IMF required a cut in credit facilities, the liberalisation of prices by 1991, the freeing of interest rates, removal of subsidies, freezing public sector wages, opening up the market to imports and the acceleration of privatisations (Ayubi 2008: 355). These measures allowed for an agreement to be signed with the World Bank to facilitate the involvement of private business in the economy. Foreign industrial investment was particularly favoured by a number of inducements which included infrastructural and exporting facilities, tax exemptions and repatriation rights. All of this was achieved by passing a number of legislative acts which incorporated the 'dictat' of international organisations in the period between 1986 and 1989 (Ayubi 1990, 1991, 1993, 2008: 355). Further impetus to the restructuring process was given by the association agreement signed by Tunisia with the EU in 1995 to establish an area of industrial free trade committing the country to reduce tariff barriers in twelve years (Owen 2004: 117).[1]

Overall, the substantial privatisation plans did not meet with great success. This was mainly due to the lack of a strong local entrepreneurial business class and the limited financial capacity of the Tunisian private sector. Here, as in Egypt, or maybe even more so, the entrepreneurial bourgeoisie was particularly tiny and mostly dependent on government protection and subsidy. Thus, instead of benefiting from the restructuring programme, it succumbed to it, with nearly 400 local private companies closing down in 1987 and almost seven hundred in 1988. This was exacerbated by the liberalisation of imports, the collapse of the exchange rate and the increase in interest rates (Ayubi 1993, 2008: 356).

Some of the targets included in the programme were eventually met and macroeconomic indicators seemed to improve (Richards and Waterbury 1998; Hakimian and Moshaver 2001). Economic growth from 1987 to 1992 was 4.3 per cent compared with 2.8 per cent for the previous five years. Tunisian real GDP growth in the 1990s averaged 4.6 per cent, whereas in the 1980s it had been 3.2 per cent, and continued to fare well in the following decade until the Arab Spring (Figure 5.1).

Inflation fell from 8.2 per cent in 1987 to 5.8 per cent in 1992 (Consumer price annual per cent change – World Bank database). Foreign reserves recovered for good, never to reach again such low levels as those of 1985 and 1986 (Figure 5.2).

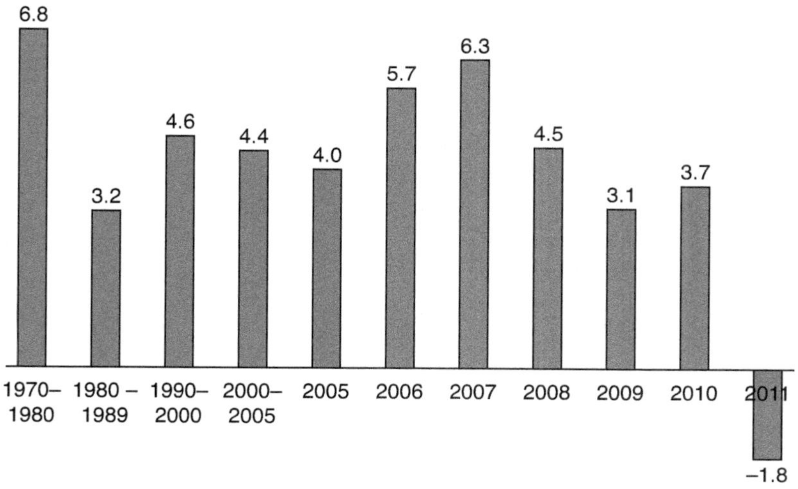

Figure 5.1 Tunisia – real GDP growth 1970–2011
Source: World Bank 2010

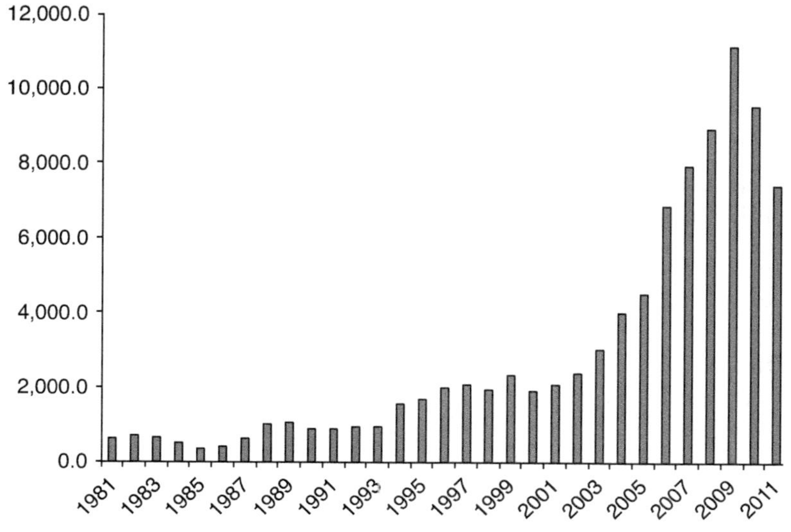

Figure 5.2 Tunisia – foreign reserves including gold, 1981–2011 (US$ millions at current prices and current exchange rates)
Source: UNCTAD database

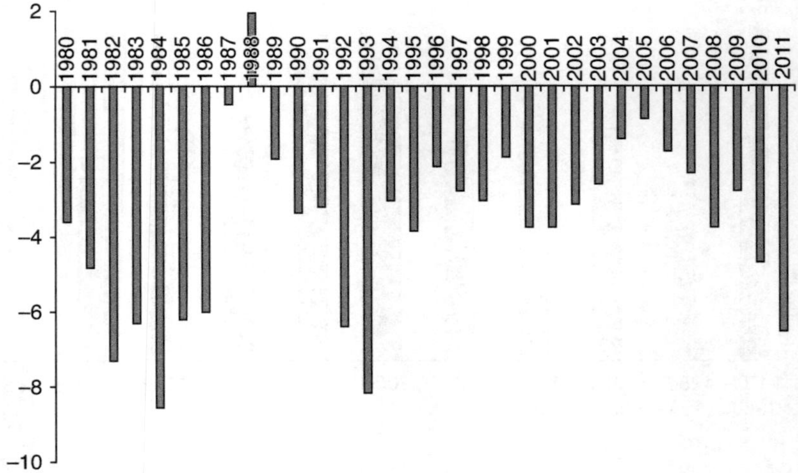

Figure 5.3 Tunisia – net balance of payments as a percentage of GDP, 1980–2011
Source: UNCTAD database

Even the balance of payments improved in the immediate aftermath of the loan, recording a surplus in 1988, although it started worsening again in the early 1990s (Figure 5.3).

However, as we will further elaborate below, the integration of Tunisia into the global political economy failed to become a reality.

The integration of Tunisia into the global political economy

In line with the theoretical background set out so far, the degree of integration of Tunisia into the global political economy will be assessed by looking at the performance of its share of global FDI stocks and inflows, the level of mergers and acquisitions and various other indicators of openness of the economy as well as production for exports (Mittlemann 2000; Dicken 2011).

As already underlined in Chapter 4, North Africa is clearly lagging behind in terms of share of global FDI especially if compared with other developing regions of the world, such as South and Eastern Asia or Latin America.

As far as Tunisia is concerned, its percentage share of global FDI stock has never stopped declining from around 0.5 per cent in 1980 to little more than 0.15 per cent in 2011 (Figure 5.4).

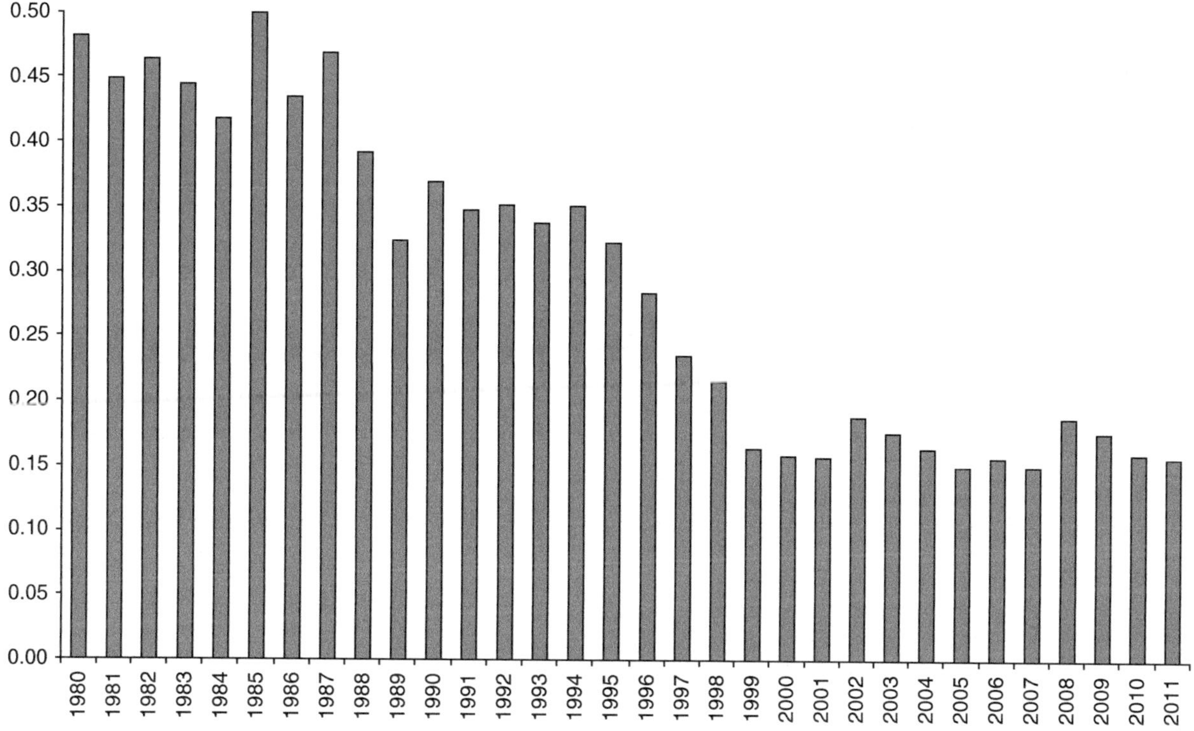

Figure 5.4 Tunisia – average percentage share of world total FDI stock, 1981–2011

Source: UNCTAD database

The overall programme of restructuring of the Tunisian economy was indeed ineffective in integrating Tunisia into the global political economy, as the percentage of global FDI stock in the country moved from an already unimpressive 0.42 per cent in the decade between 1970 and 1980 to 0.29 per cent in the period 1990 to 2000, to almost nil in the first decade of the 2000s (Figure 5.5).

The situation is very similar when looking at the performance of FDI inflows in the last three decades. If in the 1980s Tunisia could count on around 0.25 per cent of global FDI inflows, in the 1990s, after the substantial restructuring programme sponsored by the IMF, the country's share of Global FDI inflows had decreased to 0.144 per cent and in the first decade of the 2000s the average was even lower at 0.117 per cent. With the revolution the share of FDI inflows became virtually zero (0.075 per cent) (Figure 5.6).

Just to give some terms for comparison, from the second half of the 2000s FDI inflows have almost constantly been outperformed by remittances. These remittances have mainly come from permanent migrants in European countries, as further elaborated in the next section (Figure 5.7). This can hardly be considered a success for a country which undertook a substantial programme of liberalisation and restructuring of the economy with the aim of attracting foreign business. On the contrary, increased reliance on financial transfers from workers abroad is a clear sign of marginalisation from the global political economy.

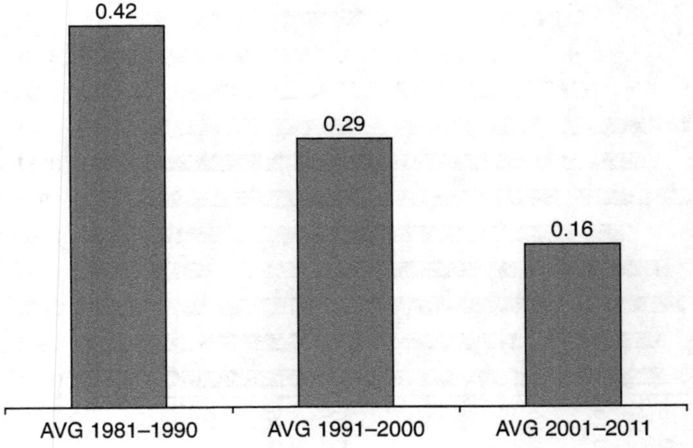

Figure 5.5 Tunisia – average percentage share of world total FDI stock, decades 1981–2011

Source: UNCTAD database

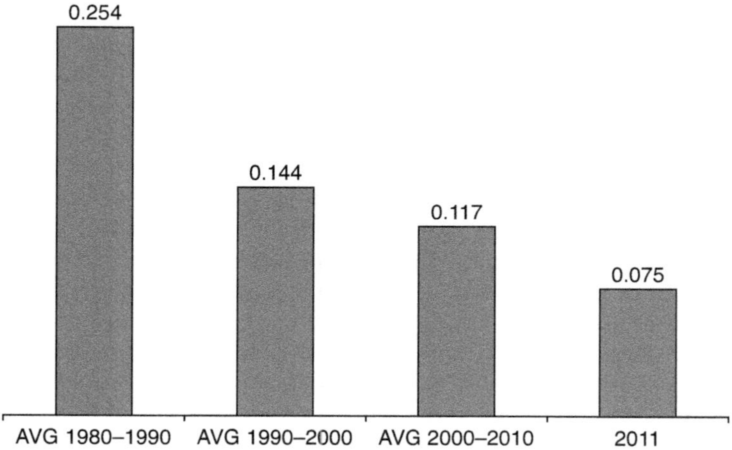

Figure 5.6 Tunisia – average percentage share of world total FDI inflows, decades 1981–2011

Source: Elaboration of the author on data by UNCTAD website http://www.unctad.org/Templates/Page.asp?intItemID=1584&lang=1 as accessed on 14 May 2013

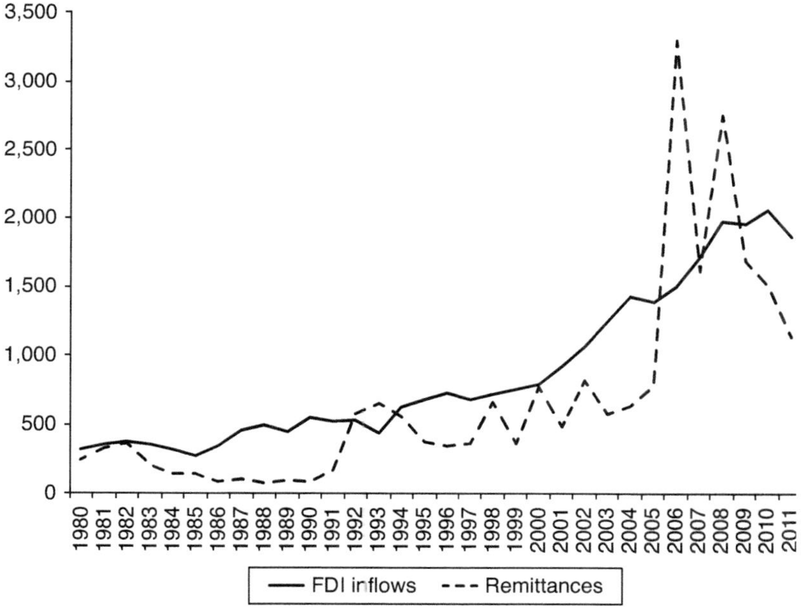

Figure 5.7 Tunisia – comparison remittances/FDI inflows, 1980–2011 (US $ millions at current prices)

Source: Elaboration of the author on data by UNCTAD website http://www.unctad.org/Templates/Page.asp?intItemID=1584&lang=1 as accessed on 13 May 2013

Another indicator of integration into the global political economy often used in the literature is the percentage share of mergers and acquisition sales over world total. Well, in the case of Tunisia this indicator has constantly been around zero in the last two decades (Table 5.1).

In other words, despite the attempts of the regime to attract international capital to the country, this strategy has been mostly a failure.

If foreign capital did not feel the attraction of the policies devised by the regime and suggested by international organisations to restructure the Tunisian economy, it is worth looking at the performance of Tunisian exports to see whether at least these have helped the country to increase its degree of integration in the global economy.

With respect to this, it is astonishing how, according to the data provided by UNCTAD, Tunisia's percentage share of world total merchandise exports has remained stable in the last thirty years at around 0.1 per cent (Figure 5.8). This denotes a very poor performance indeed.

In terms of trade openness, Tunisian trade as a percentage of purchasing power GDP actually decreased in the decade of the 1990s, moving from 28.4 per cent to 25.5 per cent (Table 5.2).

One might ask what comprises the bulk of Tunisia's GDP. According to data from UNCTAD, the economic structure of Tunisia has relied heavily on services. These represented around 60 per cent of total GDP

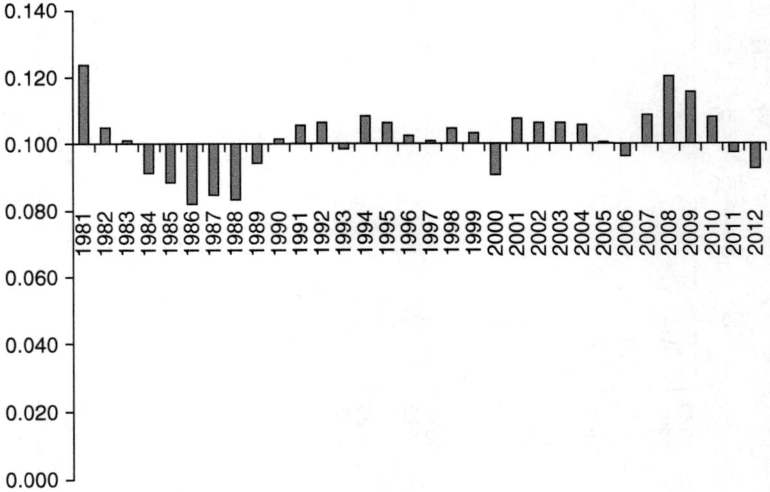

Figure 5.8 Tunisia – percentage share of total world merchandise exports, 1981–2012
Source: UNCTAD database

Table 5.1 Value of cross-border M&A by region/economy of seller, 1990–2011 (US$ millions)

Region/ economy	1990	1991	1992	1993	1994	1995	1996	1997	1998	1999	2000
World	98903	21094	48106	43623	91769	112527	142557	180751	406427	630807	905214
Tunisia	–	–	–	14	–	–	2	–	415	11	298
	0	0	0.0	0.0	0.0	0.0	0.0	0.0	0.1	0.0	0.0

Region/ economy	2001	2002	2003	2004	2005	2006	2007	2008	2009	2010	2011
World	429374	248446	182874	227221	462253	625320	1022725	706543	249732	344029	525881
Tunisia	45	78	–	–	46	2313	–	122	4	9	–
	0.0	0.0	0.0	0.0	0.0	0.4	0.0	0.0	0.0	0.0	0.0

Note: Cross-border M&A sales are calculated on a net basis as follows: Sales of companies in the host economy to foreign TNCs (–) Sales of foreign affiliates in the host economy. The data cover only those deals that involved an acquisition of an equity stake of more than 10%. The data refer to the net sales by the region/economy of the immediate acquired company.

Source: UNCTAD cross-border M&A database (www.unctad.org/fdistatistics)

Table 5.2 Trade as a percentage PPP GDP for Middle Eastern countries, 1990–1999

	1990	1999
Algeria	19.9	14.3
Bahrain	128.3	76.5*
Egypt	8.9	9.1
Iran	15.4	8.4
Israel	45.9	52.4
Jordan	34.2	29.4
Lebanon	45.1	30.9*
Morocco	15.9	18.6
Saudi Arabia	45.9	36
Syria	22	10.4
Tunisia	28.4	25.2
Turkey	13	16.2
UAE	85.3	106.7
Yemen	25.9	34.1
Middle East	23.5	16.8

*1998

Source: World Bank (2001). *The Little Data Book*. World Bank, Washington DC

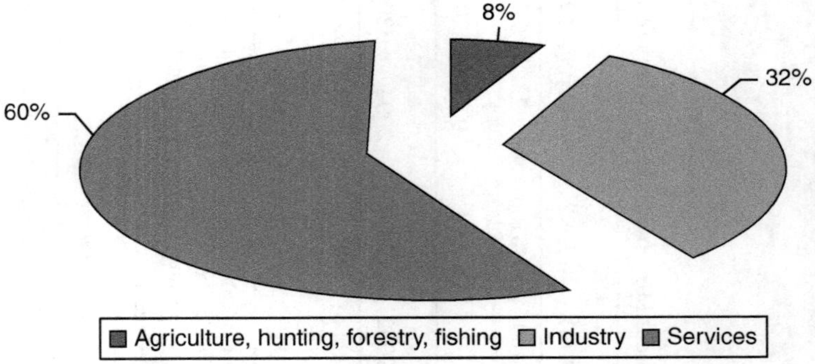

Figure 5.9 Tunisia – economic structure, 2011

Source: Elaboration of the author on data by UNCTAD website www.unctad.org

in 2011, which was more or less stable from the previous three decades. An increasingly substantial role had been played by tourism up until the revolutionary events of 2010 and 2011. In 2010, 23 per cent of total services were represented by wholesale and retail trade, restaurants and hotels (Figures 5.9 and 5.10).

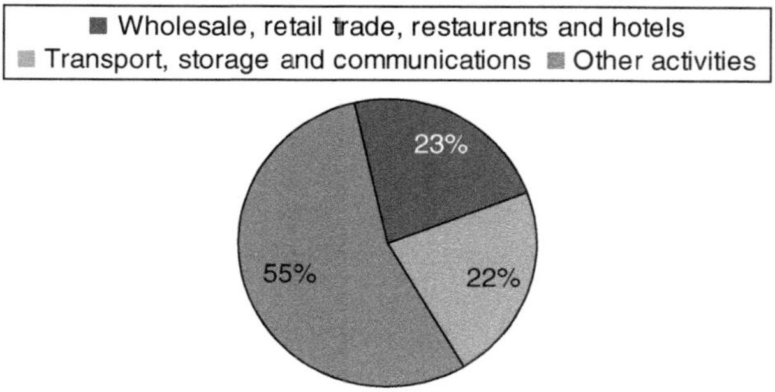

Figure 5.10 Tunisia – economic structure, composition of services, 2010
Source: Elaboration of the author on data by UNCTAD website www.unctad.org

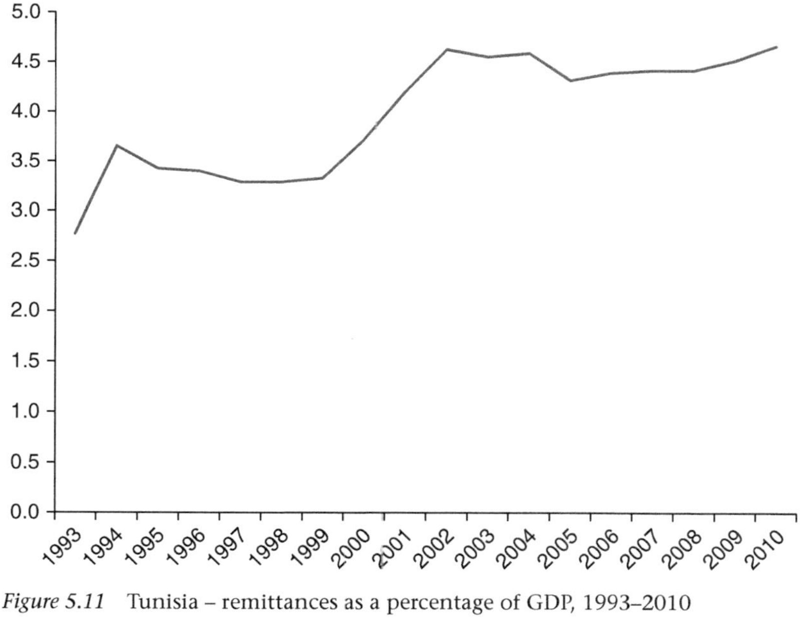

Figure 5.11 Tunisia – remittances as a percentage of GDP, 1993–2010
Source: UNCTAD database

As already mentioned, the composition of Tunisia's GDP, as well as the survival of many Tunisian households (Fourati 2009; Boubakri 2011), was increasingly reliant on remittances from migrants abroad, especially in the EU and other developed countries outside the MENA region, as further elaborated in the next section (Figure 5.11).

Workers' remittances have indeed been constantly rising over the last decade in Tunisia, both in absolute terms and as a percentage of GDP. Moreover from the late 1990s they have out-performed net levels of official development aid by at least two times (and often much more than even that, see Figure 5.12). Finally one should always remember that official data on remittances substantially underestimate total inflows of money from migrants abroad as their transfers usually happen through unofficial channels (Boubakri 2011).

In the light of the above considerations, the relation between migration and marginalisation deserves more attention, in line with the relevant literature (Dicken 2011; Mittleman 2000; Sassen 1998, 1999, 2006; Overbeek 1999, 2000; Hibou et al. 2011).

Marginalisation and extra regional migration: the case of Tunisia

The extent to which Tunisia has been progressively marginalised from the global political economy is further revealed by the analysis of the most sensitive issue in the relationship between Tunisia and Europe: the issue of extra-regional migration, especially to Europe (Dodge and Higgot 2002; Zahlan 1999). As already noted in a previous chapter of this

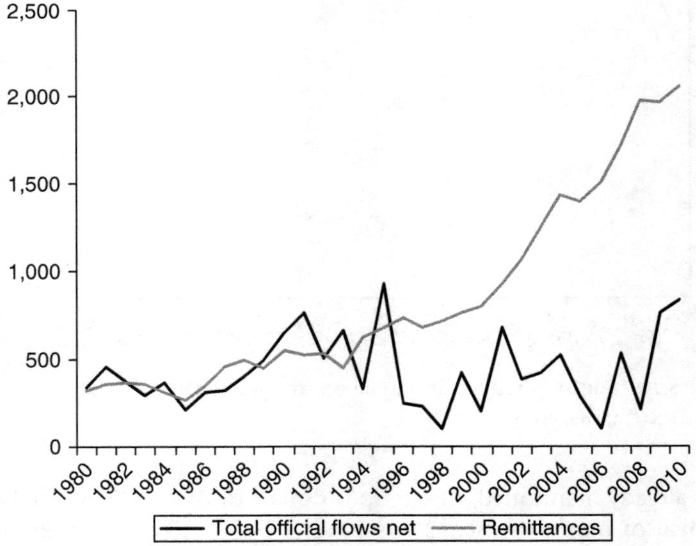

Figure 5.12 Tunisia – remittances and net official aid flows, 1980–2010 (US$ millions at current prices and current exchange rates)

Source: UNCTAD database

book, migration has progressively monopolised the Euro-Mediterranean dialogue and the policies implemented by the European Union vis-à-vis its Southern Mediterranean neighbours.

It is indeed undeniable that the number of Tunisians abroad has been constantly on the rise in the last decade, with an increase of the total number of emigrants registered in Tunisian Consulates abroad increasing from 763,890 in 2001 to 1,098,200 in 2009 (Table 5.3). Most importantly for the purposes of this study, the dynamics of Tunisian migration are such that extra-regional migration to more developed countries, especially European ones, has prevailed over intra-regional migration (Fargues 2007; Fargues and Fandrich 2012). Indeed, the number of Tunisians moving to European countries in 2009 was 911,400, around 83 per cent of the total, with the majority choosing to go to France, Italy and Germany. This is opposed to only 106,500 migrants in the Maghreb region and 48,400 residing in the rest of the Arab world (Table 5.3). It is important, although obvious, to underline that these figures usually underestimate the real number of migrants as they do not include irregular ones.

The importance of extra-regional migration in the case of Tunisia is clearly corroborated by the composition of its remittances and their evolution over recent years. Tunisia attributes great importance to the issue of remittances, given that at the end of 2010 it was estimated that around 10 per cent of the total Tunisian population was living abroad (Bel Haj Zekri 2010). Moreover, in 2006 total transfers from emigrants abroad increased to 2,010 million dinars, which put remittances in the third place as a source of foreign currency in Tunisia. In the period between 2000 and 2005 the evolution of remittance flows from abroad recorded an annual average growth of 10.61 per cent. In the previous five years, this had been around 9 per cent (Fourati 2009: 1).

What is most important for our analysis is that the almost totality of the remittances to Tunisia comes from countries outside the MENA region and in particular from Europe. In 2006 the transfers of Tunisians residing in European countries amounted to 1,784 million Tunisian dinars, which represented a staggering 88.8 per cent of total transfers in that year. This should be compared to a mere 175.7 million dinars coming from Arab countries, which only represented 8.8 per cent of total transfers. Other world countries, including Canada and the US, only accounted for 2.4 per cent of total remittances, around 50 million dinars in 2006. This is a trend which has been confirmed by the data referring to the whole decade between 1995 and 2006 (Fourati 2009: 2). Indeed, in this period the percentage of remittances coming from European countries remained

Table 5.3 Tunisia – number of migrants registered by Tunisian Consulates abroad

Countries of residence	**2001**	**2002**	**2003**	**2004**	**2005**	**2006**	**2007**	**2008**	**2009**
Albanie	11	11	11	n.d.	n.d.	n.d.	n.d.	n.d.	n.d.
Allemagne	44,143	45,904	53,925	56,000	70,200	72,100	80,336	82,600	85,500
Angleterre + Irlande	3,168	3,293	3,512	4,200	5,900	5,900	5,621	6,500	6,700
Autriche	4,720	5,057	5,190	5,500	4,400	5,100	5,896	5,900	6,100
Belgique	16,305	16,982	17,084	17,200	15,200	17,800	18,430	19,400	20,800
Bosnie	20	20	20	n.d.	n.d.	n.d.	n.d.	n.d.	n.d.
Bulgarie	11	11	n.d.	n.d.	n.d.	n.d.	83	n.d.	n.d.
Danemark	861	975	975	n.d.	n.d.	n.d.	1,169	n.d.	n.d.
Espagne	1,290	1,300	1,360	n.d.	n.d.	n.d.	2,371	n.d.	n.d.
Finlande	535	535	535	n.d.	n.d.	n.d.	790	n.d.	n.d.
France	470,459	480,067	493,028	511,200	535,600	551,700	555,347	578,000	598,500
Grèce	443	438	458	n.d.	n.d.	n.d.	632	n.d.	n.d.
Hollande	6,642	7,058	7,058	7,300	7,000	8,000	8,129	8,200	8,400
Hongrie	66	66	66	n.d.	n.d.	n.d.	99	n.d.	n.d.
Islande	8	8	8	n.d.	n.d.	n.d.	n.d.	n.d.	n.d.
Italie	78,581	89,896	101,042	112,300	113,800	127,100	142,972	141,900	152,700
Malte	173	177	177	n.d.	n.d.	n.d.	260	n.d.	n.d.
Norvège	877	1,156	1,187	n.d.	n.d.	n.d.	1,176	n.d.	n.d.
Pologne	241	211	210	n.d.	n.d.	n.d.	488	n.d.	n.d.
Portugal	61	61	49	n.d.	n.d.	n.d.	140	n.d.	n.d.
République Tchèque	257	325	319	n.d.	n.d.	n.d.	595	n.d.	n.d.
République Slovaque	30	30	30	n.d.	n.d.	n.d.	n.d.	n.d.	n.d.
Roumanie	56	56	n.d.	n.d.	n.d.	n.d.	947	n.d.	n.d.
Russie + Ukraine	666	1,037	1,406	n.d.	n.d.	n.d.	2,267	n.d.	n.d.
Suède	5,630	6,003	6,156	6,600	6,800	7,100	7,153	7,600	7,700
Suisse	6,909	6,909	6,909	9,600	10,700	11,000	11,533	12,300	13,100

Turquie	272	343	345	n.d.	n.d.	n.d.	352	n.d.	n.d.
Yougoslavie	16	244	600	n.d.	n.d.	n.d.	17	n.d.	n.d.
Autres pays d'Europe	n.d.	n.d.	n.d.	8,700	9,500	9,700	n.d.	11,500	11,900
Total Europe	642,451	668,173	701,660	738,600	779,100	815,500	846,803	873,900	911,400
Algérie	12,367	13,249	13,554	13,900	14,600	14,800	77,877	15,900	16,400
Libye	47,751	53,601	60,023	67,300	71,500	71,500	15,637	83,600	87,200
Maroc	4,000	4,000	4,082	4,100	4,200	4,200	4,255	3,000	2,900
Mauritanie	351	351	451	n.d.	n.d.	n.d.	340	n.d.	n.d.
Total Maghreb	64,469	71,201	78,110	85,300	90,300	90,500	98,109	102,500	106,500
Arabie Saoudite	n.d.	n.d.	n.d.	15,500	18,200	18,300	19,214	20,000	18,600
Bahreïn	356	420	534	n.d.	n.d.	n.d.	887	n.d.	n.d.
Djibouti	1	1	1	n.d.	n.d.	n.d.	63	n.d.	n.d.
Egypte	1,395	1,500	1,600	n.d.	n.d.	n.d.	1,753	n.d.	n.d.
Emirats Arab Unies	n.d.	n.d.	n.d.	6,500	7,300	7,300	10,838	12,400	13,800
Irak	570	291	252	n.d.	n.d.	n.d.	176	n.d.	n.d.
Jordanie	370	370	350	n.d.	n.d.	n.d.	490	n.d.	n.d.
Koweït	702	802	758	n.d.	n.d.	n.d.	1,596	n.d.	n.d.
Liban	781	849	849	n.d.	n.d.	n.d.	840	n.d.	n.d.
Oman	n.d.	n.d.	n.d.	n.d.	n.d.	n.d.	2,257	n.d.	n.d.
Palestine	452	452	452	n.d.	n.d.	n.d.	272	n.d.	n.d.
Qatar	n.d.	n.d.	n.d.	3,500	3,700	3,700	3,706	5,900	3,100
Soudan	37	30	33	n.d.	n.d.	n.d.	99	n.d.	n.d.
Syrie	1,693	1,964	1,850	n.d.	n.d.	n.d.	2,195	n.d.	n.d.
Yémen	71	87	87	n.d.	n.d.	n.d.	160	n.d.	n.d.
Autres pays arabes	31,828	25,120	32,050	8,900	9,400	9,800	n.d.	12,400	12,900
Total autres pays arabes	38,256	31,886	38,816	34,400	38,600	39,100	44,546	50,700	48,400
Afrique du sud	31	61	64	n.d.	n.d.	n.d.	n.d.	n.d.	n.d.
Cameroun	35	46	35	n.d.	n.d.	n.d.	36	n.d.	n.d.

Continued

Table 5.3 Continued

Countries of residence	2001	2002	2003	2004	2005	2006	2007	2008	2009
Congo	n.d.	n.d.	n.d.	n.d.	n.d.	n.d.	22	n.d.	n.d.
Cote d'Ivoire	142	187	108	n.d.	n.d.	n.d.	135	n.d.	n.d.
Ethiopie	19	28	28	n.d.	n.d.	n.d.	38	n.d.	n.d.
Gabon	129	64	67	n.d.	n.d.	n.d.	120	n.d.	n.d.
Guinée	65	65	75	n.d.	n.d.	n.d.	n.d.	n.d.	n.d.
Guinée Bissau	5	5	5	n.d.	n.d.	n.d.	n.d.	n.d.	n.d.
Guinée équatoriale	n.d.	n.d.	n.d.	n.d.	n.d.	n.d.	5	n.d.	n.d.
Kenya	n.d.	n.d.	n.d.	n.d.	n.d.	n.d.	3	n.d.	n.d.
Mali	34	42	42	n.d.	n.d.	n.d.	n.d.	n.d.	n.d.
Nigeria	11	12	7	n.d.	n.d.	n.d.	28	n.d.	n.d.
RD Congo	16	290	489	n.d.	n.d.	n.d.	22	n.d.	n.d.
Sénégal	122	133	142	n.d.	n.d.	n.d.	263	n.d.	n.d.
Tchad	5	n.d.	0	n.d.	n.d.	n.d.	38	n.d.	n.d.
Rwanda	n.d.	n.d.	n.d.	n.d.	n.d.	n.d.	23	n.d.	n.d.
Autres	16	22	87	n.d.	n.d.	n.d.	n.d.	n.d.	n.d.
Total Afrique	630	955	1,149	n.d.	n.d.	n.d.	733	n.d.	n.d.
Chine	74	89	88	n.d.	n.d.	n.d.	147	n.d.	n.d.
Corea du sud	n.d.	n.d.	n.d.	n.d.	n.d.	n.d.	31	n.d.	n.d.
Inde	7	12	15	n.d.	n.d.	n.d.	11	n.d.	n.d.
Indonésie	31	22	130	n.d.	n.d.	n.d.	296	n.d.	n.d.
Iran	27	29	48	n.d.	n.d.	n.d.	32	n.d.	n.d.
Japon	279	311	238	n.d.	n.d.	n.d.	575	n.d.	n.d.
Malaise	38	38	38	n.d.	n.d.	n.d.	n.d.	n.d.	n.d.
Pakistan	33	33	57	n.d.	n.d.	n.d.	37	n.d.	n.d.
Philippines	6	6	6	n.d.	n.d.	n.d.	n.d.	n.d.	n.d.
Thaïlande	24	24	24	n.d.	n.d.	n.d.	n.d.	n.d.	n.d.
Autres	9	21	25	n.d.	n.d.	n.d.	n.d.	n.d.	n.d.

Total Asie	528	585	669	n.d.	n.d.	n.d.	1,129	n.d.	n.d.
Argentine	9	8	9	n.d.	n.d.	n.d.	15	n.d.	n.d.
Australie	156	156	620	n.d.	n.d.	n.d.	644	n.d.	n.d.
Brésil	40	23	24	n.d.	n.d.	n.d.	35	n.d.	n.d.
Canada	10,531	11,545	12,347	13,200	11,600	11,600	13,220	14,200	15,300
Etats-Unis	6,820	9,348	9,800	10,800	11,400	13,400	12,913	13,400	13,700
Autres	n.d.	n.d.	n.d.	n.d.	n.d.	n.d.	5	n.d.	n.d.
Total Amérique et Océanie	17,556	21,080	22,800	24,000	23,000	25,000	26,832	27,600	29,000
Autres pays	n.d.	n.d.	n.d.	2,600	2,800	3,000	n.d.	3,100	2,900
Total	763,890	793,880	843,204	884,900	933,800	973,100	1018,152	1057,800	1098,200

Source: CARIM south database web-site: http://www.carim.org/index.php?callContent=59&callTable=1803 as accessed on 24 May 2013

stable at around 90 per cent of the total, which is pretty remarkable (see Table 5.4 below).

In 2009, the remittances coming from Europe were again around 88 per cent of total remittances to Tunisia with around 2,323 million Tunisian dinars, according to the data of the Tunisian Central Bank (higher amounts are provided by UNCTAD, Boubakri 2011). Looking at the countries providing the highest amount of transfers, European countries fare amongst the most important ones, with France first, followed by Germany and Italy (Table 5.5).

The reality of extra-regional migration from Tunisia especially towards Europe prompted the Tunisian Government to adopt a well-defined policy-making strategy towards migration in the period before the revolution (Appleyard 1999). Experts point to the existence of two axes in Tunisian migratory policy in the frame of the Economic and Social plan 2010–2014. One was directly aimed at promoting legal migration through agreements with European and non-European countries outside the MENA region (such as Canada, Australia etc.). The other axis was to strengthen the links with Tunisians abroad with the aim of encouraging them to invest in the country and sustain its development (Bel Haj Zekri 2010).

Neither of the two axes, however, seems to have worked effectively (Hibou et al. 2011).

In particular, on the side of regulating the migratory process, despite the passing by the Regime of Organic Law 2004–6 of 3 February 2004 (which was aimed at amending Law 75–40 of 14 March 1975 about passports and travel documents), irregular migration from Tunisia

Table 5.4 Evolution of remittances from Tunisians residing abroad according to country of residence, 1995–2006

Group of countries	Amounts in millions of Tunisian dollars				Percentages			
	1995	2000	2005	2006	1995	2000	2005	2006
European countries	641.2	987.0	1610.0	1784.0	90.1	90.5	89.1	88.8
Arab countries	55.4	84.3	155.6	176.7	7.8	7.7	8.6	8.8
Other countries	15.2	19.8	41.3	49.2	2.1	1.8	2.3	2.4
Total	711.8	1091.1	1806.9	2009.9	100	100	100	100

Source: Banque Central de Tunisie

Table 5.5 Remittances by expatriates by country of origin of the remittances, 2004–2009 (millions of Tunisian dinars)

Countries where remittances come from	2004	2005	2006	2007	2008	2009
Germany	255.8	257.7	297.8	335.4	365.5	399.1
Austria	17.6	18.4	20.4	22.3	25.5	27.9
Belgium	45.2	45.5	49.1	53.8	60.5	63.8
France	907.9	909.3	994.4	1,071.0	1,169.5	1,270.7
Netherlands	21.6	22.9	24.1	26.7	30.6	33.6
Italy	235.8	244.2	275.2	309.8	339.9	356.8
United Kingdom-Ireland	17.4	18.9	22.0	21.9	28.1	31.7
Sweden	14.4	15.1	16.7	18.1	20.8	23.6
Switzerland	46.4	46.7	51.4	56.2	64.1	68.7
Other European countries	30.8	31.3	32.9	37.8	41.4	47.1
Algeria	3.6	3.7	4.1	4.5	5.3	5.8
Saudi Arabia	54.6	55.5	64.1	72.5	78.8	90.7
United Arab Emirates	18.3	19.0	22.3	23.9	34.4	45.0
Libya	32.4	34.1	37.5	41.1	47.1	50.2
Morocco	4.8	5.0	5.5	6.0	6.9	7.2
Qatar	12.2	12.7	14.0	15.4	17.5	21.2
Oman	10.7	11.3	12.7	14.0	15.6	19.4
Other Arab countries	13.3	14.3	16.5	18.0	18.9	22.0
Canada	15.1	15.9	17.4	19.0	23.4	25.7
United States	9.6	9.8	12.7	13.6	22.6	20.7
Other countries	9.4	9.9	13.2	17.5	19.5	21.7
Total	1,776.9	1,801.2	2,004.0	2,198.5	2,435.9	2,652.6

Source: Central Bank of Tunisia

continued unhindered.[2] For example, in 2008, Tunisians became, for the first time, the largest nationality group of irregular migrants landing on the Italian island of Lampedusa. Their number was 6,762 which included 52 women and 184 minors. This was higher than the number of undocumented migrants from Nigeria (6,084 migrants, including 1,787 women and 351 minors). It has been estimated that in 2008, Tunisians represented two-thirds of North African nationals (i.e. from the Maghreb and Egypt) who irregularly entered Italy through the island (Boubakri 2011).

Overall, experts do not envisage a slowing of the level of legal and irregular extra-regional migration in the years following the Arab Spring. This seems to be a dynamic that has already been established for decades as a consequence of the growing marginalisation of Tunisia from the global political economy (Boubakri 2011: 17; Fourati 2008; Bel Haj Zekri 2010). Indeed, many highly-skilled young Tunisians are expected to flee the country in the coming years, further adding to the already established phenomenon of brain drain (Boubakri 2011).

The data available in the literature shows that the number of highly-skilled migrants abroad had been increasing by around 38 per cent in 2007 and 2008 vis-a-vis the average of the period between 2001 and 2007 (Fourati 2010). The majority of them have headed towards European countries, first France and then Germany and Italy (see Table 5.6). Overall, the share of extra-regional brain drain has always been above 80 per cent in the first decade of the 2000s.

The main determinant of brain drain is highly related to the marginalisation of Tunisia. As elaborated in Chapter 4, Tunisia is lagging progressively more and more behind in terms of the technological skills necessary to enter new global productive chains. This dramatically reduces the possibility for highly-skilled personnel to find appropriate jobs in the country, thus leading to an increased incidence of brain drain (Bel Haj

Table 5.6 Tunisia – evolution of brain drain according to country of destination, 2001–2008

Destination country	**May01–May02**	**May01–May02 per cent**	**May05–May06**	**May05–May06 per cent**	**May06–May07**	**May06–May07 per cent**	**May07–May08**	**May07–May08 per cent**
France	2930	50.3	2620	45.6	3070	54.2	3650	45.6
Germany	490	8.4	540	9.4	970	17.1	620	7.8
Italy	320	5.5	330	5.7	410	7.2	830	10.4
Other European Countries	720	12.3	630	11.0	260	4.6	500	6.3
Gulf countries	530	9.1	630	11.0	280	4.9	140	1.8
Other Arab countries	500	8.6	320	5.6	490	8.7	1440	18.0
Other countries	340	5.8	680	11.8	180	3.2	820	10.3
Total	5830	100	5750	100	5660	100	8000	100

Source: Elaboration of the author based on data by Fourati (2010: 12)

Zekri 2010). Indeed, looking at the evolution of the Tunisian labour market in the last three decades, it emerges clearly how highly-skilled labour has been increasingly unable to find gainful working positions in it. The unemployment rate of workers with a degree in higher education increased almost ten-fold from 1984 to 2008, from as little as 2.3 per cent in 1984 to as high as 21.6 per cent in 2008 (Table 5.7). On the contrary, in the same period, both illiterate workers and workers with only primary education have seen a decrease in their unemployment rates, from 15.2 to 5.7 per cent and from 22.4 per cent to 12.3 per cent respectively.

This dynamic clearly demonstrates the impoverishment of the skills employed by the Tunisian labour market in a period in which, on the contrary, an up-skilling of the labour force was required to be able to catch up with the globalisation process. In turn, unemployment or, more precisely, the difficulty in finding an appropriate working activity for the highly skilled, represents the main determinant of brain drain (Bel Haj Zekri 2010: 6).

Furthermore, it is also debatable whether the growing patriotism following the revolution will encourage Tunisians residing abroad to increase their investment in the country of origin to limit the effects of marginalisation and brain drain (Abdelfatta 2011).[3]

Although it is clearly too early to reach any firm conclusions, migratory flows from Tunisia following the Arab Spring seem to confirm the already established profile of the Tunisian migrant. A survey by the Observatoire National de la Jeunesse conducted in 2005 showed that the percentage of young Tunisians (between 15 and 29 years of age) that were envisaging migrating abroad, independent of their gender, level of education, socio-economic status or job opportunities, rose from 25 per cent in 1996 to 75.9 per cent in 2005. Many (around 15 per cent) even openly declared that they were ready to resort to undocumented migration to move to a foreign country.

Table 5.7 Tunisia – evolution of the unemployment rate by level of education (per cent)

	1984	1994	1999	2004	2005	2006	2007	2009
Illiterate	15.2	16.2	11.9	12.7	7.8	8.0	5.9	5.7
Primary	22.4	19.2	18.9	15.7	15.7	15.2	13.5	12.3
Secondary	11.0	13.0	16.4	14.7	14.9	14.3	15.4	15.3
Higher	2.3	3.8	8.6	10.2	14.8	17.5	19.0	21.6
Total	16.4	15.8	16.0	14.2	14.8	14.3	14.1	14.2

Source: Bel Haj Zekri (2010: 6)

This profile is confirmed by the characteristics of Tunisian migrants to Italy immediately after the revolution (Bel Haj Zekri 2010). Between January and June 2011, around 25,800 Tunisians were reported to have arrived in Italy irregularly. Their profile was the same as reported by the survey of 2005; they were mainly young people, generally between 20 and 30 years of age but sometimes as young as between 13 and 17. They mostly moved from the poorest towns of Tunisia in the centre west (Sidi Bouzid, Thala, Kasserine, Gafsa) and the south (Gabes, El Hamma, Zarzis, Tataouine), as well as the poorest quarters of the big cities such as Tunis and Sousse. Most tellingly, their profile was the same as the young Mohammed Bouazizi whose immolation by setting fire to himself sparked the Tunisian revolution. They were generally from large families, composed of four to eight members. These families would be sustained by only one breadwinner, earning between 4 and 8 dinars a day (between 2 and 4 euros) in precarious jobs without social security or employment rights (Bel Haj Zekri 2010).

When asked about their motivations to leave a country now liberated from the grip of dictatorship, they answered that they could only choose between immolating themselves like Bouazizi or undertaking the irregular migratory journey to Italy for which they had to pay an amount of money between 500 and 1,000 euros, a very high fee to pay by their deprived families. Some of them even used the money extended to them as compensation for the wounds inflicted on them during the revolution (around 1,500 euros) to pay for their passage to Europe (Ben Achour and Ben Jemia 2011).

It seems clear that political liberation did not represent for them the end of their condition which, as this chapter has attempted to demonstrate, originated in the discrepancy between the performance of the Tunisian economy and the global political economy. In a way, their decision to leave Tunisia after the revolution illustrated the extent to which their discontent was not so much a function of their political repression, but of their economic marginalisation. Paradoxically, they used their newly acquired freedom to leave the country and it seems unlikely that this haemorrhage will stop in the future.

Conclusion

The rhetoric about Tunisia spread by international organisations, most notably the World Bank and the International Monetary Fund, but to some extent also the European Union, had endorsed the idea of the

Tunisian economic miracle. Tunisia was singled out as the 'Mediterranean dragon', the example to follow in terms of economic growth, implementation of structural reforms, liberalisations and privatisation to achieve macroeconomic stability.

Despite the fact that the Tunisian economy seemed to have reacted well to the strong restructuring cure administered by the IMF at the end of the 1980s, the reality was that the programme failed to achieve the objective of integrating the country into the global political economy. On the contrary, its relative marginalisation increased over the course of the following two decades. This further aggravated the internal contradictions of neo-liberal restructuring and produced growing discontent. In the realm of civil society, as analysed in Chapter 3, discontent cemented an alliance between the impoverished middle class and the lower strata of society in the name of a political Islam that had been brutally repressed by Ben-Ali's regime.

Marginalisation from globalisation also increased the numbers of those who were prepared to undergo irregular migration to escape the country and the region, perhaps forever. This was especially true for those growing sections of the highly-skilled labour force which were increasingly unable to find a job appropriate to their skill level. They were as a result more and more willing to flee Tunisia in search of better opportunities in Europe. This process clearly did not stop with the newly acquired political freedom from the authoritarian regime. On the contrary, extra-regional migration after the revolution reproduced exactly the same patterns as before, further adding to the conclusion that discontent in Tunisia was not political, but economic.

Indeed, the thousands of young Tunisians arriving on the Italian shores in the few months after the liberation of the country from Ben Ali presented similar socio-economic and demographic characteristics as the ones who had left the country before and were migrating for exactly the same reasons. Moreover, they mostly presented a similar profile as that of Bouazizi, although they decided to manifest their discontent in a different way to him. Paraphrasing the claim of one migrant, they could either do as Bouazizi or leave the country by any means, including irregular ones. They were many 'Bouazizis' whose decision to escape was clearly not influenced by the political liberation of the country.

It is debatable whether these are strong bases on which to build a new Tunisia, but this is outside the scope of this analysis which now turns to the other allegedly successful revolution in the region, the Egyptian one.

Notes

1. For the text of the association agreement see website http://ec.europa.eu/trade/policy/countries-and-regions/countries/tunisia/ as accessed on 9 May 2013
2. See for example: Hibou (2003); Bayart (2007); Meddeb (2008).
3. For a thorough analysis of return migration and investment see Cassarino (2000).

References

Abdelfatta, D. (2011). *Impact of Arab Revolts on Migration.* CARIM Analytic and Synthetic Notes 2011/68, EUI, Florence.

Appleyard, R. (ed.) (1999). *Emigration Dynamics in Developing Countries, Volume IV: The Arab Region.* Ashgate, London.

Ayubi, N. (1990). 'Arab Bureaucracies: Expanding sizes, changing roles', in Giacomo Luciani (ed), *The Arab State*. Routledge, London.

Ayubi, N. (1991). *The State and Public Policy in Egypt since Sadat.* Ithaca Press, Reading.

Ayubi, N. (1993). 'The "Fiscal crisis" and the "Washington consensus": Towards an explanation of the Middle East liberalisations', in Blin, L. (ed.), *L'Economie Egyptienne*. L'Harmattan, Paris.

Ayubi, N. (2008). *Overstating the Arab State: Politics and Society in the Middle East.* IB Tauris, London.

Bayart, J.F. (2007). *Global Subjects. A Political Critique of Globalisation*, trans. by Andrew Brown. Polity Press, Cambridge.

Bel Haj Zekri, A. (2010). *Le Cadre socio-politique de la migration hautement qualifiée en Tunisie*. CARIM AS 2010/38, CARIM-EUI, Florence.

Ben Achour, S. and Ben Jemia, M. (2011). *Revolution Tunisienne et Migration Clandestine Vers Europe: Reactionnes Europeennes et Tunisiennes.* CARIM AS 2011/65, CARIM-EUI, Florence.

Boubakri, H. (2011). *Migrations et developpement. Reflexion et analyse a partir du cas de la Tunisie.* CARIM AS 2011/55, CARIM-EUI, Florence.

CARIM (2008). Euro-Mediterranean Consortium for Applied Research on International Migration, European University Institute, RSCAS, San Domenico in Fiesole, Florence, website http://www.carim.org/ as accessed on 3 September 2008.

Cassarino, J.P. (2000), *Tunisian New Entrepreneurs and their Past Experiences of Migration in Europe*. Ashgate Publishers, Aldershot.

Clement Moore, H., and Springborg, R. (2010). Globalization and the Politics of Development in the Middle East. Cambridge University Press.

Dicken, P. (2011). *Global Shift: Mapping the Changing Contours of the World Economy*, (6th ed.). Guilford Press, New York.

Dodge, T. and Higgot, R. (2002). *Globalisation and the Middle East.* The Royal Institute of International Affairs, London.

Fargues, P. (ed.) (2007). *Mediterranean Migration, 2006–2007*. European University Institute, RSCAS, San Domenico in Fiesole, Florence.

Fargues, P. and Fandrich, C. (2012). *Migration after the Arab Spring*. MPC Research Report 2012/09, Florence: EUI.

Fawcett, L. and Sayigh, Y. (1999). *The Third World beyond the Cold War: Continuity and Change*. Oxford University Press, Oxford.

Fourati, H. (2008). *Consultation de la jeunesse et desire d'emigration chez le jeunes en Tunisie 1996–2005*. CARIM AS 2008/47, CARIM-EUI, Florence.

Fourati, H. (2009). *Les Transferts des Tunisiens a l'étranger et leurs impacts sur le neveau de vie des ménages directement beneficiaries 1995–2005*. Carim notes d'analyse de synthese 2009/27, CARIM-EUI, Florence.

Fourati, H. (2010). *La migration hautement qualifiée depuis et vers la Tunisie*. CARIM AS 2010/18, CARIM-EUI, Florence.

Hakimian, H. and Moshaver, Z. (2001). *The State and Global Change: The Political Economy of Transition in the Middle East and North Africa*. Curzon Press, Richmond.

Hamid, S. (2011). 'Tunisia: The birthplace of the revolution', in Pollack, K.M. (ed.), *The Arab Awakening : America and the Transformation of the Middle East*, e-book, accessed 9 May 2013, http://kcl.eblib.com/patron/FullRecord.aspx?p=795889, pp. 111–116.

Hibou, B. (2003). 'Le Partenariat en réanimation bureaucratique', and more generally the special number 'Les faces cachées du Partenariat euroméditerranéen', *Critique internationale*, n° 18, April 2003

Hibou, B. (2011). *The Force of Obedience: The Political Economy of Repression in Tunisia*. Polity Press, Cambridge.

Hibou, B., Meddeb, H. and Hamdi, M. (2011). *Tunisia after 14 January and Its Social and Political Economy. The Issues at Stake in a Reconfiguration of European Policy*. Euro-Mediterranean Human Rights Network (EMHRN), June 2011, p. 92

Meddeb, H. (2008). *Ambivalence de la politique migratoire en Tunisie*. FASOPO, Paris, Mimeo.

Mittleman, J.H. (2000). *The Globalisation Syndrome: Transformation and Resistance*. Princeton University Press, Princeton.

Overbeek, H. (1999). *The Budapest Process: Internationalisation of Migration Control*, Paper presented to the 40th Annual Conference of the International Studies Association, February 1999, Washington D.C., Mimeo, pp. 16–20.

Overbeek, H. (2000). 'Globalisation, sovereignty and transnational regulation: Reshaping the governance of international migration', in Gosh, B. (ed.), *Managing Migration: Time for a New International Regime*. Oxford University Press, Oxford.

Owen, R. (2004). *State, Power and Politics in the Making of the Modern Middle East*. Routledge, London.

Owen, R. and Pamuk, S. (1999). *A History of Middle East Economies in the 20th Century*. Harvard University Press, Cambridge, MA.

Perkins, K. (2004). *A History of Modern Tunisia*. Cambridge University Press, Cambridge.

Pollack, K.M. (2011). *The Arab Awakening : America and the Transformation of the Middle East*, e-book, accessed 9 May 2013, <http://kcl.eblib.com/patron/FullRecord.aspx?p=795889>.

Richards, A., and Waterbury, J. (1998). A political Economy of the Middle East. Westview Press.

Sassen, S. (1998). *Globalisation and Its Discontents: Essays on the New Mobility of People and Money*. The New York Press, New York
Sassen, S. (1999). *Guests and Aliens*. The New York Press, New York.
Sassen, S. (2006). *Territory, Authority, Rights: From Mediaeval to Global Assemblages*. Princeton University Press, Princeton, NJ.
Zahlan, A.B. (1999). 'Labor migration and economic integration in the Middle East', in Hudson, M.C. (ed.), *Middle East Dilemma*. Tauris and Co. Ltd, New York, pp. 259–279.

6
Egypt: From Liberalisation to Marginalisation

Introduction

At this point it is important to ascertain to what extent Egypt, the second country experiencing political turmoil leading to regime change during the events of the Arab Spring, has been excluded or marginalised from the global political economy.

In Chapter 3 we have already underlined the extent to which the country is lagging behind in terms of catching up with the technological skills and capacities necessary to fully gather the benefits of globalisation.

Here the analysis moves to the economic dimensions of marginalisation using the indicators traditionally identified in the literature as revealing the most in terms of marginalisation from or integration into the global political economy (Dodge and Higgot 2002; Hakimian and Moshaver 2001; Fawcett and Sayigh 1999). These are represented by the level and value of FDI stocks and inflows and their performance over time, processes of market integration reflected in Mergers and Acquisitions, and trade openness specifically aimed at increasing exports.

Of course, these indicators will be brought together with other suitable ones to provide a broader picture of the degree of the country's integration into the global economy. Amongst them, the level and evolution over time of remittances from Egyptian permanent emigrants is considered as an important indicator of marginalisation and brain drain.

Before proposing such an empirical analysis, however, the next section will provide an account of the steps undertaken by Egypt to liberalise and open its economy.

The mother of all liberalisations!

The literature portrays the case of Egypt as the 'mother of Arab liberalisations' (Ayubi [1999] 2008: 339; Similarly Owen and Pamuk 1999).

Sadat, in 1974, inaugurated the liberalisation and privatisation programme with his 'open door policy', the *infitah* (Owen 2004: 116). In 1974, the Egyptian government adopted the 'Old Egyptian Investment Law' (Law no. 43, 'On Arab and Foreign Investment and Free Zones') with the aim of attracting foreign investment in Egypt either alone or in association with Egyptian business. In 1989, this law was reformed with the adoption of Investment Law no. 230. The implementation of the infitah was, however, very sluggish. On one side the second oil boom at the end of the 1970s provided the government with enough money to limit international pressure for the implementation of the liberalisation process. On the other hand, liberalisation provoked many discontents and impoverished the population and therefore needed to be slowed down to avoid the political risks of radical restructuring. The peak of the programme of privatisation was indeed formally achieved only in 1987 when the Parliament finally passed a bill allowing for the sale of a number of public properties (Owen 2004: 116; Ayubi 2008: 346).

In May 1997, a new law was passed, the Law of Investment Guarantees and Incentives, which cancelled any previous regulations relating to foreign investment. It was enforced by the Prime Minister's Decree no. 2108. Finally, in October 1999, the old 1883 Commercial Code was replaced by a new one (Khyeda 2007: 73–104).

At the roots of this process of opening the economy was the aim of increasing foreign investment (Khyeda 2007: 73–104). As already noted in a previous chapter, this was a strategy based on an alliance between the Egyptian State and international capital which did not enjoy the full support of the local middle class. In principle, the Egyptian middle classes might have favoured the open door policy and the liberalisation process. However, the way that it was implemented in practice was unfavourable to the middle classes and exacerbated their progressive marginalisation from the levers of power that had already provoked their discontent (Ayubi 1990, 1991, 1993, 2008). In fact, this preference for the 'open door policy' made local industry more fragile by exposing it too suddenly to external competition which it could not withstand (Ayubi 2008: 339). Indeed, the preferred formula for the implementation of the infitah in Egypt was one of joint ventures between the

Egyptian public sector and foreign multinational corporations (Ayubi 2008: 334).

Paradoxically, however, despite the existence of a clear strategy of state elites to attract international capital, foreign direct investments only arrived in Egypt to a limited extent, as further detailed in the next section. In the majority of cases Egypt witnessed one-off acquisitions, such as the sale for US$1.6 billion of the Bank of Alexandria, taking place in October 2006, or the private equity deal transferring the family-owned Amoun Pharmaceutical into US hands for US$450 million (Khyeda 2007).

Instead, as detailed in Chapter 4, the economic stabilisation of Egypt was mostly made possible by external aid, disbursed by foreign countries with principally geopolitical/strategic considerations in mind. For example, in the course of the first Iraq war in 1990–1991, Egypt received about $3.9 billion, while the US and the Gulf states cancelled some $12.9 billion worth of debts, thus substantially reducing debt-servicing burdens (Ayubi 2008: 346–347).

Not even the fact that the Egyptian government had embarked on a substantial programme of macroeconomic adjustment during the 1990s helped to attract FDIs. This programme, agreed with the IMF, was part of a broader package aimed at cancelling half of the Egyptian public debt (Owen 2004). Starting from May 1991, the package scheduled a cancellation of 15 per cent of the debt by October 1992; another 15 per cent was to be erased with the implementation of the second agreement with the IMF between November 1992 and April 1993. The remaining amount would be cancelled from May 1993 to November 1994. However, the IMF imposed as a condition to its credit extension[1] (amounting to 60 per cent of Egyptian contributions to the fund) the implementation of structural macroeconomic reforms according to the guidelines of the IMF and the World Bank (Ayubi 2008: 346–347; Owen 2004: 117).

Table 6.1 presents an overview of the lending arrangements between the Egyptian government and the IMF, including starting dates and amounts for the period between May 1984 and June 2008.

The economic stabilisation programmes attached to the IMF loans, the related structural reforms, privatisations and liberalisations, debt relief and foreign aid, coming especially from the US, all seemed to help Egypt maintain its macroeconomic performance. Indeed, although decreasing somewhat during the decades of the 1970s and 1980s, in the course of the 1990s the real GDP increased on average by around 5 per cent. Growth continued to be sustained throughout the 2000s until before the turmoil of 2011 (Figure 6.1 below).

Table 6.1 Egypt – History of lending arrangements with the IMF from 1 May 1984 to 30 June 2008 (thousands of SDRs)

Facility	Date of arrangement	Date of expiration or cancellation	Amount agreed	Amount drawn	Amount outstanding
Standby arrangement	11 October 1996	30 September 1998	271,400	0	0
Extended fund facility	20 September 1993	19 September 1996	400,000	0	0
Standby arrangement	17 May 1991	31 May 1993	234,400	147,200	0
Standby arrangement	15 May 1987	30 November 1988	250,000	116,000	0
Total			1,155,800	263,200	0

Source: IMF (2008)

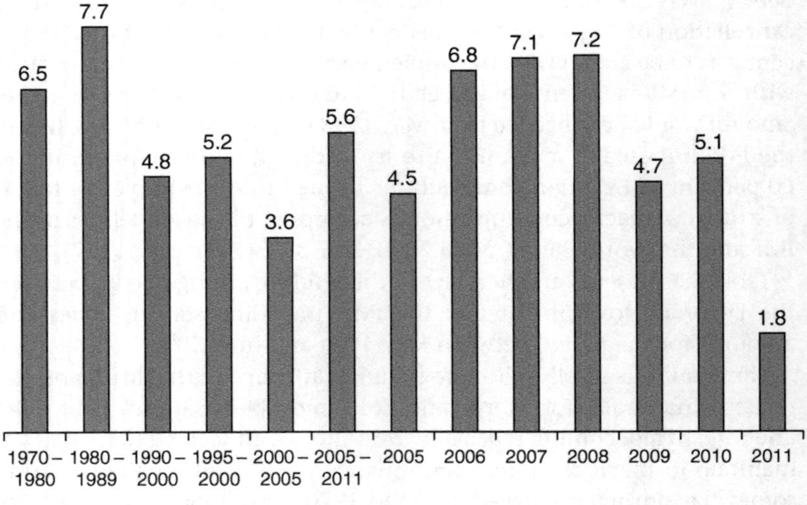

Figure 6.1 Egypt – annual average growth rates of real GDP, 1970–2011

Source: Elaboration by the author on data from UNCTAD website http://www.unctad.org/Templates/Page.asp?intItemID=1584&lang=1 as accessed on 7 May 2013

Other macroeconomic indicators improved by various degrees in the period, such as for example the level of foreign reserves (Figure 6.2), the size of the external debt (Figure 6.3) and the fiscal balance (Figure 6.4), which all improved over the course of the 1990s. According to the data provided by UNCTAD, the amount of total reserves in Egypt, including gold, increased by nine times between 1990 and 1998, before levelling in the first years of 2000 (Figure 6.2) and skyrocketing just before the Revolution of 25 January. The Egyptian current account experienced some substantial surpluses in the first half of the 1990s which however turned into deficits in the second half of the 1990s, but improved again just before the start of the global financial crisis (Figure 6.3). Even cash deficits as a percentage of GDP were contained over the course of the 1990s, although they deteriorated in the 2000s (Figure 6.4).

As one would expect given the nature and content of the IMF conditionality, inflation decreased substantially during the 1990s, with the GDP deflator moving from almost 20 per cent in 1992 to almost 0 in 1999 (Figure 6.5).

Price stability allowed the government to peg the exchange rate of the Egyptian pound to the US dollar during this period, with all foreign exchange transactions taking place within a ±3 per cent range around a central rate which was announced by the Central Bank of Egypt (Figure 6.6).[2] Again, the aim was to attract as much FDI as possible.

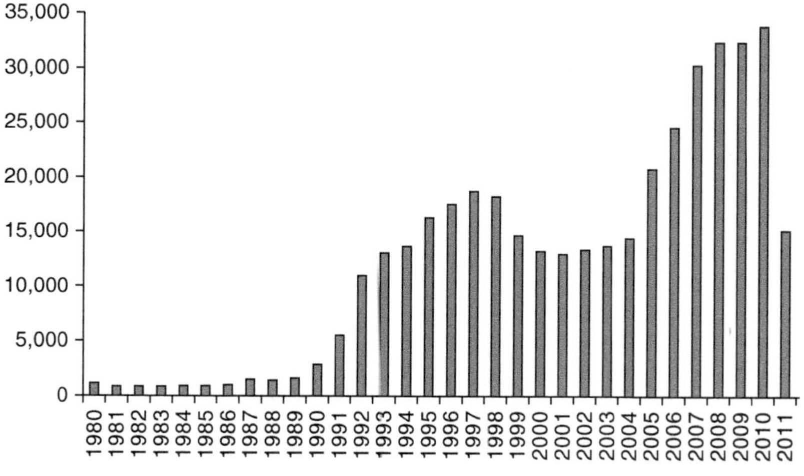

Figure 6.2 Egypt – total reserves including gold, 1980–2011 (US$ millions current prices current, exchange rates)

Source: Elaboration by the author on data from UNCTAD website http://www.unctad.org/Templates/Page.asp?intItemID=1584&lang=1 as accessed on 7 May 2013

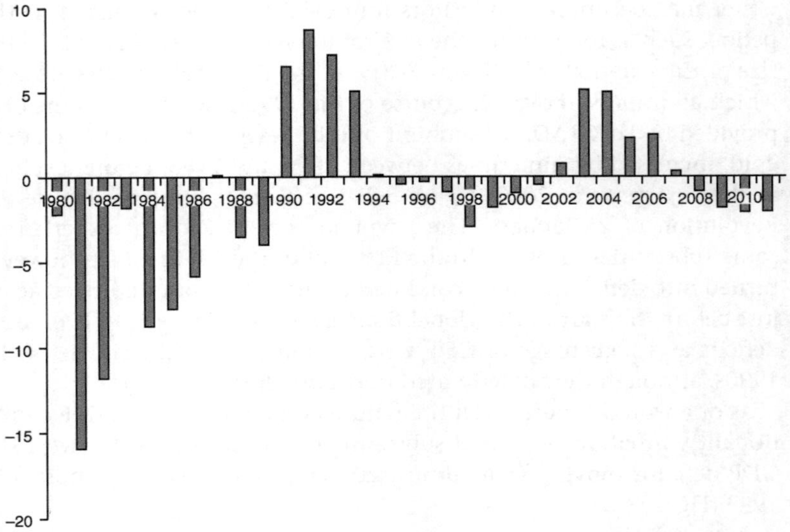

Figure 6.3 Egypt – current account net, 1980–2011(percentage of GDP)

Source: Elaboration by the author on data from UNCTAD website http://www.unctad.org/Templates/Page.asp?intItemID=1584&lang=1 as accessed on 7 May 2013

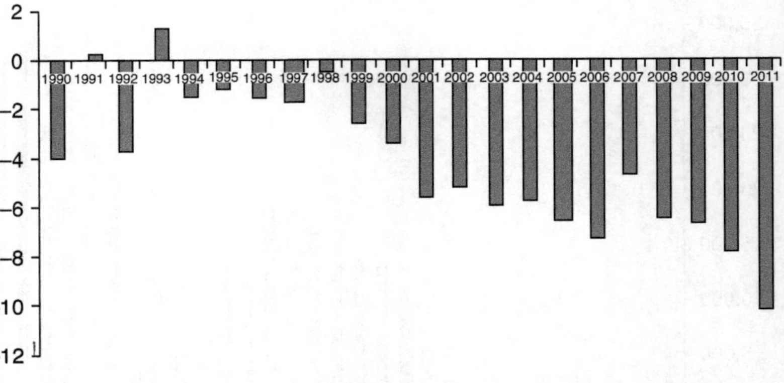

Figure 6.4 Egypt – cash surplus/deficit, 1990–2011 (percentage of GDP)

Source: Elaboration by the author on data from the World Bank website http://web.worldbank.org/WBSITE/EXTERNAL/DATASTATISTICS/0,,menuPK:232599~pagePK:64133170~piPK:64133498~theSitePK:239419,00.html as accessed on 7 May 2013

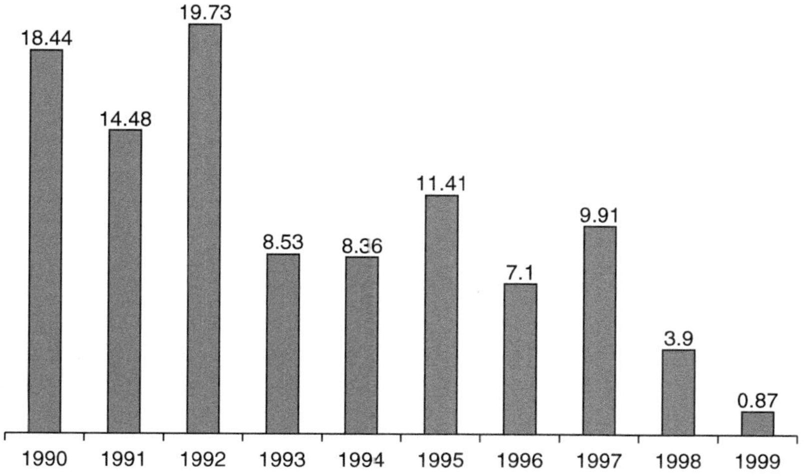

Figure 6.5 Egypt – inflation, GDP deflator, 1990–1999 (annual percentage)

Source: Elaboration by the author on data from the World Bank website http://web.worldbank.org/WBSITE/EXTERNAL/DATASTATISTICS/0,,menuPK:232599~pagePK:64133170~piPK:64133498~theSitePK:239419,00.html as accessed on 7 May 2013

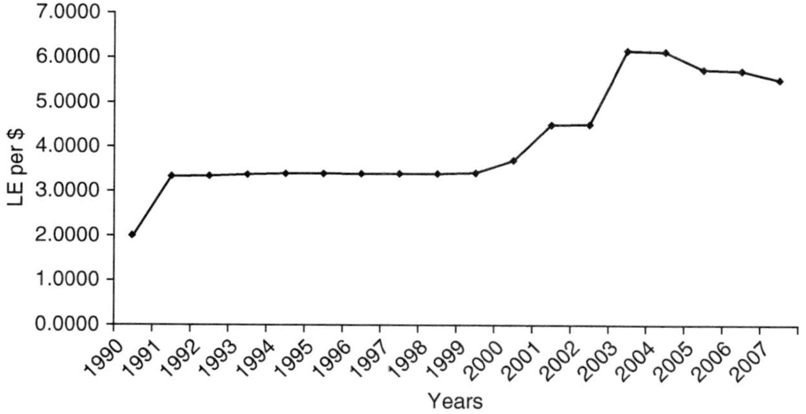

Figure 6.6 Egyptian pound (LE) exchange rate in US$, 1990–2007

Source: Elaboration by the author on data from the IMF, International Financial Statistics website http://www.imfstatistics.org/imf/ as accessed on 7 May 2013

Despite the relative macroeconomic stability experienced by Egypt in the course of the 1990s, a substantial programme of privatisation and the Egyptian government's commitment to structural reforms and economic adjustment, Egypt failed to attract more than a very limited level of foreign investment and the path to liberalisation seemed, in practice, to lead to marginalisation.[3]

The marginalisation of Egypt

Macroeconomic indicators of marginalisation

An assessment of the degree of economic marginalisation of Egypt, despite liberalisation measures aimed at increasing its participation in the global political economy, starts from its share of total global FDI and the evolution of this indicator over the years preceding the Arab Spring. In Chapter 4 we have already noticed that, in spite of the dramatic increase of world FDI stock since 1980, the largest share continues to be held by developed nations. Amongst developing regions, Asia is the one with the highest increase in the share of total FDI, whereas North Africa's portion has actually been declining in the last 30 years (Chapter 4).

In the case of Egypt, the declining trend in the percentage of total FDI stock from the 1980s until the second half of the 2000s was very marked, with the lowest levels registered at the beginning of the new millennium (Figure 6.7).

In general, the stock of FDIs in Egypt was never more than 0.6 per cent, but after the structural reform programme of the 1990s it declined to a level which was never above 0.4 per cent and even reached a low of 0.2 per cent in 2004 (Figure 6.7). This is hardly a success story in terms of opening up of the Egyptian economy to foreign capital as was originally envisaged at the start of the infitah.

Looking at the average for each decade between 1981 and 2010 it appears even more clearly how the trend has irrefutably been a declining one. Indeed if in the decade of the 1980s the percentage share of Egyptian total FDI stock was an already tiny 0.53 per cent, in the 1990s it decreased to 0.4 per cent and in the 2000s to a minuscule 0.29 per cent (Figure 6.8).

Not dissimilarly, the percentage of total FDI inflows going to Egypt has been declining steadily since the 1980s. Not surprisingly, this reached a negative level in 2011, after the Arab Spring (Figure 6.9). It is worth noting that the slight increase in FDI inflows in the period between 2004 and 2009 is due to the expansion in the oil sector and a boom in privatisations (Nassar 2009: 9).

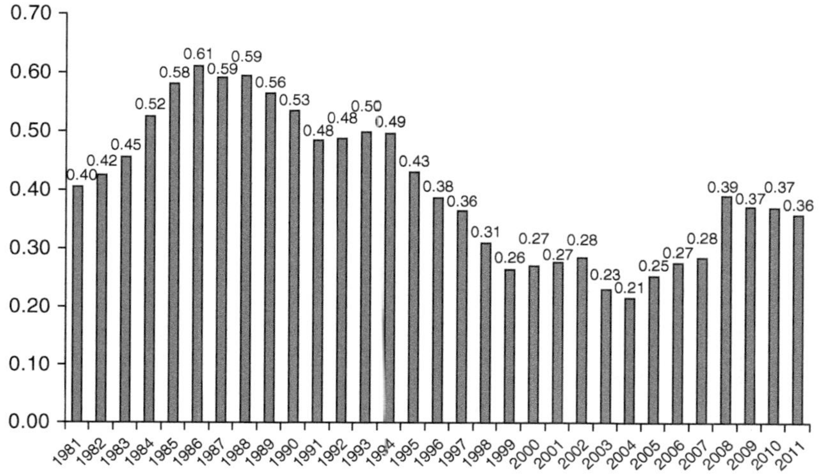

Figure 6.7 Egypt – average percentage share of world total FDI stock, 1981–2011

Source: Elaboration by the author on data from UNCTAD website http://www.unctad.org/Templates/Page.asp?intItemID=1584&lang=1 as accessed on 30 April 2013

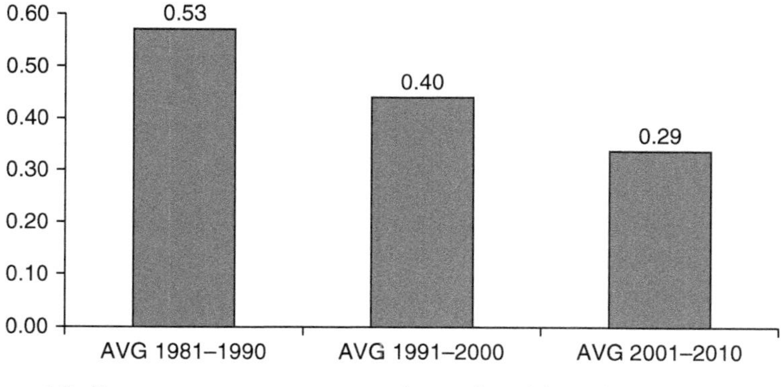

Figure 6.8 Egypt – average percentage share of world total FDI stock, decades 1981–2010

Source: Elaboration by the author on data from UNCTAD website http://www.unctad.org/Templates/Page.asp?intItemID=1584&lang=1 as accessed on 30 April 2013

Even more telling is the fact that, in absolute terms, the level of FDI inflows for the whole liberalisation and structural reform period, from the 1980s to the mid-2000s, was always a fraction of the level of migrants' remittances. At its lowest point FDI was recorded at only US$237.4 million, in 2003 (Figure 6.10).

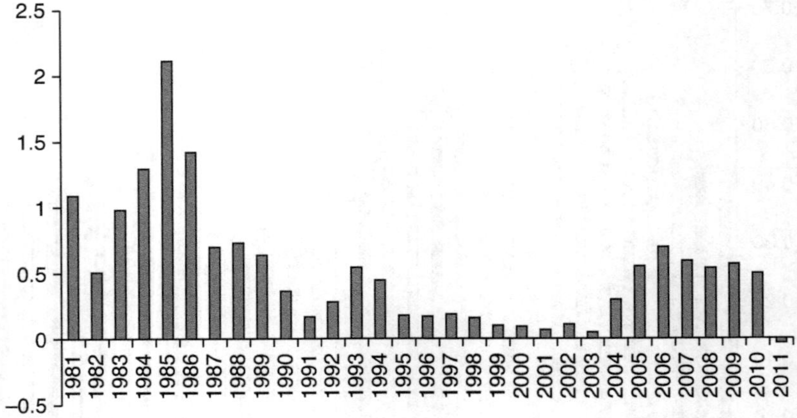

Figure 6.9 Egypt – average percentage share of world total FDI inflows, 1981–2011

Source: Elaboration bythe author on data from UNCTAD website http://www.unctad.org/Templates/Page.asp?intItemID=1584&lang=1 as accessed on 30 April 2013

In the case of Egypt, not only is the level of FDI limited, but Western portfolio investment in company shares quoted on regional stock markets is also minimal, if not negative. Net portfolio investment in Egypt in the fiscal year 2001–2002 amounted to $45.3 million, and the first three quarters of the 2002–2003 financial year saw a net outflow of $206 million.[4]

Turning to mergers and acquisitions, the percentage share of sales over the world total is negligible in Egypt (0.2 on average for the past two decades) (Table 6.2).

In order to assess the effect on trade openness of the structural reforms adopted by the Mubarak government in the course of the 1990s under the pressure of the IMF, it is worth looking also at the figures relating to trade as a share of purchasing power parity GDP (PPP GDP). The figures refer to the sum of exports and imports divided by PPP GDP. During the period considered these figures fell in most countries in the Middle East, and in the region as a whole. As reported in Chapter 4, very few countries in the region opened up after the restructuring programmes, while the majority underwent a closure of their economies. In particular Egypt remained remarkably stable moving from 8.9 per cent in 1990 to 9.1 per cent in 1999 (Table 5.2, Chapter 4).

The graph below shows how Egypt's trade openness, measured by UNCTAD as the average imports and exports as a percentage of GDP,

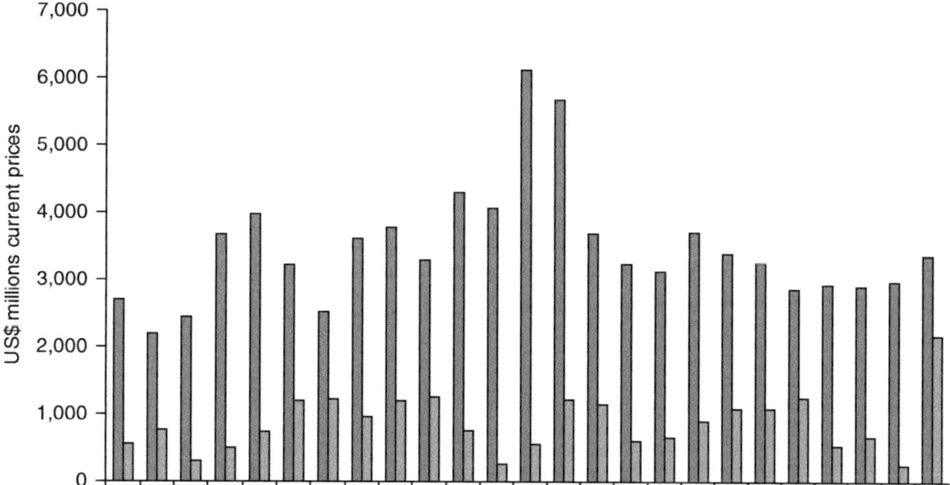

	1980	1981	1982	1983	1984	1985	1986	1987	1988	1989	1990	1991	1992	1993	1994	1995	1996	1997	1998	1999	2000	2001	2002	2003	2004
Egypt-remittances	2696	2181	2439	3666	3963	3212	2506	3604	3770	3293	4284	4054	6104	5664	3672	3226	3107	3697	3370	3235	2852	2911	2893	2961	3341
Egypt-FDI inflows	548.3	752.6	293.6	490	729.1	1178	1217	947.7	1190	1250	734	253	459	1207	1133	595.2	636.4	886.9	1076	1065	1235	509.9	646.9	237.4	2157

Figure 6.10 Egypt – comparison remittances/FDI inflows, 1980–2005 (US$ millions at current prices)

Source: Elaboration by the author on data from UNCTAD website http://www.unctad.org/Templates/Page.asp?intItemID=1584&lang=1 as accessed on 30 April 2013

Table 6.2 Value of cross-border M&A by region/economy of seller, 1990–2011 (US$ millions)

	1990	1991	1992	1993	1994	1995	1996	1997	1998	1999	2000	
World	98,903	21,094	48,106	43,623	91,769	112,527	142,557	180,751	406,427	630,807	905,214	
Egypt	–	–	131	177	17	10	163	1	109	700	1,091	
% of World total	0	0	0.27218	0.40634	0.0185	0.0088	0.1144	0.0003	0.02673	0.11101	0.15061	
	2001	**2002**	**2003**	**2004**	**2005**	**2006**	**2007**	**2008**	**2009**	**2010**	**2011**	**AVG%**
World	429,374	248,446	182,874	227,221	462,253	625,320	1,022,725	706,543	249,732	344,029	525,881	
Egypt	188	374	378	24	1,478	2,976	1,713	15,895	993	195	609	
% of World total	0.04384	0.15061	0.20660	0.01058	0.31967	0.47589	0.16746	2.24973	0.39752	0.05668	0.11573	0.23969

Source: UNCTAD cross-border M&A database(www.unctad.org/fdistatistics)

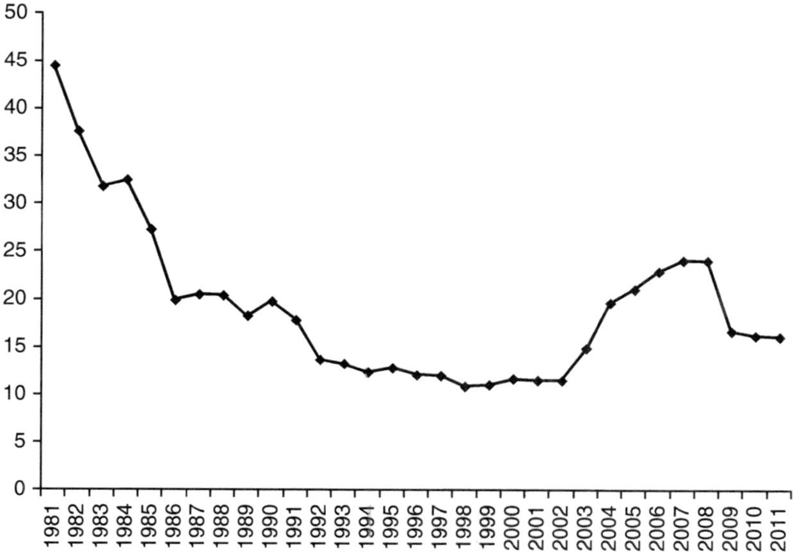

Figure 6.11 Egypt – trade openness: average imports and exports as a percentage of GDP

Source: UNCTAD database

decreased substantially from 1981 to 2011, falling from around 45 per cent to a mere 16 per cent (Figure 6.11).

Indeed, in the decade between 1993 and 2004, although the value of exports increased, the Egyptian economy relied heavily on tourism, remittances from Egyptians living abroad, revenues from the Suez Canal, and oil.

The situation did not substantially change in the following years. The Central Bank of Egypt reports that in the period between 1999 and 2007, the main sources of foreign exchange in Egypt were exports, tourism and travel receipts, oil revenues, remittances and Suez Canal duties. FDI inflows represented on average only 9 per cent of the total amount of foreign currency received (Figure 6.12). This is substantially less than remittances (12 per cent) and tourism (17 per cent) and very similar to Suez Canal dues (8 per cent).

The literature (Nassar 2009) ranks the most significant sources of foreign currency in Egypt according to their stability in the decade between 1999 and 2007 as follows:

1. Suez canal dues
2. Remittances
3. Travel and tourism receipts
4. Exports of goods
5. Official transfers
6. Petroleum exports
7. FDI

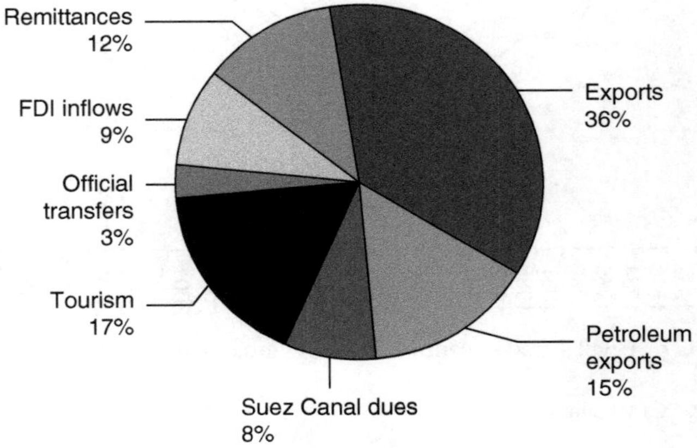

Figure 6.12 Egypt – foreign exchange inflows, 1999–2007
Source: Central Bank of Egypt (2007), elaboration by the author

Table 6.3 Egypt – Sources of foreign currency inflows, 1993/94–2002/03 (US$ millions)

	Petroleum exports	Suez Canal duties	Travel and tourism receipts	Official transfers	FDI inflows	Exports	Remittances*
1993–94	1772.1	1990.3	1779.3	813.6	1320.8	3337.3	4866.11
1994–95	2176	2058.4	2298.9	918.6	782.7	4957	4325.41
1995–96	2226	1884.7	3009.1	723.6	626.9	4608.5	3522.2
1996–97	2578	1848.9	3646.3	889.6	769.7	5345.4	3690.87
1997–98	1728.4	1776.4	2940.5	882.6	1103.9	5128.4	3873.02
1998–99	999.7	1771	3235.1	1096.7	710.6	4445.1	3465.9
1999–00	2272.9	1780.8	4313.8	932.4	1656.1	6387.7	3711
2000–01	2632.4	1842.5	4316.9	769.3	509.4	7078.2	2926.4
2001–02	2381	1819.8	3422.8	1143.6	428.2	7120.8	2907.87
2002–03	3160.8	2236.2	3796.4	663.6	700.6	8205.2	2689.25

*(at constant prices 1999/2000)
Source: Egyptian Ministry of Foreign Trade Bulletin Various Issues

Clearly neither exports of goods nor FDI represented the most stable source of foreign currency before the change of regime. This was the case, instead, for both tourism and remittances. Both, therefore, deserve more attention.

UNCTAD data suggests that almost 50 per cent of Egypt's GDP in 2010 was generated by the services sector with tourism as the most important contributor (Figures 6.13 and 6.14).

It is debatable whether this will continue after the change of Mubarak's regime. Data for 2011 present a decline in the role played by tourism services in the wake of the Arab Spring, but this alone is certainly not enough to reach any conclusions in this respect.

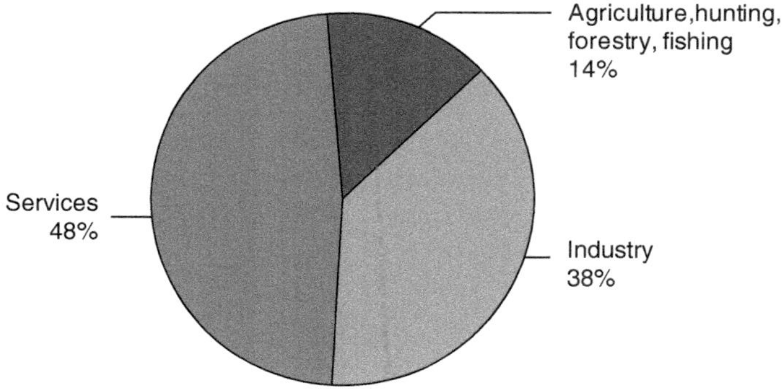

Figure 6.13 Egypt – economic structure, 2010
Source: Elaboration bythe author on data from UNCTAD website www.unctad.org

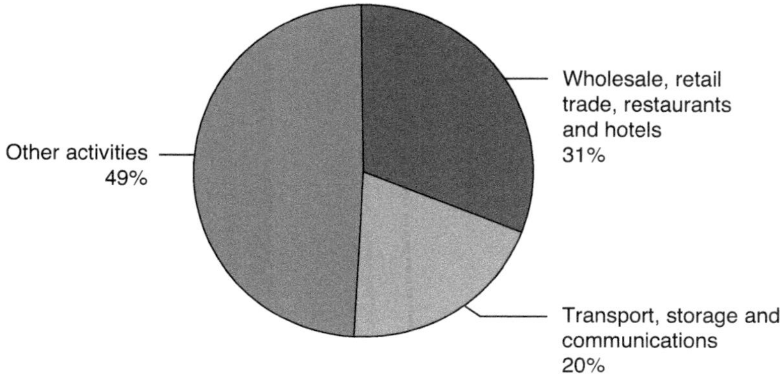

Figure 6.14 Egypt – economic structure, composition of services, 2010
Source: Elaboration by the author on data from UNCTAD website www.unctad.org

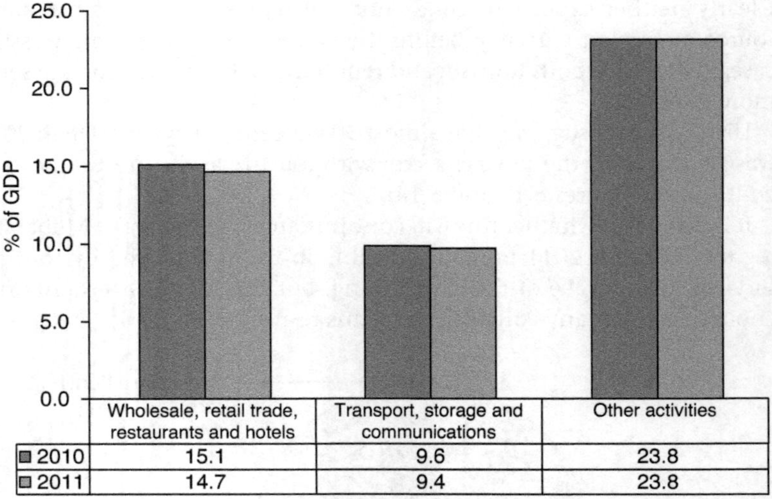

Figure 6.15 Egypt – composition of services, 2010–2011 (percentage of GDP)
Source: Elaboration by the author on data from UNCTAD website www.unctad.org

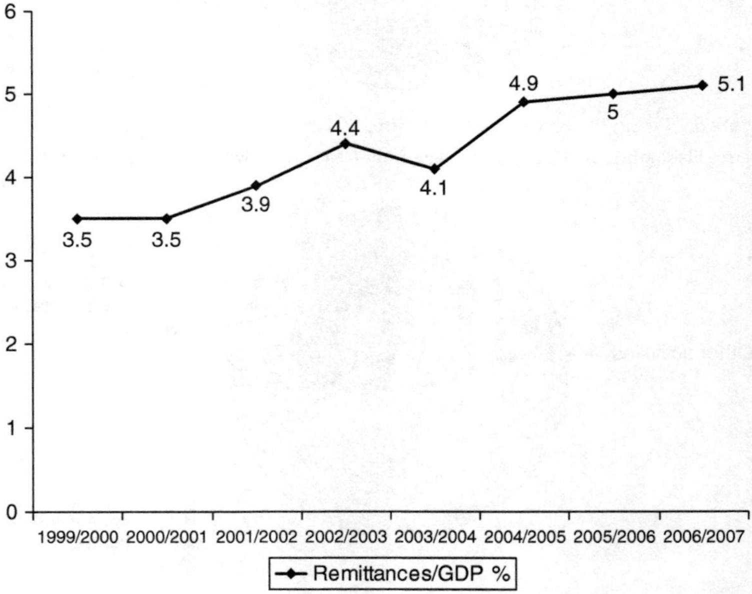

Figure 6.16 Egypt – remittances as a percentage of GDP, 1999–2007
Source: Nassar 2009

As far as remittances are concerned, their percentage contribution to GDP in the period between 1999–2007 has increased, showing the importance of migration out of Egypt as a source of foreign currency for the state and of income for families (similarly Nassar 2009: 22) (Figure 6.16). Moreover, as the official data on remittances do not include those that follow alternative routes into the country, the estimates of real impact of remittances on GDP should be at least doubled (Nassar 2009: 22).

The importance of workers' remittances for the Egyptian economy is clearly demonstrated by the fact that in the last three decades, workers' remittances have always been higher than official development assistance and official aid (Figure 6.17).

In the wake of the Arab Spring, Egyptian remittances recorded their highest level in the history of Egypt, reaching $12.6 billion for the financial year 2010–2011 (Abdelfattah 2011: 9).

The data reported above point to another important indicator of the marginalisation of Egypt from the global political economy, as indicated by transnationalist scholars (Dicken 2011; Mittelman 2000; Sassen 1998, 1999, 2006; Overbeek 1999, 2000): the question of the relation between marginalisation and extra-regional migration, that is to say, migration

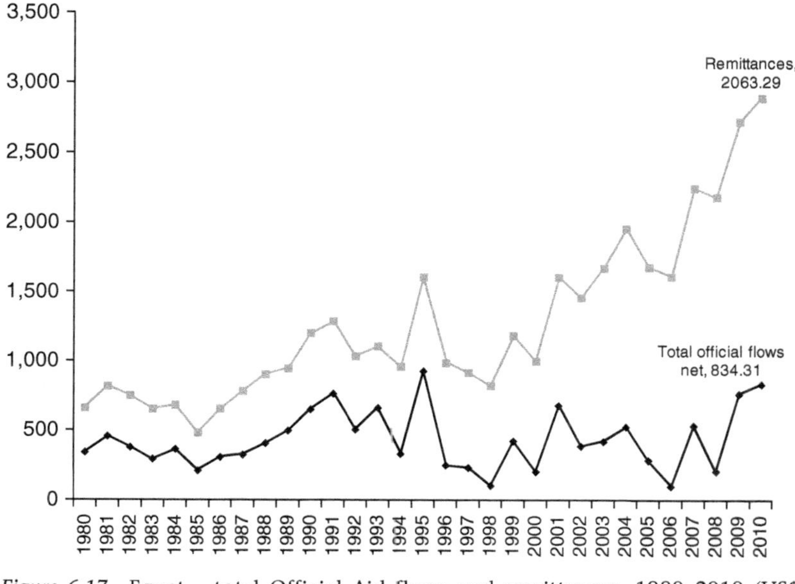

Figure 6.17 Egypt – total Official Aid flows and remittances, 1980–2010 (US$ millions at current prices and current exchange rates)

Source: UNCTAD database

outside the MENA area. This deserves closer attention, especially after the Arab Spring. To this we turn in the next section of the chapter.

Other indicators of marginalisation: extra-regional migration and brain drain

There have been various phases in the development of migratory flows out of Egypt. Scholars (Appleyard 1999; Feiler 2003; Dessouki 1982; Amin 2000; Zohry and Harrell-Bond 2003) generally refer to five phases. To this it may be necessary to add a sixth one starting after the Arab Spring, although it is still debatable whether the political change will actually make any difference in terms of emigration trends (Table 6.4).

The first wave, before 1974, was a consequence of the economic, political and social changes that Egypt underwent after Nasser took power, but it was limited in terms of numbers and social characteristics. Indeed, the social composition of migrants in this phase was almost totally represented by the upper classes, especially professionals and capitalists, who were threatened by Nasser's nationalisation and property-seizing measures. Emigration was a consequence of the revolution and of its impact on the Egyptian social structure, especially in terms of substitution of the previous elite with the new, Nasserite one (Binder 1978; Keppel 1999). The main countries of destination of this first wave of migration were Canada and the USA (Amin 2000: 96–97). Thus, migration from Egypt in the 1960s was a very limited phenomenon both in terms of scale and of scope (Choucri 1978).

Migratory flows out of Egypt became a sizeable phenomenon only in the 1970s, especially after the inauguration of the infitah in 1974 (Seccombe 1985; Sell 1987; Ibrahim 1982: 65). This coincided with the

Table 6.4 Egyptian migration phases

Phase 1: Before 1974 'The early phase of migration'	Very limited migration, mostly highly skilled or politically determined
Phase 2: 1974–1984 'The expansion phase'	Expansion of temporary migration in the Arab oil-producing countries
Phase 3: 1984–1988 'The contraction phase'	Contraction of migration to the Arab world
Phase 4: 1988–1992 'The deterioration phase'	Significant flow of return migrants from the Gulf area to Egypt
Phase 5: 1992–2011 'The recent phase'	Significant increase of permanent migration to the more developed world
Phase 6: 2011– 'After the Arab Spring'	Anything changes?

first oil shock, which facilitated intra-regional migration from resource-poor MENA countries to wealthy members of the OPEC which were experiencing sudden job shortages. In 1975, there were an estimated 1.6 million migrant workers in the labour-importing countries of Bahrain, Kuwait, Libya, Oman, Qatar, Saudi Arabia and the United Arab Emirates, of which 1.1 million were of Arab origin (Zahlan 1999). In 1970 the Egyptian Central Agency for Public Mobilisation and Statistics (CAPMAS) estimated the number of Egyptian abroad to be a mere 70,000. In 1976, the number of Egyptian emigrants had become a staggering 1.4 million (Zohry and Harrell-Bond 2003). This migratory wave was however almost exclusively intra-regional and of a temporary nature, involving mainly young, unskilled or semi-skilled male workers leaving Egypt and heading to the oil-rich countries of the Gulf or Libya, first after the 1973 boom in oil prices, and again after the second increase in oil prices in 1979 (Amin 2000: 96–97).

The literature then identifies a contraction in the number of migrants from Egypt between 1984 and 1988 due to the reduction of oil revenues induced by the beginning of the Iran–Iraq war. This contraction was followed by a true collapse of intra-regional migration in the second half of the 1980s provoked by the Iran–Iraq war, the fall of oil prices, the declining demand for construction workers in Arab countries, and the policy of replacing foreign labour with nationals in the Arab Gulf States (Zohry and Harrell-Bond 2003; contra Zahlan 1999). This state of affairs was exacerbated after the first Gulf war, producing a significant return migration from the Gulf area to Egypt (Talani 2010). As a result of the war, about two million people, including more than two-thirds of Kuwait's citizens and more than a million foreign workers, were displaced from Kuwait, Iraq and Saudi Arabia (Russell 1992). By the conclusion of the war, virtually all Egyptian immigrants in Iraq and Kuwait returned to Egypt or were displaced to other countries in the region (Russell 1992: 721). The ILO estimates a reduction of around 21.5 per cent in the Egyptian emigrant population between 1989 and 1991, from 1,964,000 in 1989 to 1,541,000 in 1991 (ILO 2008).

The following period is identified in the literature as a truly new phase in the development of outward migration from Egypt, and one which is related to its increasing marginalisation from the global political economy (Talani 2010).

This phase is characterised by a marked increased in extra-regional permanent migration. Between 1990 and 1998, the number of permanent migrants to developed countries increased on average by 83 per cent. In particular, permanent migration to Europe increased by around 125 per cent (from 225,251 to 506,028 migrants) whereas intra-regional temporary migration increased by only 68 per cent.

This trend towards an increase in permanent migration, especially to Europe, was confirmed in the following decade, from 1998 to 2008. Data from Egyptian consulates abroad shows a marked increase in the total number of Egyptian registered as permanent migrants in Europe, from 508,598 to 780,841 (an increase of more than 53 per cent). Looking only at the official consular data, migration from Egypt increased overall by

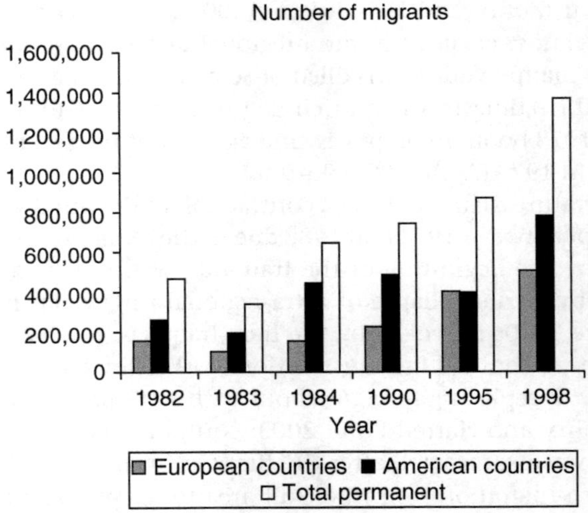

Figure 6.18 Egyptians abroad, permanent US/Europe, 1992–1998
Source: Elaboration by the author on data by the Egyptian Ministry for Manpower and Emigration as reported by CARIM (2008)

Table 6.5 Egyptian migration, 1998–2008

Country of residence	1998	2008
Total African countries	1,278	2,445
Total Asian countries	3,203	6,073
Total Oceanian countries	83,450	106,000
Total American countries	780,821	790,799
Total European countries	508,598	780,841
Total Arab countries	3,601,859	4,789,359
Main total	4,979,209	6,475,517

Source: Consular records (Ministry of Manpower and Emigration)
Updated: 4 May 2012

at least 30 per cent in the last decade. Of course these figures grossly underestimate the real number of Egyptians abroad because they do not include any estimates for irregular migration (Zohry 2007).

Another important characteristic of this new, marginalisation-induced wave of migration from Egypt was that it did not only include unskilled or semi-skilled migrants, as the previous ones, but also involved skilled or highly skilled labour.[5] Indeed, looking at the characteristics of Egyptian workers abroad, it is clear that they are on average more educated than the non-migrant population (Table 6.6).

The little data available shows that the number of Egyptian migrants who did not receive any formal education is more than 20 per cent less than in the non-migrant population. On the other hand, the migrants that received secondary education exceed the number of non-migrants who received it by more than 20 per cent. Furthermore, the percentage of migrants with a university degree or a higher level of education is 21.2 per cent while that of non-migrants with a similar level of education is only 14.5 per cent. These indications of brain drain are confirmed by the employment dynamics of Egyptian migrants abroad.

Looking at the figures relating to the occupation categories of Egyptian workers in Arab countries from 1985 to 2002, a clear tendency towards an increase in the numbers of highly qualified migrants emerges. Indeed, while the percentage of work permits granted to scientists and technicians was 20.4 per cent in 1985, this number had doubled in 2002 (41 per cent) Also, the number of managers has increased, whereas there were 10 per cent fewer production workers and clerical workers lowered from 8.8 per cent to 1.5 per cent (Table 6.7).

Table 6.6 Educational level of migrants and non-migrants at last emigration (migrants) or five years ago (non-migrants), 1997 (per cent)

Educational level	**Migrants**	**Non-migrants**
Non formal education	15.4	37.7
Incomplete Primary	18.7	18.5
Primary	7.8	8.8
Preparatory	4.2	4.9
Secondary	32.7	15.7
University or Higher	21.2	14.5
Total (%)	**100**	**100**
Number	1,121	3,672

Source: Ministry of Manpower and Emigration as reported by CARIM (2008), updated 7 February 2005

Moreover, permanent migration to more developed countries has always represented a source of brain drain as it has mainly involved more educated workers (ILO 2008). As extra-regional permanent migration has been on the rise in recent times, brain drain also has increased. Indeed, according to recent data, more than 77 per cent of Egyptians heading to OECD countries or to the USA have completed their tertiary education, around 19 per cent their secondary education, and only 4 per cent have only their primary education. As far as the kind of professions which are involved in the brain drain, Nassar reports that at the beginning of the 2000s, 18.3 per cent of highly skilled migrants from Egypt were employed in medical sciences, 32.2 per cent were engineers, 36.5 per cent were in working in social sciences, 8 per cent in basic sciences, and 5 per cent in agriculture (Nassar 2005: 8)

Table 6.7 Work permits granted to Egyptians in Arab countries, by occupation and year – 1985, 1990, 2002 (per cent)

Occupation	**1985**	**1990**	**2002**
Scientists and technicians	20.4	40.2	41.0
Managers	0.3	0.3	2.4
Clerical workers	8.8	8.0	1.5
Sales and services	18.5	17.3	12.7
Agriculture, animal husbandry and fishing	8.9	5.3	8.6
Production workers	43.0	28.9	33.8
Total	**100**	**100**	**100**

Source: Ministry of Manpower and Emigration as reported by CARIM (2008), updated 7 February 2005

Table 6.8 Permanent migrant flows by level of education in the period 2000–2007

	PhD	**Masters**	**High diploma**	**University**	**Intermediate**	**No qualifications**	**Total**
2000	8	12	8	243	233	32	536
2001	5	14	12	322	334	31	718
2002	10	10	11	274	323	24	652
2003	4	2	2	167	104	14	293
2004	3	16	9	200	115	14	357
2005	5	15	9	196	180	20	425
2006	4	12	7	210	124	11	368
2007	3	10	10	198	145	7	373
Total	42	91	68	1810	1558	153	3722

Source: CAPMAS (2007)

Similar considerations relating to the extra-regional permanent migration dynamics of highly skilled Egyptian workers who have headed to more developed OECD countries also confirm the hypotheses made in the theoretical section of this book. That is to say: the marginalisation of Egypt and of the MENA region from the global political economy reduces the possibilities of employing highly skilled personnel in the country, thus further adding to its marginalisation. The country seems to have entered a vicious circle which is becoming more and more difficult to break (IOM 2005).

Has the Arab Spring modified the characteristics of Egyptian outward migration? Although it is clearly too early to assess the impact of the events of 2011 on emigration flows from Egypt, the few studies conducted so far seem to confirm a continuation of the previous trend, in the sense that post-2011 extra-regional migration present characteristics similar to the previous phase (Abdelfattah 2011; Hafez and Ghaly 2012; Fargues and Fandrich 2012; Fargues 2007).

A study conducted by two scholars of the Center for Migration and Refugee Studies of the American University in Cairo in 2012 examined perceptions of Egyptian migration after the Arab Spring. Professors, political activists, political party founding members, analysts and experts were asked for their opinion on the future of migration and migratory policy in Egypt. As could have been expected, migration did not figure as one of the top priorities in the post-revolution political climate. What emerged, however, was a general consensus that migration, and especially migration of the highly skilled, will inevitably continue even at a faster rate than before because 'push factors exist and I think increased after the revolution'. (Hafez and Ghaly 2012: 11).

Furthermore, and risking circular reasoning, the push factors which lead the youth to leave Egypt before the uprisings, including economic marginalisation, have also been recognised as the roots of the Arab Spring itself (Abdelfattah 2011: 8). The International Organization for Migration (IOM 2011) was one of the first institutions to carry out a survey of the motivations for migration after the events of 25 January 2011. Of 750 Egyptians interviewed, 79 per cent of the respondents stated that their biggest problem was employment, 43 per cent claimed that the level of wages and salaries was too low and the other major problems cited were corruption, security, education and health. Contrary to expectations, the political and economic stability of Egypt were not perceived as problems and more than 50 per cent of the respondents were optimistic about the political and economic security of Egypt in the future. Those who wished to migrate because of the revolution of 2011 totalled only 15 per cent of the respondents, while the others were either willing to migrate or had already taken the decision to migrate before the revolution. The main push factors continued to be a lack of job opportunities and bad living conditions (IOM 2011).

Comparing these results with the Survey of Young People in Egypt (SYPE) carried out in 2009 by the Population Council, for which 15,000 Egyptians between the ages of 10 and 29 were questioned, we find that the numbers are very consistent. The percentage of potential migrants in the pre- and post-revolution surveys is very similar, and also before the Arab Spring a lack of job opportunities was the main push factor. Moreover, this was not dissimilar from the result of a Push and Pull Factors Survey covering several countries in addition to Egypt, conducted in the year 2000. Overall, the literature seems convinced that economic motivations are the main push factors in pre- and post-revolution surveys, although for certain categories such as the Copts, the Christians and certain segments of the elite, instability and a lack of security are new push factors that will need to be taken into account (Abdelfattah 2011: 8).

More in general, permanent extra-regional migration does not seem to have been affected by the Arab Spring, but appears to be following previous trends and the main changes in flows have happened within the region (Fargues and Fandrich 2012).

Conclusion

Concluding, the discussion in this chapter points to the fact that, rather than catching up with the process of globalisation, Egypt appears to be increasingly marginalised from the global political economy. Egypt is indeed one of the MENA area countries experiencing a decrease in its share of FDI stock in the last three decades. Despite a policy of liberalisation and privatisation, inaugurated in 1974 with the infitah of Sadat, Egypt failed to become attractive to foreign investors. Instead, both its share of FDI stock and its share of FDI inflows in the last thirty years have substantially decreased. The country has also been marginalised in terms of mergers and acquisitions, and its trade openness has remained at the same very low level throughout the 1990s.

Paradoxically, this has happened even though the country had successfully implemented substantial restructuring and stabilisation programmes under the auspices of the IMF and the World Bank. Overall, it would be fair to say that the country moved from liberalisation directly to marginalisation, providing a clear example of the fact that the adoption of neo-liberal policies does not necessarily lead to more integration in the global political economy.

As a result, after decades of liberalisation, privatisation and economic restructuring, Egypt continues to rely heavily on remittances as one of its most stable sources of GDP, and these are coming more and more from the most developed countries, first of all the US and increasingly also from Europe. Indeed, permanent extra-regional migration of especially skilled and highly skilled migrants is on the rise, and this signals the growing marginalisation of the country from the core economies. Such a pattern constitutes a vicious circle which the Arab Spring does not seem to have been able to break, but could have even made worse.

Notes

1. Lending arrangements, which are similar to a line of credit, are approved by the IMF Executive Board to support a country's adjustment programme. The arrangement requires the member to observe specific terms in order to be eligible to receive a disbursement. The IMF lends under Stand-by and Extended arrangements, and, at reduced rates, under Poverty Reduction and Growth Facility arrangements. See IMF (2008).
2. The crisis following 11 September 2001 led to a marked devaluation of the Egyptian pound (see Figure 5.6). Hence, from January 2003, the Egyptian pound was allowed to float. On 1 February 2005, Egypt's exchange rate was reclassified to a conventional peg from a managed float with no predetermined path for the exchange rate. Since July 2007, the de facto exchange arrangement has been akin to a managed float. See IMF (2008).
3. For reasons why FDI did not materialise, see Ayubi 1999: 341.
4. See IMF (2008).
5. Highly skilled workers are defined as those studying or having studied towards a University degree or possessing equivalent experience in a given academic field (IOM 2005).

References

Abdelfattah, D. (2011). *Impact of Arab Revolts on Migration.* CARIM Analytic and Synthetic Notes 2011/68, EUI, Florence.

Amin, G. (2000). *Whatever Happened to Egyptians?* The American University in Cairo Press, Cairo.

Appleyard, R. (ed.) (1999). *Emigration Dynamics in Developing Countries, Volume IV: The Arab Region.* Ashgate, London.

Ayubi, N. (1990). 'Arab Bureaucracies: Expanding Sizes, Changing Roles', in Luciani, G. (ed.) *The Arab State*, Routledge, London.

Ayubi, N. (1991). *The State and Public Policy in Egypt since Sadat.* Ithaca Press, Reading.

Ayubi, N. (1993). 'The "Fiscal Crisis" and the "Washington Consensus": Towards an Explanation of the Middle East Liberalisations', in Blin, L. (ed.) *L'Economie Egyptienne*, L'Harmattan, Paris.

Ayubi, N. (1999–2008). *Overstating the Arab State: Politics and Society in the Middle East.* IB Tauris, London.

Binder, L. (1978). *In a Moment of Enthusiasm: Political Power and the Second Stratum in Egypt.* University of Chicago Press, Chicago and London.

CARIM (2008). Euro-Mediterranean Consortium for Applied Research on International Migration, European University Institute, RSCAS, San Domenico in Fiesole, Florence, website http://www.carim.org/ as accessed on 3 September 2008

Central Bank of Egypt (2007). *Economic Review*, 47(4), 2006–2007.

Choucri, N. (1978). *Migration Processes Among Developing Countries: The Middle East.* MIT, Cambridge, MA.

Dessouki, A.E.H. (1982). The Shift in Egypt's Migration Policy 1952–1977. *Middle Eastern Studies*, 18(1), 53–68.

Dicken, P. (2011). *Global Shift: Mapping the Changing Contours of the World Economy* (6th ed.). Guilford.

Dodge, T., and Higgot, R. (2002). *Globalisation and the Middle East.* The Royal Institute of International Affairs, London.

Egyptian Ministry for Manpower and Emigration (2008). At: http://www.emigration.gov.eg/MigrationLaw/EgyptianMigrationLaw.aspx, accessed on 7 July 2008.

Fargues, P. (ed.) (2007). *Mediterranean Migration, 2006–2007.* European University Institute, RSCAS, San Domenico in Fiesole, Florence.

Fargues, P., and Fandrich, C. (2012). *Migration after the Arab Spring.* MPC Research Report 2012/09, EUI, Florence.

Fawcett, L., and Sayigh, Y. (1999). *The Third World Beyond the Cold War: Continuity and Change.* Oxford University Press, Oxford.

Feiler, G. (2003). *Economic Relations between Egypt and the Gulf Oil States, 1967–2000: Petro Wealth and Patterns of Influence.* Sussex Academic Press, Brighton.

Hafez, H. and Ghaly, A. (2012). *The Arab Spring and Migration in Egypt: One Year on: Impacts, Perceptions and Attitudes.* MPC Research Report 2012/05, EUI, Florence.

Hakimian, H., and Moshaver, Z. (2001). *The State and Global Change: The Political Economy of Transition in the Middle East and North Africa.* Curzon Press, Richmond.

Ibrahim, S.E. (1982). *The New Arab Social Order: A Study of the Social Impact of the Oil Wealth.* Westview Press, Boulder, CO.

ILO [International Labour Organization] (2008). At: http://laborsta.ilo.org/cgi-bin/brokerv8.exe, accessed on 22 July.

IMF [International Monetary Fund] (2008). At: http://www.imf.org, accessed on 23 July.

IOM [International Office for Migration] (2005). *World Migration 2005.* IOM, Cairo.

IOM (2011). *Egypt after January 25: Survey of Youth Migration Intentions Cairo, May 2011.* Cairo: IOM

Kepel, G. (1999). 'Toward a Social Analysis of Islamist Movements', in Binder, L. (ed.) *Ethnic Conflict and International Politics in the Middle East.* University Press of Florida, Florida, US, pp. 181–207.

Khyeda, S. (2007). Foreign Direct Investment in the Middle East: Major Regulatory Restrictions. *Insight Turkey*, 9(2), 73–104.

Mittelman, J.H. (2000). *The Globalisation Syndrome: Transformation and Resistance.* Princeton University Press, Princeton.

Nassar, H. (2005). *Migration, Transfers and Development in Egypt.* European University Institute, RSCAS, Research Reports 2005/01.
Nassar, H. (2009). *Migration and Financial Flows: Egypt in the MENA Area.* European University Institute, CARIM, Research Reports 2009/20.
OECD [Organisation for Economic Co-operation and Development] (2008). *International Migration Statistics.* At: http://www.oecd.org/home/0,2987,en_2649_201185_1_1_1_1_1,00.html as accessed on 3 September 2008.
Overbeek, H. (1999). *The Budapest Process: Internationalization of Migration Control.* Paper presented to the 40th Annual Conference of the International Studies Association, 16–20 February 1999, Washington D.C., mimeo.
Overbeek, H. (2000). 'Globalisation, Sovereignty and Transnational Regulation: Reshaping the Governance of International Migration', in Gosh, B. (ed.) *Managing Migration: Time for a New International Regime,* Oxford University Press, Oxford.
Owen, R., and Pamuk, S. (1999). *A History of Middle East Economies in the 20th Century.* Harvard University Press, Cambridge, MA.
Owen, R. (2004). *State, Power and Politics in the Making of the Modern Middle East.* Routledge.
Russell, S.S. (1992). International Migration and Political Turmoil in the Middle East. *Population and Development Review,* 18(4), 719–727.
Sassen, S. (1998). *Globalization and Its Discontents: Essays on the New Mobility of People and Money.* The New Press, New York.
Sassen, S. (1999). *Guests and Aliens.* The New Press, New York.
Sassen, S. (2006). *Territory, Authority, Rights: From Medieval to Global Assemblages.* Princeton University Press, Princeton NJ.
Seccombe, I.J. (1985). International Labor Migration in the Middle East: A Review of Literature and Research, 1974–84. *International Migration Review,* 19(2), 335–352.
Sell, R. (1987). *Gone for Good? Egyptian Migration Processes in the Arab World.* Cairo Papers in Social Sciences, The American University in Cairo Press, Cairo.
Talani, L.S. (2010). *From Egypt to Europe.* I.B. Tauris, London.
UNCTAD [United Nations Conference on Trade and Development] (2008). Globalisation and Development. At: http://www.unctad.org/Templates/StartPage.asp?intItemID=2874&lang=1, accessed on 28 July.
Zahlan, A.B. (1999). 'Labor Migration and Economic Integration in the Middle East', in Hudson M.C. (ed.) *Middle East Dilemma.* Tauris and Co. Ltd, New York, pp. 259–279.
Zohry, A. (2007). Egyptian Irregular Migration to Europe. *Migration Letters,* 4(1), 53–63.
Zohry, A., and Harrell-Bond, B. (2003). *Contemporary Egyptian Migration: An Overview of Voluntary and Forced Migration.* University of Sussex working papers, C3.

7
Libya: The Political Economy of Isolation

Introduction

Only a few days after the Egyptian revolution had achieved its climax with the fall of Hosni Mubarak, Libyans started a battle to topple their own dictator. However, contrary to the cases of Egypt and Tunisia, in Libya the battle was destined to last much longer as Ghadhafi refused to release power. Eventually the revolutionaries managed to achieve their aims only thanks to the intervention of NATO, which helped them take control of Tripoli six months after the beginning of the struggle, in late August 2011 (Boyle 2013).

The refusal of Ghadhafi to step down and the exacerbation of hostilities between the different factions in Libya led to a much more violent outcome of the revolution than in Egypt and Tunisia. However, this was not the only difference between the events in these countries.

Factors peculiar to Libya played a major role in shaping these events, and were destined to play a very important role also after the end of the hostilities. First and foremost is the fact that, contrary to the other two cases of the Arab Spring, Libya is not a resource-poor MENA country, but can count on all the advantages and disadvantages of being a major oil-producing country. This also means that the political economy background in which the events of the Arab Spring unfolded in Libya was pretty dissimilar to that of neighbouring Egypt and Tunisia.

Oil is certainly a curse for the developing countries which produce it. Yet it is also a blessing, allowing the rulers of those countries, whether authoritarian or not, to make different choices to those possible in resource-poor ones (Owen 2004; Ayubi 2008; Owen and Pamuk 1999).

Indeed Ghadhafi shares some of the traits of the Arab nationalist/socialist autocrats of the region, *a la* Nasser (Vandewalle 1998: 76). However, he also presents some evident differences which are reflected in the policies he implemented in his country in his four decades in power, as well as in the reaction that these provoked in the West.

In this chapter, the political economy of Libyan isolation which led to its economic marginalisation from globalisation is articulated within a context characterised by the two dimensions of Ghadhafi's unique political/economic experiment and the reactions of the West. The chapter will conclude assessing the extent of Libya's marginalisation from the global political economy.

The economic experiment of Ghadhafi

It is difficult to deny the peculiarities of Ghadhafi's Libyan experiment even in the context of the already peculiar political economy of the region. As he took power in 1969 with his Free Officers' Movement, Ghadhafi viewed his rule as a mission to completely transform the political, social and economic structure of the country. This experiment eventually led to the proclamation of the *Jamahiriyyah* ('state of the masses') in March 1977 (Owen 2004: 54; Al-Aturk 2011). It is important to notice that Ghadhafi's economic experiment was possible because, by the time he took power, Libya had become a fully fledged oil-producing country and its economy completely relied on this.

Oil had been discovered in Libya at the time of King Idris al-Sanusi, in 1959. In the wake of independence the Libyan economy was mainly agrarian and kinship was the main mechanism for economic distribution (Vandewalle 1998: 48). The economic challenges for the newly independent country were formidable. In 1951, around 90 per cent of the population was illiterate. Libya was one of the poorest countries of the world with an annual per capita income of around $25–35 and most of its population living at subsistence level (Vandewalle 2012: 51). The discovery of oil totally changed this outlook (Luciani 1990). First, the exploration fees paid by international oil companies, and then also oil revenues, shaped Libya into a classic case of a distributive state, the main function of which was to distribute oil revenues, whilst maintaining its structure of an essentially tribal society (Vandewalle 1998: 48; Vandewalle 2012: 53; Owen 2004: 53; Owen and Pamuk 1999).

Within few years Libya became the fourth most prolific producer of oil in the world (Vandewalle 2012). Given the characteristics of the 1955

Libyan Petroleum law, which limited the control of the Libyan government over the price level in favour of an increase in volumes, oil companies had an incentive to exploit Libyan oilfields to their maximum. The 1955 petroleum law, later amended, was aimed at attracting as many oil companies as possible, as it endorsed a volume-oriented as opposed to a price-oriented policy. As a consequence, in the 1960s both production and revenues increased dramatically, although not the posted price of oil, which is the basis of taxable income for producing countries (St John 2012). By 1962, there were 84 concessions operated by 19 companies, the majority of which were from the US and Britain (Vandewalle 1998: 49). In 1963 the country had achieved a total of 437 producing wells and petroleum made up around 99 per cent of the country's exports. On the eve of Ghadhafi's taking of power, in 1968, the Libyans had granted some 137 concessions to 39 Major and independent companies and overall these achieved a production of around 2.6 million barrels per day (Vandewalle 2012: 58).

The history of the industry had never seen such an abrupt expansion, which was further favoured by the closing of the Suez Canal after the June 1967 war. This made oil companies increase their production from Libya to maximise the cost savings deriving from not having to ship oil produced in the Gulf via the Cape of Good Hope (St John 2012: loc 2085 of 5346).

The consequences of these developments for the Libyan economy can hardly be overestimated. The country experienced an unprecedented economic boom which pushed per capita annual income up from \$50–60 in 1960 to around \$2,000 less than ten years later, on the eve of Ghadhafi's revolution. Based exclusively on oil production, Libyan GDP grew by around 20 per cent a year in the decade of the 1960s (Vandewalle 1998: 50).

This was the background against which Ghadhafi's economic experiment took place.

Immediately after the military's taking of power in 1969, Muhammar Ghadhafi became the *primus inter pares* of the Revolutionary Command Council (RCC) and soon thereafter its new leader. The Libyan revolutionary regime was heavily influenced by Nasser's ideology, whose Arab nationalistic and socialist components represented the bases of the political action of the new Libyan government. For Ghadhafi, Nasser was a powerful symbol of all that he wished to achieve in Libya: independence from foreigners, prosperity for the population, and the dream of Arab unity. After Nasser's death, Ghadhafi considered himself to be his main heir in the Arab world (Owen 2004: 54).

In Ghadhafi's plan for his country, oil was the means through which to obtain the aims of the revolution (Owen 2004). Many laws aimed at widening the share of the newly acquired prosperity were passed by the new regime, aimed at ensuring the wealth reached the population at large. Expenditure for education, literacy and health care dramatically increased in the first four years of Ghadhafi's rule (Owen 2004). Workers saw their minimum wages increase, interest-free loans and free housing were provided, repayment of loans was waived on the first anniversary of the revolution and workers were allowed to take a part of companies' profits (Vandewalle 1998: 72–73). The agricultural sector also greatly benefitted from Ghadhafi's economic experiment. Land which had been confiscated from the previous regimes was distributed to farmers, who could purchase what they needed at a mere 10 per cent of the real value. Land could also be bought interest free and farmers were guaranteed a salary until the farm was self-sufficient. The banking sector was nationalised, with the government taking 51 per cent control in 1970. This allowed for subsidised loans to be extended for the building of houses, especially in the countryside. Finally, small businesses could benefit from a 'Libya first' policy that required the government to contract only Libyan businesses (Vandewalle 1998: 73).

As oil was paying for similar measures, an important part of Ghadhafi's economic experiment was to take control of the oil business. Because of the policy pursued by the previous government, Libyan oilfields were being exploited to their maximum by foreign companies. In 1970, Libyan production reached the unsustainable level of around 3.7 million barrels a day. By then, oil represented the totality of Libyan exports (99.82 per cent) and made up a staggering 98.7 per cent of its revenues (Vandewalle 2012: 89).

In sum, Libya was completely dependent on international companies' exploitation of its only economic resource. However, oil was employing a mere 1 per cent of the Libyan active population and this created a very unbalanced economic structure (Vandewalle 1998: 74). Having a bigger say in the oil business was therefore a priority for Ghadhafi.

Straightforward nationalisation of crude oil production was unfeasible at the time, mainly because of the lack of expertise in the country to exploit this resource autonomously. Thus, the first step towards getting greater control of oil could only be represented by reversing the mechanism introduced by the 1955 petroleum law which had favoured volume over pricing. Accordingly, Ghadhafi's government intervened by cutting production (St John 2012). The objective was to increase prices and, consequently, the level of taxes paid by international companies. To this aim in December 1969, immediately after the revolution, the new government set up a committee to negotiate the increase of posted prices with oil companies, something which had not been addressed in the previous era of King Idris. At the same time, the regime decreased production quotas for individual companies, thus starting to gradually achieve more control over the oil industry (Vandewalle 2012: 90; St John 2012).This strategy proved successful to the extent that Ghadhafi's demands for higher prices were ratified in the Tripoli agreements signed on 2 April 1971. This set the precedent for more victories for the government against multinational companies, leading to higher prices overall and bigger shares of profits for the Libyans (Vandewalle 1998: 76).

Strengthened by the successful results of the negotiations with foreign companies, the regime moved to the second step in its endeavour to take control of its oil. This focused on increasing the role played in the oil industry by the Libyan National Oil Company (LNOC). It led to the LNOC acquiring all of the concessions that had been abandoned by multinational companies in the aftermath of the price negotiations. Despite an attempt by international oil businesses to counter Ghadhafi's actions by secretly agreeing to buy any concessions left by foreign oil companies, the government eventually won. This set the stage for its final attack on the mainly American and British oil companies.

In the period between 1971 and 1973 the Libyan government declared majority shares in all of the oil companies active in the country and on 1 September 1973 announced a 51 per cent participation in the holdings of the Majors (Vadewalle 1998: 76). On February 1974 Libya completely nationalised three US oil companies: Texaco, the Libyan American Oil Company and California Asiatic (Vandewalle 1998: XXV). The year before it had already nationalised British Petroleum (BP) (Vandewalle 2012: 173).

By the end of this period of nationalisation of foreign oil companies, Ghadhafi's economic experiment had achieved its aim of controlling the oil business whilst he was increasingly recognised in the region as the true heir of Nasser and the natural leader of pan-Arabism.

Oil prices started to climb steadily, and by the autumn of 1973 Libya had achieved \$2 billion of foreign currency reserves, enough to sustain imports for around four years in case of an international embargo. Furthermore, in 1970 the annual per capita income had reached \$2,168 (Vandewalle 2012: 91).

The amount of financial resources accumulated was used to further Ghadhafi's economic experiment (Ibrahim 1982). In 1970 the regime started to redistribute land confiscated from the Sanusi government and the Italians. In the same year, the government laid out the main features of the new Libyan industrial infrastructure. Large industrial undertakings, such as liquefaction plants and refineries, were taken over by the state. Small private business was preserved but within the economic policy framework set by the government (Vandewalle 2012: 92).

The three year Economic and Social Development plan (1973 to 1975) detailed the objectives of the regime for the economic future of Libya. It projected an annual GDP growth of 11 per cent overall and proclaimed an increased effort to develop non-oil sectors. It was especially keen on supporting new public investments in the agricultural sector with the aim to make Libya self-sufficient in terms of food production (Vandewalle 1998: 78). All of this was to be financed through oil revenues. And oil revenues skyrocketed with the 1973 oil crisis (or 'oil boom' for the Libyans) making it possible for the regime to increase its investments accordingly. New large-scale industrial endeavours were initiated, new credit was extended through the Libyan Industrial Bank to produce consumer goods internally and public money was used to finance the construction of an adequate industrial infrastructure including electricity projects and harbours. In the meantime the banking sector, the insurance companies and the hospitals had been nationalised or otherwise put under the government's control (Vandewalle 1998: 79).

The two oil booms of the 1970s brought an estimated $95 billion in revenues to the country, a substantial amount of financial resources for Ghadhafi to sustain his revolutionary experiment (Vandewalle 1998: 83; Owen 2004: 55). The transformation of the country in the first decade after the revolution was astonishing. In the political realm, people were made directly responsible for running state institutions through an innovative system of committees and congresses. From the economic point of view, the changes were even more revolutionary with the outlawing of all private economic activity. The wealth accumulated through the Libyan oil industry paid for ambitious welfare state programmes, large-scale industrial projects and governmental contracts (Owen 2004: 55).

In this context, Ghadhafi brought forward his plan to build a Jamahiriyyah through an 'Everlasting Revolution' (*al-Fatih Abadan*) whose ideological foundations were laid down in the famous 'Green Book' *al-Kitab al-Akhdar* (Owen 2004: 54).

It cannot be denied that, in this process, the state had acquired a vital role in the Libyan economy. In line with the theoretical outline of this book, it is now essential to evaluate whether and how in the following years this role was put under discussion (Mittelman 2000; Overbeek 1999, 2000).

The political economy of isolation and the role of the west

A Libyan proverb tellingly says:

> 'If your pocket gets empty, your faults will be many'. (Vandewalle 1998: cover)

The extent to which the incapacity of Arab autocrats to maintain the same level of expenditure in the wake of the challenges of globalisation brought waves of discontent that eventually fuelled the protests known under the name of the Arab Spring has already been ascertained in the previous chapters of this book (Similarly Ayubi 2008: 394; Dodge and Higgot 2002; Hakimian and Moshaver 2001).

In the cases of Egypt and Tunisia the crisis of the state was a function of the impossibility of keeping up with the globalisation process. Yet in the case of Libya it is undeniable that the role of the West in limiting the spending capacity of the state was extremely relevant. In turn, the attitude of Western countries, especially the US, towards the Libyan regime cannot be disentangled from the way in which Ghadhafi decided to handle the question of oil.

Already in the wake of the nationalisation of American oil companies, in 1975, the US announced a series of restrictions on the purchase of strategic equipment by Libya and on the training of Libyans on specific aircrafts (Vandewalle 1998: XXVI). In February 1977 Libya was added to the list of potential enemies of the US by the Department of Defense. By the end of 1981, the US had implemented a policy to stop all imports of crude oil from Libya. Equally, all exports to Libya from the US, apart from food and medicine, were banned. In the meantime, two of the Majors abandoned Libyan oilfields: Esso Standard Libya and Esso Sirte. At the beginning of 1983 Mobil also left the country for good. Other western multinational oil companies had already reduced their production or postponed contracts that were already signed with the Libyan regime (Vandewalle 1998: 119). Although Ghadhafi desperately tried to attract the oil business back by offering discounts and incentives to companies, the Libyan economy was seriously hit by these events.

At the roots of these developments were growing concerns relating to the escalating confrontation between Libya and Western countries. On one side, there was the French opposition to the intervention of Libya in Chad (Simons 2003: 47–53). Even more important for the political economy of the country, however, was the conflict with the US. In August 1981 the US had shot down two Libyan jet fighters in the Gulf of Sidra. As already mentioned, soon thereafter the US proclaimed a total boycott of Libyan oil, a measure which alone reduced Libyan revenues by a third. In April 1986 the US bombed Tripoli and Benghazi.

Libyan production of oil clearly suffered from these events. At the end of 1981 Libya produced only 600,000 barrels per day, a decline from 1.7 million in the first quarter of the same year. Total production in 1981 was 40 per cent lower than in 1980. It is estimated that at least 500,000 barrels per day were lost, as they had previously been routinely shipped to the US. Oil revenues decreased from $21 billion in 1981, to $5.4 billion in 1986 (Vandewalle 1998: 123; Vandewalle 2012: 113).

The loss of revenues also tested the economic experiment of Ghadhafi, who had to start cutting back on public expenditure. In March 1987 the regime passed a set of economic reforms which are known as the first Libyan *Infitah* (Vandewalle 1998). On the eve of the first two waves of the Libyan Infitah, the percentage of the population which was directly working for the state was estimated at 70–75 per cent. As the amount of revenues that could be used to maintain this formidable state apparatus had been steadily decreasing in the aftermath of the US boycott, Ghadhafi had to pass a set of reforms aimed at limiting the intervention of the state in the economy. The content of the reforms was threefold: they were aimed firstly at cutting state expenditures, secondly at limiting public subsidies and thirdly at promoting private involvement in industrial, agricultural and commercial businesses (Vandewalle 1998: 151).

The first set of reforms was implemented between 1987 and 1990. Between 1987 and 1988 the government introduced the idea of *tashrukkiya*, or collective management, allowing for the creation of cooperatives and thus reintroducing the private sector into a Libyan economic system which had been totally nationalised with the 1978 law on 'wage earners, not employees' (Vandewalle 1998: 151). As a consequence, one year later around 140 small and medium enterprises were entrusted to self-management committees and could no longer rely on public subsidies. The ban on retail trade was lifted too, and souks all around the country were allowed to open again. Between 1988 and 1990, the government liberalised the import/export sectors, allowed private practices for professionals and eliminated subsidies on a series of agricultural products, whilst also stating publicly that farmers could freely sell their goods in the markets (which already happened in practice). In an effort to attract more revenues, the government established Oilinvest, a holding aimed at increasing Libyan refining capacity and marketing its oil in Europe (Vandewalle 1998: 152).

With the second wave of reforms the liberalisation process acquired momentum. In an attempt to attract as much foreign investment as possible, Ghadhafi supported a clear division of labour between the state and the private sector. This was the first time such a division had been suggested since the start of the revolution. In the spring of 1993 Ghadhafi proposed measures introducing special guarantees for foreign capital, promoting foreign companies' involvement in the Libyan tourist industry and allowing for the convertibility of the Libyan dinar. Some of these measures were adopted by the General People's Congress (GPC) in 1994, including those related to facilitating foreign investment. Other laws were passed to enable private companies to open foreign currency accounts and import equipment from abroad, as well as a law allowing for the creation of more private companies through access to credit from state and commercial banks. At the same time, the regime acted more decisively on cutting public expenditure by proposing the decentralisation of expenditure, a reduction in the number of public employees and greater fiscal responsibility of local authorities (*mahalla*) (Vandewalle 1998: 152–153).

Although not all of the measures proposed by Ghadhafi were eventually adopted by the General People's Congress or implemented, it is clear that the regime had been forced to change its approach to the running of the Libyan economy.

This desperate attempt to attract foreign business in the country, as well as the cutting of public expenditure and the revival of the private sector, were all ensuing from the isolation from the international context which Libya had been increasingly suffering. After the systematic cutting of all diplomatic and trade relations with his regime, not to mention the bombings of Tripoli and Benghazi, Ghadhafi tried to recover from the deep economic and political crisis in which his country had plunged by proposing a programme of structural reforms (Vandewalle 2012: 152).

However the situation did not change for the better. Immediately after the announcement of the first wave of the Infitah, which could perhaps be interpreted as a sign of weakness by the rest of the world, the isolation of Libya became, if possible, deeper and was catalysed by the Lockerbie issue.

Given the impact that the Lockerbie events will have on the political economy of Libyan isolation, it is important to recall how they occurred. In the evening of 21 December 1988, a bomb brought down Pan American World Airways jumbo jet flight PA 103 going from London's Heathrow airport to New York's JFK. The incident happened over Lockerbie and caused the death of all the passengers and members of the flight crew, totalling some 259 people, as well as another 11 persons killed on the ground. Together with an attack on a French DC-10 aircraft (UTA 772) on 19 September 1989, the Lockerbie terrorist attack soon became the reason for the imposition of more sanctions on the already struggling Libyan economy (Simons 2003: 141; Boyle 2013).

In breach of existing international law, in particular the Montreal Convention of 1971, Washington and London demanded that two Libyan suspects were extradited to the US or the UK, despite the fact that no extradition treaty existed between Libya and the two countries at the time. In fact, extradition was against Libyan law and the Montreal convention reinforced the right of Libya not to extradite the suspects but put them under trial at home (Simons 2003: 144). Ignoring the right attributed to Libya by international law, the US and Britain reverted to other devices to obtain extradition of the two Libyan suspects, including threats of unilateral sanctions and of recourse to force, and the generation of anti-Libyan resolutions in the UN Security Council (Boyle 2013: loc 2280 of 4949).

Three years after the Lockerbie events, on 14 November 1991, Washington and London announced that the bombing had been the responsibility of the two Libyans. To obtain their extradition, Washington hinted at the possibility of imposing international sanctions on the country and even recurring to military action if Ghadhafi refused to surrender the two suspects. A few days later, on 27 November, the US and the British government asked the Libyan government to accept full criminal and financial responsibility for the bombing, despite the fact that no trial had been conducted as yet. In compliance with the Montreal Convention, Libya arrested the two suspects and put them on trial in December 1991. The US and the UK refused to recognise the legitimacy of the Libyan handling of the case and approached the UN Security Council which, under the British Presidency, adopted the first resolution designed to address the Lockerbie issue (Boyle 2013: loc 2280 of 4949). On 21 January 1992 the UN Security Council unanimously adopted resolution 731, which

> condemned the destruction of PA 103 and UTA 772, strongly deplored the fact that the Libyan government had not yet responded, urged the Libyan government to respond, requested the Secretary General to seek Libyan cooperation and urged all states individually and collectively to encourage the Libyan government to respond fully and effectively to the requests.[1]

Predictably, Ghadhafi refused to hand over the suspects, and this resulted in an escalation of the pressure by the UN Security Council. On 31 March 1992 the Council passed resolution 748, which further added to the isolation of Libya by banning all flights to and from the country, reducing the size and scope of Libyan diplomatic and consular missions and imposing a total arms embargo. Yet this too failed to convince Ghadhafi to extradite the two alleged terrorists. In November 1993 the UN Security Council adopted a new resolution: SCR 883. This represented a serious blow to the Libyan economy and included the freezing of a huge number of Libyan assets abroad, the strengthening of the measures included in SCR 748, and the banning of the export to Libya of a wide range of equipment including those necessary for the production of oil (UNSC 2013). The undeclared aim was to stop the Libyan oil industry altogether. This objective could not be totally achieved, given the dependence of European countries on Libyan oil, but oil revenues were substantially hit by the sanctions (Simons 2003).

Moreover, if the US had not managed to impose a global oil embargo on Libya through the UN resolutions, it went very close to achieving it with the passing of the Iran and Libyan Sanctions Act (ILSA) in August 1996. This included provisions of sanctions on foreign companies investing more than $40 million in the oil industry of Libya. A dispute ensued with Europe over the legality of these terms (Vandewalle 2012: 171).

The whole of the Libyan economy suffered from this wide-ranging sanctions regime, rendering completely vain the reforms of the Libyan Infitah (Simons 2003: 148–156; similarly Vandewalle 2012: 156).

The consequences of the sanctions were dire for the Libyan population (Vandewalle 2012: 152). A report of the Libyan mission to the UN denounced the humanitarian, economic and social damage caused by the UN Security Council Resolutions. It was estimated that 15,750 people died because they could not be evacuated by air for treatment abroad and that the impossibility of obtaining medicines by air produced thousands of stillbirths and hundreds of maternal deaths. In the economic sphere, the regime imposed by the sanctions produced an estimated $5 billion of losses in Libyan industry and mineral sectors by early 1998. In the same year, a UN fact-finding mission to Libya found that in the aftermath of the sanctions Libya's GDP had shrunk, FDIs were reduced, inflation had increased and the unemployment level had moved from less than 1 per cent in 1992 to more than 12 per cent in 1996 (UNSC 2013). Vandewalle (2012) reports that, as a consequence of the imposition of multilateral sanctions, as well as the ILSA, in the period concerned between 1992 and 1999, the Libyan economy grew by only 0.8 per cent a year and the country's per capita GDP decreased from $7,311 to $5,896. In the year 1998 alone, export earnings collapsed to $7 billion (Vandewalle 2012: 155). The sectors which were impacted the most were health and social services and the agricultural and transportation sectors. The level of poverty also worsened considerably (Simons 2003: 157).

The damaging effects of the various waves of sanctions were sizable. They made the overall economic structure of the country far weaker and unable to cope with the pressures of modernisation, especially of the oil industry which, indeed, became far less productive during the 1990s. It is estimated that the oilfields taken over from the American companies and operated by the LNOC experienced a decline in production of around 8 per cent a year (Vandewalle 2012: 157). Overall, the imposition of multilateral sanctions as a consequence of the Lockerbie issue struck a deadly blow to an economy already weakened by years of conflict and embargos with the US.

However, the embargo was having some consequences also for the US and the UK, with oil companies of these countries eager to gain again access to Libyan reserves (Simons 2003). Hence the decision to try the two suspects of the Lockerbie bombing on neutral terrain, in the Netherlands under Scottish law. This decision was adopted through yet another UN resolution: SCR 1192 (UNSC 2013). When the two suspects appeared in front of the Scottish judges in the Netherlands, in April 1999, the UN froze its sanctions, and finally lifted them in 2003. However the US continued its unilateral embargo, imposed by the ILSA. Despite this, some Western trade with Libya resumed and the threat of military action against the country disappeared for the time being, only to appear again in the wake of the Arab Spring (Simons 2003: 158–164).

We have already noted how the US had been, until the implementation of the ban on imports of Libyan crude oil in 1982, the single largest importer of Libyan oil. Yet by 1988 all Majors and independent US producers had left the country, following the implementation of the US ban and the US government's decision in 1986 to order all American companies and citizens to leave the Jamahiriyyah.[2] The French parastatal oil company, Elf Aquitaine, also abandoned Libya in the 1980s as a result of the French–Libyan dispute over Chad, although the French company Total had remained. Of the non-US Major companies, BP had been nationalised already in 1973 (Vandewalle 2012: 159).

Consequently, Libya had to target other European countries for the sale of its oil production. With the banning of imports of all products from the Ras el-Unuf refinery the country established solid trade relations with Germany and Italy, and started trade with new partners such as Turkey and Brazil. At the same time, Libya sought to offset declining oil production with the development of its enormous and almost totally unexploited natural gas reserves. These moves consolidated the new international trade relations of the country which, in 1993, signed a contract with the Italian energy company AGIP-ENI for a $5.5 billion joint venture to develop the Western Libyan gas project. The project had to be abandoned for the time being given the dispute between Europe and the US on the legality of the ILSA (Vandewalle 2012: 153).

It was clear, however, that old economic ties with the US, France and the UK, were, in the course of the whole Lockerbie period, being substituted by new ones with different trade partners such as Italy and Germany. Thus, when the UN's multilateral sanctions were frozen in April 1999 these were the countries which benefited the most from the new investment climate in Libya. This was especially so because the normalisation of diplomatic and trade relations with the US would not happen until 2007 (IMF 2009) although all U.S. Libya-specific trade sanctions would be lifted in September 2004 (IMF 2005: 5).

The rift between the US and the UK, on one side, and most of the rest of the international community on the other, had indeed been exacerbated by the outcome of the Lockerbie trial, which acquitted one suspect (Fhimah) and condemned, also in appeal, the other (al-Magrahi) (Boyle 2013). It was hard not to suspect that the whole Lockerbie affair had been deeply influenced by the strong domestic interests of the US and the UK (Simons 2003; Vandewalle 2012: 171).

It is indeed difficult to deny that, as this history of the political economy of isolation reveals, oil, and energy in general, have played an incredibly relevant role in the dynamics of the relations between the West and Libya. And they continue to do so.

In 2000, 2001 and 2002, the Jamahiriyyah was still ranked amongst the most attractive oil and gas sites in the world by the experts of international energy companies. This was due to the fact that around three quarters of its territory had not been explored yet and that its enormous gas resources were almost completely unexploited. However the political situation of the country and the uncertainties related to Ghadhafi's international status still represented a barrier to foreign investment (Vandewalle 2012: 177).

Paradoxically, the events of September 2001 and the American war against terror gave new steam, and new sources of income, to a regime which had however by then lost its hegemonic grip over an increasingly antagonistic civil society.

Although in August 2001 the US Congress had renewed until 2006 the unilateral sanction regime imposed through the ILSA, Ghadhafi appeared from the onset more an ally than an enemy of the US war on terror, contrary to many other countries in the MENA region and certainly contrary to the feelings of many people in the area (Vandewalle 2012: 171). His final renunciation of Weapons of Mass Destruction in 2003 opened the doors to reconciliation with the West and to foreign investment. Moreover, a few months before, the General People's Congress had adopted measures to inaugurate a new phase of the Infitah. This was preceded by the decision taken in 2002 to peg the dinar to the SDR (Special Drawing Rights) and to liberalise external trade to make the investment climate of the country more attractive (IMF 2003; 2009).[3] In the following years, the General People's Congress adopted a number of neo-liberal style economic directives based on the recommendations of the IMF which, for the first time in its history, the country had consulted to restructure its economy from 29April until 15 May 2003 (IMF 2003; 2006). On this occasion, the Libyan authorities had agreed with IMF staff that:

> Higher growth rates and diversification of the Libyan economy could only be achieved through deregulation, a significant scaling down of the dominant role of the public sector, and the development of the private sector. (IMF 2005: 4)

In the period of 2004 and 2005 structural reforms included a significant streamlining of the tariff schedule, the partial liberalisation of interest rates, the broadening of both the privatisation program and the scope for foreign investments, and the launching of the privatisation of a major public bank. The Libyan authorities were acting on the basis of a Medium Term Strategy prepared by IMF staff to reform the Libyan economy (IMF 2006: 3).

In 2006 the measures adopted to restructure the economy included the elimination of most import monopolies and the partial liberalisation of foreign direct investment (FDI) in the non-oil sector (IMF 2007: 3; Figure 7.1 below).

- Reduction of the floor on non-oil FDI from US$50 million to US$1.5 million.
- State import monopolies are limited to petroleum products and weaponry.
- Import bans for religious, health and ecological reasons restricted to ten products.
- Merger of 21 regional banks and development of a plan to restructure the public commercial banks.
- Acceleration of efforts to strengthen banking supervision and modernise the payment system.
- Establishment of a Large Taxpayers Office (LTO).
- Establishment of the LIA to centralise oil revenue management.
- Reduction of the consumption tax to 15–25 percent, exemption of all intermediate goods from the consumption tax, and some capital and intermediate goods from the 4 percent import service fee.
- Opening of 51 offices across the country to expedite approval of business permits.
- Downward adjustment of electricity tariffs for domestic use by enlarging the lowest tariff's bracket.
- Establishment of a negative list for non-oil FDI limited to retail and wholesale trade, and importation.
- Issuance of a decree requiring that all FDI in the non-oil sector be undertaken through joint ventures with a minimum Libyan participation of 35 percent.
- The ministry of planning's national accounts unit has been reactivated, and field surveys have been developed.

Figure 7.1 Libya – structural reforms implemented, 2006
Source: IMF (2007: 8)

In 2007, in order to implement a long-due increase in the wages of the public sector, which had been frozen since 1981, the Libyan government agreed with the IMF to reduce the subsidies budget by about 23 per cent. The other condition to obtain IMF consensus on the wage increase was the implementation of a plan to streamline the public sector, terminating the jobs of around a third of total Libyan State employees (300,000 out of around 910,000). Finally the Libyan authorities agreed that the wage increase would be gradual, as requested by the IMF, and effective only after the official termination of redundant staff (IMF 2007: 10).

This emphasis on the reduction of public expenditure and restraint in public finance by the IMF was at odds with the fact that Libya was not experiencing any fiscal crisis at the time. In fact, the country constantly enjoyed two digit surpluses of its annual fiscal position over GDP (Table 7.1).

In sum, even Ghadhafi had finally decided to bow to the international pressures for the adoption of neo-liberal practices in the wake of

Table 7.1 Libya – basic financial indicators, 2004–2008 (US$ millions)

	2004	2005	2006	Prel./2007	Proj./2008
Central government finances revenue	53.6	62.9	65.1	61.4	66.3
Of which: Hydrocarbon	46.4	58.5	60.2	55.2	60.9
Expenditure and net lending	39.7	32.1	29.5	35.2	31.4
Of which: Capital expenditure	16.2	18.2	16.2	21.0	18.0
Overall position (surplus)	13.9	30.9	35.5	26.2	35.0

Source: IMF (2008: 17)

the collapse of the Libyan economy following decades of isolation and sanctions. In doing so, the regime was clearly attempting to address the dire state of the Libyan economy which, with a 30 per cent unemployment rate, was starting to pose also social and political problems (Vandewalle 2012: 186; IMF 2003). However the dismantling of the state apparatus implied political risks as well as some economic gains which as detailed below, did not materialise to the extent necessary for Ghadhafi to regain hegemony over the Libyan population (Ayubi 2008: 394).

Very differently from what had happened after Ghadhafi'srevolution, equality was not an aim of the newly inaugurated Infitah policies. Workers employed in the public sector still received barely survival wages in cities which, thanks to the liberalisations, were now experiencing much higher costs of living and, especially, housing (Vandewalle 2012: 197). Indeed, before the limited and heavily conditioned increase in 2007, wages had been frozen for more than two decades at the dismal level of 250 to 300 dinars a month, even for highly qualified workers (IMF 2003). Moreover, international pressures to cut expenditures, especially from the IMF, managed to convince Ghadhafi to put on hold the Wealth Distribution Programme. This was a Programme which had been devised in March 2008 to distribute part of the oil wealth to the people while, at the same time, reducing the size of the government (IMF 2009:4).

The grievances of an exhausted population, as already discussed in Chapter 3, were increasingly being heard in Libyan Islamic quarters which, despite decades of repression, still managed to survive in the country. As in other countries in the area, most notably Egypt and Tunisia, religion had become the only consolation after years of political and economic deprivation (Kawcynski 2011 loc 4249 of 5524). The widespread protests in Benghazi in connection to the famous issue of the anti-Mohammed Danish cartoons and the way in which the regime responded to them in 2006,[4] are a clear demonstration of this.

To conclude, on the eve of the Arab Spring Libyans' discontent with Ghadhafi's regime was irremediable (Kawcynski 2011; Vandewalle 2012). At its roots there was the progressive impoverishment of the Libyan middle class, following the reduction of state subsidies and wages (similarly Ayubi 2008: 394). In turn, the crisis of the 'distributive state' ensued from years of exclusion of the country from the international consortium as a consequence of the way in which Ghadhafi had decided to handle the oil business. The hegemonic power of the Leader of the revolution and of his extravagant ideology had vanished (Vandewalle 2012) and the cuts imposed to the state by the newly inaugurated, IMF-sponsored Infitah would not help in restoring it. To this it must be added, for the case of Libya, the underlying tribal rivalries which were never settled by the substantially failed efforts at state-building of both King Idris and Ghadhafi (Vandewalle 1998, 2012; Owen 2004: 53–55; Boyle 2013; Al-Aturk 2011).

In the following section we will explore the extent to which the political economy isolation of Libya resulted in its economic marginalisation from the global political economy.

Assessing Libya's economic marginalisation

As emerges clearly from the analysis above, the assessment of Libyan marginalisation from the global political economy cannot be disentangled from the political steps taken by the West to isolate Ghadhafi for a great part of the 1980s and 1990s. Bombings and years of embargos and commercial warfare did obviously impact the Libyan economy which, following the booms of the 1970s, plunged into crisis in the following two decades. Recovery did take place once the country could enjoy more relaxed international trade relations. However, the events of 2011 produced the complete disarray of the Libyan economy with a loss of GDP of around 60 per cent, clearly related to the halting of crude oil extraction during the civil war (IMF 2013: 5).

The oil industry did however resume in 2012,with the implication that the IMF estimated a percentage growth of GDP of around 105 per cent despite the fact that instability and security continued to pose serious problems (IMF 2013: 4).

Indeed, the IMF expected hydrocarbon output to reach pre-conflict levels in 2013, while in the non-hydrocarbon sectors improvement

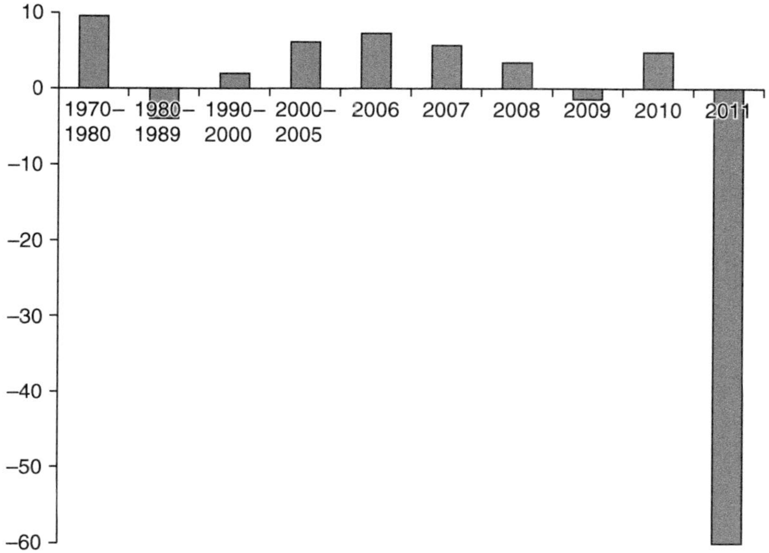

Figure 7.2 Libya – real GDP growth rates annual, 1970–2011
Source: UNCTAD

depended on reconstruction and private demand, both heavily compromised by the fact that well-armed militias still held considerable power and controlled much of the Libyan territory (IMF 2013: 4).

The political dimension of Libyan marginalisation is obviously very important in order to make sense of the main indicators of integration into the globalisation process already identified in the theoretical discussion and assessed in the cases of Tunisia and Egypt.

Overall, in the case of Libya it is hard to talk about a path of integration of the country into the global political economy.

Looking at the percentage of total FDI stock from the 1980s until 2011, although the partial political rehabilitation of Ghadhafi in the early 2000s did bring some foreign capital back into the country, the share of total FDI stock never even reached 0.1 per cent, substantially decreasing from the already tiny 0.25 per cent recorded in 1980. It is worth noting that the first two waves of the Libyan Infitah, although aimed at increasing the stock of FDIs in the country, clearly failed to achieve their objectives as the share of global FDI stock heavily decreased in the course of the 1990s to reach almost zero in the second half of the decade. The third wave of the Infitah in the 2000s only

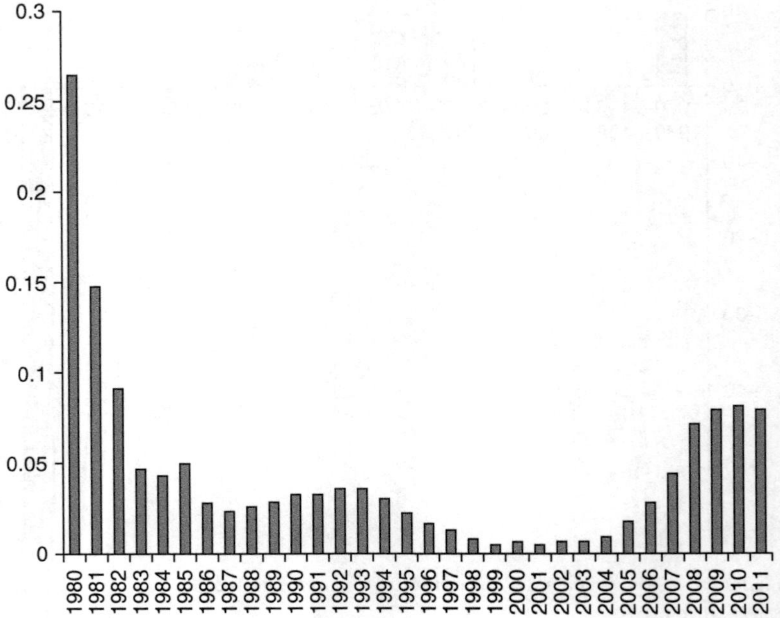

Figure 7.3 Libya – average percentage share of world total FDI stock, 1981–2011

Source: Elaboration by the author on data from UNCTAD website http://www.unctad.org/Templates/Page.asp?intItemID=1584&lang=1 as accessed on 30 April 2013

marginally improved the situation of FDIs in the country and certainly not to the extent expected, given its aggressive character (Figure 7.3).

Similar conclusions can be drawn by looking at the average percentage share of the world total FDI stock by decades from 1980s to the 2000s (Figure 7.4).

This trend is confirmed by the figures relating to the share of total FDIs inflows reaching Libya in the last three decades.

Investment and disinvestment by foreign companies in Libya is related to its unique economic resource of oil. Because of this it is not particularly surprising that Ghadhafi's policy of nationalisation of the oil industry from the beginning of the 1970s and the ensuing retaliation measures taken by Western countries, especially the US and the UK, brought the country's share of total world FDI inflows to, at best, close to zero, if not much below it (Figure 7.5).

Again, the figures in Figure 7.5 show the extent to which the structural reform programme devised by Ghadhafi at the end of the 1980s

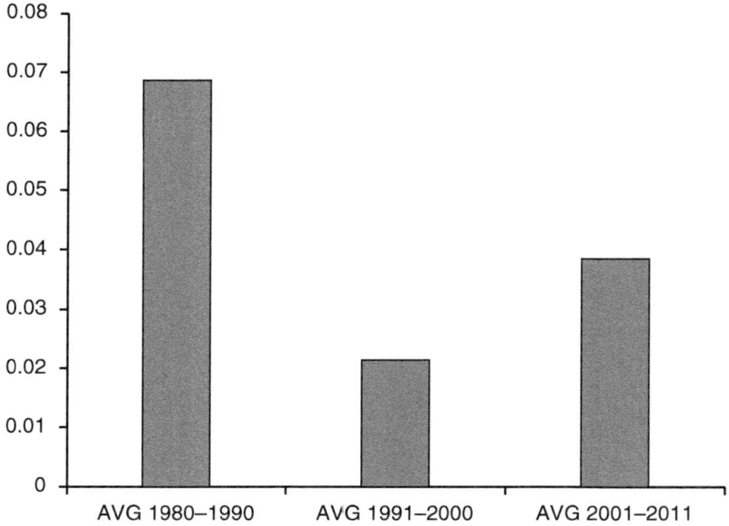

Figure 7.4 Libya – average percentage share of world total FDI stock, decades 1980–2011

Source: Elaboration by the author on data from UNCTAD website http://www.unctad.org/Templates/Page.asp?intItemID=1584&lang=1 as accessed on 30 April 2013

and beginning of the 1990s to attract foreign business and revenues was unsuccessful. A similar conclusion can be drawn by looking at the figures relating to the trade account, which, precisely at the time of the first two waves of the Infitah, went back into deficit, recording a fall of 7 per cent in 1988 and of 4 per cent in 1993 (UNCTAD 2013).

In terms of mergers and acquisitions it is not even worth providing a percentage of the world total. In fact they were zero until the normalisation of diplomatic relations with the US and the EU in 2006 and 2007, when they became marginally above zero. In absolute terms they were 1 in 2006, 200 in 2007, 307 in 2008, 145 in 2009, 91 in 2010 and 20 in 2011 (UNCTAD 2013).

Neither is there much to say as far as trade openness is concerned: for most of the four decades in which Ghadhafi was in power the country was under some form of embargo. To be sure, also during the Arab Spring, on 17 March 2011, the UN Security Council froze Libya's foreign assets. The UN-imposed sanctions were lifted only on 16 December 2011.

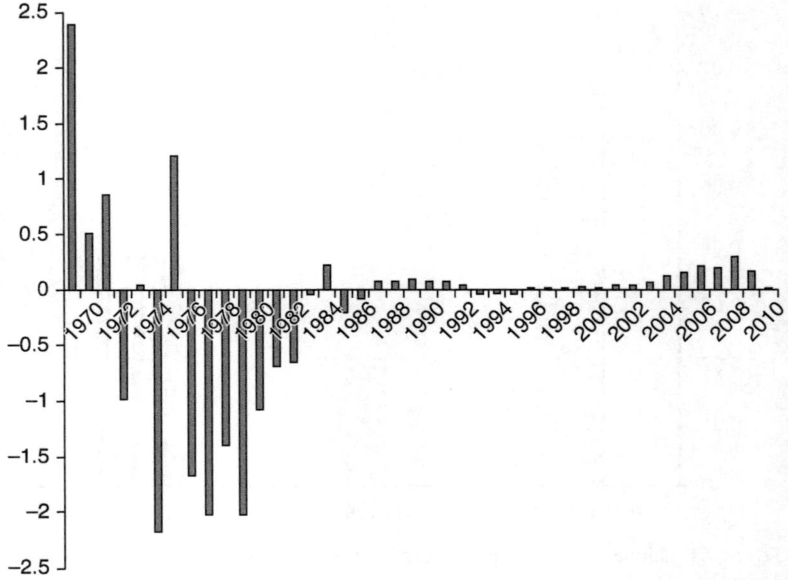

Figure 7.5 Libya – average percentage share of world total FDI inflows, 1970–2011
Source: Elaboration by the author on data from UNCTAD website http://www.unctad.org/Templates/Page.asp?intItemID=1584&lang=1 as accessed on 30 April 2013

Conclusion

As with Tunisia and Egypt, albeit for different reasons and within a totally different political economy background, Libya has been marginalised from the global political economy in the last three decades.

The discovery of oil at the end of the 1950s proved both a blessing and a curse for the country especially after Ghadhafi's assumption of power.

On the one hand, it was mainly because of the unprecedented wealth provided by the exploitation of Libyan oilfields that Ghadhafi's economic and political experiment was possible. On the other hand, however, the need for Ghadhafi to control the oil business to finance his projects brought the country to decades of isolation and conflict. This, in turn, meant the final defeat of Ghadhafi's extravagant ideals and the economic marginalisation of Libya from the global political economy.

Not even the sudden change of emphasis from nationalisation to economic liberalisation brought about by the economic difficulties ensuing from its diplomatic isolation managed to make the country significantly more attractive to foreigners. Only once isolation was relaxed at the beginning of the 2000s did some investment take place, but this did not manage to placate the discontent of the Libyans.

The crisis of the state was, in the case of Libya, the crisis of the distributive state. The distributive state had initially sustained Ghadhafi's economic experiment, but the long conflict with the West, especially the US and the UK, brought the progressive disappearance of the resources available to Ghadhafi to economically support the population. This affected his capacity to keep his hegemonic leadership over the country. In turn, the conflict with Western countries cannot be totally disconnected from the way that Ghadhafi had decided to handle the oil business through nationalisations and taking control of the industry.

This is not the place to attempt any evaluation of the relations between the West and Ghadhafi's Libya. It seems clear, however, that the economic fate of the country cannot be disentangled from the political economy of isolation as discussed in this chapter.

Notes

1. Simons (2003: 148–149).
2. For chronology of these events see Vandewalle (2012: 159).
3. On 1 January 2002 the authorities adopted a conventional fixed peg to the SDR at a rate of LD1 = SDR 0.608. In June 2003 the exchange rate was devalued by 15 per cent to LD1 = SDR 0.5175. From 14 February 1999 to 31 December 2001 a dual exchange rate system was in place with an official exchange rate pegged to the SDR and a special exchange rate pegged to the US dollar. In June 2003 the authorities eliminated the restrictions that gave rise to multiple currency practices. See IMF (2009).
4. See BBC website: http://news.bbc.co.uk/1/hi/world/middle_east/4688602.stm as accessed on 28 June 2013.

References

Al-Aturk, A. (2011). 'Libya: From Revolt to State Building', in Pollack, K. M. (ed.) *The Arab Awakening : America and the Transformation of the Middle East*, e-book, accessed 9 May 2013, http://kcl.eblib.com/patron/FullRecord.aspx?p=795889, pp.117–127.

Ayubi, N. (2008). *Overstating the Arab State: Politics and Society in the Middle East.* IB Tauris, London.

BBC web site: http://news.bbc.co.uk/1/hi/world/middle_East/4688602.stm as accessed on 28 June 2013.

Boyle, F.A. (2013). *Destroying Libya and World Order.* Clarity Press, Atlanta.

Dodge, T., and Higgot, R. (2002). *Globalisation and the Middle East.* The Royal Institute of International Affairs, London.

Hakimian, H., and Moshaver, Z. (2001). *The State and Global Change: The Political Economy of Transition in the Middle East and North Africa.* Curzon Press, Richmond.

Ibrahim, S.E. (1982). *The New Arab Social Order: A Study of the Social Impact of the Oil Wealth.* Westview Press, Boulder, CO.

IMF (2003). *The Socialist People's Libyan Arab Jamahiriya: 2003 Article IV Consultation.* Staff Report, IMF, Washington, website: http://www.imf.org/external/pubs/ft/scr/2003/cr03327.pdf accessed on 27 June 2013.

IMF (2005). *The Socialist People's Libyan Arab Jamahiriya: 2004 Article IV Consultation.* Staff Report, IMF, Washington, website: http://www.imf.org/external/country/lby/index.htm?type=56 as accessed on 28 June 2013.

IMF (2006). *The Socialist People's Libyan Arab Jamahiriya: 2005 Article IV Consultation.* Staff Report, IMF, Washington, website: http://www.imf.org/external/country/lby/index.htm?type=56 as accessed on 28 June 2013.

IMF (2007). *The Socialist People's Libyan Arab Jamahiriya: 2006 Article IV Consultation.* Staff Report, IMF, Washington, website: http://www.imf.org/external/country/lby/index.htm?type=56 as accessed on 28 June 2013.

IMF (2009). *The Socialist People's Libyan Arab Jamahiriya: 2009 Article IV Consultation.* Staff Report, IMF, Washington, website: http://www.imf.org/external/country/lby/index.htm?type=56 as accessed on 28 June 2013.

IMF (2013). website: http://www.imf.org/external/pubs/ft/scr/2013/cr13150.pdf as accessed on 1 July 2013.

Kawczynski, D,, (2011). *Seeking Gaddafi: Libya, the West and the Arab Spring.* Biteback Publishing ltd.

Luciani, G. (ed.) (1990). *The Arab State.* Routledge, London.

Mittelman, J.H. (2000). *The Globalisation Syndrome: Transformation and Resistance.* Princeton University Press, Princeton, NJ.

Overbeek, H. (1999). *The Budapest Process: Internationalisation of Migration Control.* Paper presented to the 40th Annual Conference of the International Studies Association, 16–20 February 1999, Washington D.C., mimeo.

Overbeek, H. (2000). 'Globalisation, Sovereignty and Transnational Regulation: Reshaping the Governance of International Migration', in Gosh, B. (ed.) *Managing Migration: Time for a New International Regime.* Oxford University Press, Oxford.

Owen, R. (2004). *State, Power and Politics in the Making of the Modern Middle East.* Routledge.

Owen, R., and Pamuk, S. (1999). *A History of Middle East Economies in the 20th Century.* Harvard University Press, Cambridge, MA.

Simons, G. (2003). *Libya and the West: From Independence to Lockerbie.* Centre for Libyan Studies, Oxford.

St John, R.B. (2012). *Libya: From Colony to Revolution.* Oneworld, Oxford.

UNSC (2013). Repertoire of the Practices of the Security Council, website: http://www.un.org/en/sc/repertoire/subsidiary_organs/sanctions_and_other_committees.shtml as accessed on 26 June 2013.

UNCTAD (2013). website http://www.unctad.org/Templates/Page.asp?intItemID=1584&lang=1 as accessed on 30 April 2013.

Vandewalle, D. (1998). *Libya since Independence: Oil and State-building.* Cornell University Press, Ithaca and London.

Vandewalle, D. (2012). *A History of Modern Libya.* Cambridge University Press, Cambridge.

Conclusion

The aim of this book was to discuss the events of the Arab Spring within the context of traditional International Political Economy approaches to globalisation. More specifically, starting from a transnationalist IPE approach, a qualitative definition of globalisation was adopted (Mittelman 2000; 2004; Sassen 1988, 1991, 1996; Dicken 1998, 2003). From this standpoint, globalisation was defined as a qualitatively new phenomenon, whose main components have been represented by an unprecedented increase of foreign direct investment (FDI), the marginalisation of certain areas of the globe, including the MENA area, and the growing incapacity of the nation state to control its economy, territory and people (Van der Pijl 2011; Overbeek 1999, 2000; Cox 1981, 1996; Sassen 1996; Mittelman 2000: 25–26). While the parallel phenomenon of regionalisation, both *de jure* and *de facto*, allows some regions of the world to limit the disruptive impact of global restructuring by reconfiguring a new 'spatial fix' at the regional level, marginalised areas of the world are left with no further layers of governance above the nation state. As a result they face social unrest and political instability.

From the transnationalist perspective, the engine of global restructuring is technological innovation. This produces structural transformations both in the realm of financial activities and in the productive sphere (Overbeek 1995, 2000; Dicken 1999, 2003), thus also radically modifying socio-economic relations and alliances (Gramsci 1975, 1999; Sassen 1988, 1991, 1996).

In the case of the MENA area, the geographical reallocation of production, or more precisely the lack of it, is what frames its progressive marginalisation from the global political economy. In some regions of the globe, the creation of Export Processing Zones, a policy of mergers and acquisitions or straightforward FDI allow for a virtuous circle of catching up with the global core (Mittelman 2000; Dicken 2003). These regions enjoy a substantial reallocation of labour-intensive production with a related increase of GDP and employment rates, as well as a marked improvement to the standards of life of their middle classes, although accompanied with inequalities and contradictions. However, this has not happened everywhere in the globe. Rather, it is a phenomenon which characterises the so-called triad of the Americas, Europe and Asia, whereas the rest of the world, including the MENA area, is increasingly left at the margins of the global political economy (Mittelman 2000; Overbeek 1999, 2000).

Hence, this contribution has considered the MENA area as a clear example of a lack of regionalisation. Moreover, given the focus of the book on the Arab Spring, the three countries successfully undergoing regime change in 2011, Tunisia, Egypt and Libya, are considered to have been progressively marginalised from the globalisation process. Consequently, they have each undergone a crisis of legitimacy rooted in the crisis of the nation state to govern the economy. Chapter 3 elaborated on the socio-economic dimension of marginalisation in theoretical terms and in relation to the three countries considered. In particular, the chapter underlined the extent to which these countries were not integrated in the technological dimension of globalisation and this was reflected in the underdevelopment of their educational system, labour structures and civil societies. The interplay between civil society and regime change was also explicitly tackled in this chapter.

Summing up, from the theoretical point of view, the following dimensions of globalisation are relevant to frame the discussion of the Arab Spring:

- The lack of regionalisation of some areas of the world, most notably the MENA area.
- The progressive marginalisation of the areas of the world which are not integrated in the globalisation process.
- The ensuing crisis of the nation state in marginalised countries and the resulting intensification of social and ethnic conflicts (Pellerin and Overbeek 2001).
- The increasing precariousness of living standards for the middle classes in marginalised countries.

This theoretical framework leads to three paradoxes, as addressed earlier in the book:

- The paradox of regionalisation within globalisation.
- The paradox of marginalisation within globalisation.
- The paradox of the empowerment of civil society and social capital in the unfolding of the crisis of the nation state.

Regionalisation (or lack thereof)

Starting with the first paradox, it seems difficult to deny that, from whichever theoretical perspective we approach this issue, regionalisation is an ongoing process. It is however also undeniable that it is not a phenomenon which interests all areas of the globe in the same way, if at all.

Realists, for example, although they still deny that globalisation exists, do emphasise that a process of division of the global political economy into the three macro-regions of Europe, the Americas and Asia, dominated by hegemonic nation states, is under way. Similarly, intergovernmentalists attribute a heuristic value to the interests of the most powerful states, especially their economic interests, in order to understand and explain the processes of both *de jure* and *de facto* regionalisation. As a consequence, from this theoretical standpoint, integration is not a given, but reflects the interests of leading countries within each region. Moreover, regional integration does not necessarily lead to convergence as it is the expression of power relations with the weakest countries' interests subordinated to the ones of the hegemonic nation states.

On the other hand, liberal institutionalists do not see the process of regionalisation as antagonistic to that of globalisation, but as complementary to it. By all means, the globe may be interested by the creation of three macro-economic regions, as underlined by realists. However this is not in contradiction with the creation of a true global political economy because the liberalisation processes implied by globalisation do not allow for the establishment of protected trade areas and institutional regional blocs. Moreover, the existing international governance system is increasingly inadequate to cater for the needs and fundamental rights to equity and justice of the entirety of humanity. This leads to a neo-functional need to establish a new cosmopolitan institutional order providing for a cosmopolitan political community, a sort of Kantian *Res Publica,* which would guarantee equality and social justice.

Moving to the transnationalist camp, scholars within this tradition do not share the institutionalist utopian belief in a cosmopolitan supranational political community to come. On the contrary, in the neo-liberal regionalisation process they tend to identify the reproduction at the supranational level of the conditions necessary for capital accumulation to take place both at the national and at the regional levels. From this perspective, globalisation entails a number of contradictions, amongst which the most relevant for the analysis of the MENA area is its progressive marginalisation and its lack of regionalisation. This is compounded by the crisis of the nation state as the locus of organisation of production and of control of territory and, most importantly, people.

Thus, the theoretical analysis of the process of regionalisation confirms the idea that the Middle East and Northern Africa is one of the areas of the world where regionalisation is not taking place. Moreover, the dynamics of globalisation as addressed in the theoretical section of the book do not allow for many hopes relating to its future integration. None of the traditional mechanisms of integration identified by the main theories of regional integration are taking place in the area.

On the contrary, with the crisis of the state which, in the post-colonial Arab world, has been the main provider of support to the population and protection from the vagaries of the markets (van der Pijl 2011; Dodge and Higgot 2002), the marginalisation of the area from globalisation and the lack of any regional integration has resulted in civil societies being now left alone and unsheltered.

Marginalisation

Moving to the paradox of marginalisation, the book shows that the MENA area is not on its way towards catching up with the rest of the world. Instead, it seems that this region is being increasingly marginalised from the global political economy. By looking at all usual indicators of integration, such as the level and share of global FDIs, the number and values of mergers and acquisitions, and the performance of exports and trade openness, a picture of increasing peripherisation of the area emerges. This progressive marginalisation from the global core, in turn, does not seem to have been accompanied by more intra-regional trade integration, because this has been at best, stable, and, indeed, very low, for the last 30 years.

Even in terms of solidarity it seems that intra-regional aid in the MENA area is heavily influenced by geopolitical considerations. Despite the revival of Arab official assistance to the region in the wake of the second Iraq War, aid flows from Arab sources are currently lower than in the late 1970s and early 1980s. However, even during this period aid flows within the region were mainly redistributive in nature and official aid to the more heavily dependent countries came mainly from countries outside the region, for example the US in the case of Egypt.

The literature is therefore unanimous in assessing the dynamics of the MENA area in the global political economy as a case of (dis)integration. Moreover, the idea of the area's intra-regional integration can be defined as an oxymoron. Clearly, and as opposed to what is found in other areas of the world, the Arab region continues to appear to be fundamentally and increasingly divided and lacking both *de jure* and *de facto* integration. On the contrary, the three regions identified in the literature as the 'triad', namely Europe, the Americas and Eastern Asia, are enjoying high and increasing levels of economic and institutional integration. As already noticed, it would be inappropriate even to attribute too much importance to solidarity dynamics within the Arab region because intra-regional official aid flows are determined primarily by geopolitical considerations, are mainly redistributive in nature and are not as relevant as official aid from extra-regional countries such as the US.

The last three chapters of the book have been devoted to the assessment of the level of marginalisation of the three countries interested by the Arab Spring, starting with the case of Tunisia.

Tunisia was an unlikely candidate to start the revolutionary wave which would be known as the Arab Spring. International organisations such as the IMF, the World Bank and the EU had on various occasions underlined how the country was an example of economic virtue, as its record in terms of GDP growth, macroeconomic stability and structural reforms seemed to confirm.

Although the strong restructuring programme administered by the IMF from the end of the 1980s seemed to have produced some improvement in the performance of macroeconomic indicators of the country, the reality was that the integration of Tunisia in the global political economy was further away.

By simply having a look at the usual indicators of integration into the global political economy, it appears clearly that the country had undergone a process of (dis)integration from the start of the globalisation era. The growing discontent of civil society ensuing from economic peripherisation in turn cemented the constitution of an alternative socio-economic bloc between the impoverished middle class and the lower strata of society. This took the form of a political Islam which had managed to survive the brutal repression Ben-Ali's regime.

Further proof of the degree of marginalisation of Tunisia was given by the increasing number of its citizens who were prepared to undergo irregular migration to escape the country and the region, in the majority of cases forever. The migration phenomenon concerns not only the unskilled sections of the labour force, but, increasingly, highly skilled workers unable to be inserted in the Tunisian labour markets at a level appropriate to their abilities and expectations. This is a typical outcome of the lack of integration into globalisation.

Consequently, extra-regional migration of both unskilled and increasingly skilled labour from Tunisia, mostly towards Europe, has become an unstoppable phenomenon. These dynamics have not been modified by newly-acquired political freedom from the authoritarian regime after the Arab Spring. Instead, migratory flows have continued unhindered after the revolution, maintaining prevalently the same characteristics as before and further adding to the conclusion that discontent in Tunisia was not political, but economic. Indeed, it is striking to notice how the socio-economic and demographic profiles of the thousands of young Tunisians arriving on the Italian shores in the few months after the liberation of the country from Ben Ali were exactly the same as before the revolution. Even more tellingly, they were the same as that of Bouazizi, but manifested their discontent in a different way to him. Instead of setting fire to themselves, as Bouazizi did, they decided to leave the country by any means, including irregular ones. They were many 'Bouazizis' still fleeing the country in desperation despite its liberation from the dictator.

This is the political economy context in which the new Tunisia is today being built, and it is outside the scope of this contribution to evaluate whether it is strong enough.

Turning to Egypt, the other allegedly successful revolution in the region, the analysis in Chapter 6 concludes that the country appears to be increasingly marginalised from the global political economy. The Egyptian shares of FDI stock and inflows have been steadily decreasing in the last three decades notwithstanding a policy of liberalisation and privatisation, already started in 1974 by Sadat's "infitah". Neither do other indicators of integration, such as the number of mergers and acquisitions or the degree of trade openness, show any sign of improvement since the 1980s.

Paradoxically, this happened despite the overall successful implementation of strict restructuring and stabilisation programmes during Mubarak's regime (Roccu, 2013), as dictated by international organisations such as the IMF and the World Bank. In a nutshell, one could claim that Egypt moved directly from liberalisation into marginalisation, thus clearly showing how the adoption of neo-liberal practices does not necessarily lead to more integration in the global political economy.

On the contrary, the consequence of decades of liberalisation, privatisation and economic restructuring has been an increase in the role played by remittances as one of the most stable sources of the Egyptian GDP. This in turn demonstrates the growing importance of extra-regional migratory flows, especially towards developed countries, most commonly to the US and increasingly also to Europe. Indeed, the importance of extra-regional permanent migration of skilled and highly skilled migrants in particular for the Egyptian economy is a further demonstration of the growing marginalisation of the country from the core political economies. These dynamics do not seem to have been reversed by the Arab Spring, and in fact there is already evidence that the continuing wave of political instability could have even made them worse.

Thus, it is undeniable that in the cases of Egypt and Tunisia the incapacity of Arab autocrats to support the middle classes in the wake of the challenges imposed by globalisation brought waves of discontent that eventually fuelled the protests known as the Arab Spring (similarly Ayubi 2008: 394; Dodge and Higgot 2002; Hakimian and Moshaver 2001).

This is true, to some extent, also for the case of Libya, although there the crisis of the state was not only a function of the impossibility of keeping up with the globalisation process but was buttressed by the difficult relationship of the country with the West. This, in turn, cannot be disentangled from the way in which Ghadhafi decided to handle the question of oil.

Oil had been discovered in Libya at the end of the 1950s. It proved both a blessing and a curse for the country, especially after Ghadhafi's assumption of power. Indeed, it was mainly thanks to oil revenues that Ghadhafi could implement his unique economic and political experiment. However, this required complete control of the oil business by the Libyan regime, which was achieved through a policy of nationalisation of the industry at the expense of foreign-owned oil companies, American and British ones in particular. The outcome of this policy was decades of isolation from and conflict with the West, which eventually resulted in the collapse of Ghadhafi's extravagant ideals and in the economic marginalisation of Libya from the global political economy.

The change of economic policy making from nationalisation to liberalisation, urged by economic problems resulting from Ghadhafi's diplomatic isolation, managed to make the country significantly more attractive to foreigners. Investment eventually took place, in a very limited fashion, only at the beginning of the 2000s but this was not enough to improve the economic situation of the country and, therefore, to limit the discontent of its population.

Indeed, even Ghadhafi was forced to accept the intervention of the IMF at the beginning of the 2000s and implement a set of neo-liberal policies in an attempt to avoid the collapse of the Libyan economy after decades of isolation and sanctions. The economic situation of Libya, with a 30 per cent unemployment rate, was clearly posing also social and political problems (Vandewalle 2012: 186; IMF 2003). However this last-minute attempt to save the economy, as well as its political legitimacy, did not achieve the results necessary for Ghadhafi to regain hegemony over the Libyan population (Ayubi 2008: 394). On the contrary, the further dismantling of the Libyan state apparatus required by the IMF guidelines only exacerbated the hostility towards the regime which was further fuelled by long-standing tribal rivalries.

To conclude, the hostility of the Libyans towards the regime of Ghadhafi, on the eve of the Arab Spring, was not remediable (Kawcynski 2011; Vandewalle 2012). Its origins are to be found in the progressive worsening of the standards of life of the Libyan middle class, ensuing from the retreat of the state (similarly Ayubi 2008: 394). This crisis of the 'distributive state', in turn, was a consequence of the exclusion of the country from the global political economy, due also to the way in which Ghadhafi had decided to seize the oil and energy production business. The Leader could not count any more on any hegemonic legitimacy as the economic basis of his extravagant ideology had been destroyed (Vandewalle 2012), and the subsequent programme of expenditure reductions imposed by the IMF further limited his capacity to control his people and territory. Finally, an already tense situation was exacerbated by underlying tribal rivalries which could not be resolved by the substantially failed efforts at state building of both King Idris and Ghadhafi (Vandewalle 1998, 2012; Owen 2004: 53–55; Boyle 2013; Al-Aturk 2011).

Concluding, despite having different political economy backgrounds all three of the countries considered in this book, Tunisia, Egypt and Libya, have been marginalised from the global political economy in the globalisation era. Overall, it is difficult to deny that the MENA area is not only experiencing a growing peripherisation from the global political economy but also a substantial lack of regionalisation, both a *de jure* and *de facto*. As such, the region is a clear example of lack of regionalisation within globalisation and of economic marginalisation from the global political economy.

Civil society

One of the most interesting implications of the process of globalisation for civil society and social capital in Arab countries in general, and for the three countries considered here in particular, has been the rise and radicalisation of Islam. This has been related in this book to the economic, political and cultural marginalisation of the middle class(es) ensuing from the retreat of the state.

Although the literature about social capital generally considers religious associations as just another form of voluntary association (Putnam 2000), evidence shows that Religious Social Capital (RSC), such as faith-based organisations active in civil society, also plays an important political and economic role (Harrigan and El said 2009: 13). Moreover, the Arab world, given the distinctive characteristics of Islam, is peculiar in the extent to which social capital is generated mainly through faith-based associations.

Based on Gramsci (1975, 1999), the book hypothesised that one of the consequences of globalisation in the MENA region, especially of its impact in terms of the crisis of the nation state, has been the emergence of a new socio-economic bloc striving to achieve hegemony. This was ideologically underpinned by Islamism and cemented by a new alliance between the 'discontented' middle class(es) and the 'dispossessed' lower ones (Roccu 2012; Harvey 2008, 2010). As in the mostly statist regimes of the Middle East the middle class is mainly represented by civil servants (Ayubi 2008: 343; Clark 2004; Roccu 2012), it seems apparent that they would be discontented by the retreat of the state ensuing from neo-liberal restructuring associated with globalisation (Said 2007: 6). Indeed, neo-liberal policies in the region mainly benefited a tiny group of crony capitalists, very enmeshed with the authoritarian regimes but also mainly allied with international capital more than with local small and medium enterprises, which on the contrary were generally weak (Ayubi 2008: 180–181). The liberalisation waves adopted in the countries studied in this book, as a consequence of globalisation-induced economic restructuring, totally failed to incorporate local private small and medium entrepreneurs not connected to the regimes into the system (Roccu 2012; Ayubi 2008: 329–357).

On the other hand, the dispossessed are those who have no possessions, the starving poor, the many Bouazizis still emigrating illegally to find some hope abroad (Clark 2004: 11; Ayubi 2008: 179). Both the discontented middle classes and the dispossessed poor have been increasingly marginalised economically, politically and culturally from the authoritarian statist regimes of the countries analysed here (Roccu 2012; Ayubi 2008: 181). Thus, as already underlined and discussed in the book, globalisation-induced economic restructuring mainly affected the lower and middle classes (Ayubi 2008: 352; Heydemann 2004; Roccu 2012), further marginalising them. The outcome has been increasing protest movements, including 'Political Islam' (Ayubi 2008: 181–182).

This contribution proposes the hypothesis that in the Middle East, Islam steadily but surely became the ideological point of reference of those sections of civil society left behind by existing regimes, namely the discontented middle classes and the lower classes. Islamic societal organisations also increasingly took centre stage in the life of these classes. This phenomenon was compounded by an increasing ideological weakness of the existing power bloc that had lost its hegemonic grip on civil society, if it ever had it (Roccu, 2013; Ayubi 2008: 399). Overall, liberalisation impacted on the civil societies of the countries analysed here by creating a new socio-economic alliance between the marginalised strata, cemented by a common ideology, Islam.

Summing up, globalisation-induced economic restructuring, by either restricting the ability of the state to protect the poor and the middle classes or by causing a profound identity crisis in civil society through state repression, strengthened the hand of political Islam and undermined the legitimacy of the regimes in the resource-poor countries of the MENA area, including Egypt and Tunisia (Harrigan and El-Said 2009: 1–2; Clark 2004: 11–12; Hakimian and Moshaver 2000). This process did not take place suddenly in 2010 and 2011. In Egypt the capillary penetration of Islam in civil society was made possible through decades thanks to the capacity of faith-based organisations to create social capital and establish strong solidarity networks both within classes and between them (similarly Richards and Waterbury 1998: 348–350). In Egypt, as well as Jordan (Knowles 2005) and Yemen, it was thanks to Islamic Social Institutions (ISIs) that horizontal and vertical social networks of solidarity could be established among the discontented middle classes and the dispossessed poor ones. As a consequence, social capital in these countries fostered an Islamic view of society and of the state which represented an alternative to both the status quo and to more secular social settings. Following the transnationalists, we may indeed conclude that globalisation empowered civil society. This occurred in a very distinctive way by binding both the middle classes and the poorer strata of society more closely in the name of a vision of the state and society alternative to both the existing regimes and a more secular project. The alliance between these increasingly marginalized classes was thus cemented in the name of Islam. This is why, in Egypt, although the Muslim Brotherhood was not at the forefront of the 2011 Tahrir square protests, it nevertheless managed to obtain power soon thereafter through democratic means.

However, for Gramsci the economic dimension is essential for the aspiring hegemonic group to secure its dominant position in the social and political spheres. Therefore, if the group aspiring to achieve supremacy is unable to guarantee and preserve the economic interests of its allies, its quest for hegemony will eventually be doomed to fail. One could read the latest events in Egypt in this light, as the newly established Muslim Brotherhood-dominated government's notable failure to kick-start the economy led to new protests and the re-establishment of the *status quo*. The new military power is today, indeed, in a better position to obtain the kind of economic support allowing it to better control the economy thanks to its strong alliance with big private capital, both domestic and foreign.

It is however too early to attach the word 'end' to the Egyptian revolution. The battle for hegemony between the previous socio-economic bloc and the new alliance of the discontented and the dispossessed in the name of Islam is still going on. The Muslim Brotherhood has been repressed brutally by the new military regime of al Sisi, but has not been tamed, as the mobilisations on the streets and squares of Egyptian cities and in the countryside clearly demonstrate.

Not dissimilarly, Tunisian civil society was deeply permeated by Islamism which came to represent a strong factor of cohesion between the middle and lower classes. Differently from the Egyptian case, the brutal repression of Ben Ali's regime did not allow faith-based organisations and social capital to take control of the welfare state. Instead of eradicating religious aspirations in society, repression enlarged the sources of discontent, thus strengthening the Islamist quest for hegemony. One could come to the conclusion that the evolutions of Egyptian and Tunisian civil society are the two sides of one same coin: by adopting *de facto* opposite attitudes towards the development of Islamic Social Institutions and religious social capital, the result was the same, namely the empowerment of the Islamist counter-hegemonic claims as opposed to both the *status quo* and a more secular political project.

Summing up, Egypt and Tunisian societies turned to Islam as a counter-hegemonic project as their corrupted statist regimes failed to guarantee prosperity to the middle classes. Although, these new approaches to constitutional order based on political Islam had progressively grown into meaningful alternatives to the declining statist regimes, they too had or could in the future have the same economic problems as their predecessors. Thus the battle for hegemony continues.

The case of Libya is only partially similar to the other two cases of the Arab Spring. It is true that the analysis of the radicalisation and penetration of Islam in society as a consequence of the incapacity of the regime to continue to guarantee the prosperity of its society can be applied also to the case of Libya. However, Libya, as an oil-producing country, presents some peculiarities that need addressing. The crisis of the Libyan State was primarily a crisis of the distributive state based on oil revenues. Oil wealth had initially sustained Ghadhafi's economic experiment, but it was the long conflict with the West, especially the US and the UK, that limited the economic resources available to Ghadhafi to support the population more than the globalisation process. In turn, the conflict with Western countries found its origins in the policy of nationalisation and control of the oil industry, which Ghadhafi had decided to implement from the onset of his revolution. It is true that globalisation feeds on oil and energy and as a result, somehow, energy resources in Libya became more and more precious as the globalisation process advanced. This discussion is outside the scope of this contribution. It seems clear, however, as highlighted here, that the economic fate of Libya cannot be disentangled from the political economy of oil.

References

Al-Aturk, A. (2011). Libya: From Revolt to State Building, in Pollack, K. M. (ed.) *The Arab Awakening : America and the Transformation of the Middle East*, e-book, accessed 09 May 2013, http://kcl.eblib.com/patron/FullRecord.aspx?p=795889, pp.117–127

Ayubi, N. (2008). *Overstating the Arab State: Politics and Society in the Middle East.* IB Tauris, London.

Boyle, F.A. (2013). *Destroying Libya and World Order.* Clarity Press, Atlanta.

Clark, J., (2004). *Islam, Charity and Activism*, Indiana University Press.

Cox, R.W. (1981). Social Forces, States, and World Orders: Beyond International Relations Theory. *Millennium*, 10, 127–155.

Cox, R.W. (1996). *Approaches to World Order.* Cambridge University Press, Cambridge.

Dicken, P. (1998). *Global Shift, Transforming the World Economy*, (3rd ed.). Paul Chapman Publishing, London.

Dicken, P. (2003). *Global Shift: Reshaping the Global Economic Map in the 21st century*, (4th ed.). Sage Publications, London.

Dodge, T., and Higgot, R. (2002). *Globalisation and the Middle East.* The Royal Institute of International Affairs, London.

Gramsci, A. (1975). *Quaderni dal carcere.* Einaudi, Torino.

Gramsci, A. (1999). *Selections from the Prison Notebooks of Antonio Gramsci*. Elecbook electronic books, London.
Hakimian, H., and Moshaver, Z. (2001). The State and Global Change: The Political Economy of Transition in the Middle East and North Africa. Curzon Press, Richmond.
Harrigan, J., and El Said H., (2009). Economic liberalisation, Social Capital and Islamic Welfare Provision. Palgrave, London.
Harvey, D. (2008). The Right to the City, New Left Review 53, September–October 2008.
Harvey, D. (2010). *The Enigma of Capital and the Crises of Capitalism*. Profile Books, London.
Heydemann, S. (ed.) (2004) Networks of Privilege in the Middle East: The Politics of Economic Reforms Revisited. Palgrave Macmillan, Basingstoke.
IMF, (2003). The Socialist People's Libyan Arab Jamahiriya: 2003 Article IV Consultation – Staff Report, Washington: IMF, web-site: http://www.imf.org/external/pubs/ft/scr/2003/cr03327.pdf accessed on June 27, 2013
Kawczynski, D., (2011). Seeking Gaddafi: Libya, the West and the Arab Spring. Biteback Publishing ltd.
Knowles, W. (2005). Jordan since 1989: A Study in Political Economy. I.B. Tauris, London.
Mittelman, J.H. (2000). *The Globalisation Syndrome: Transformation and Resistance*. Princeton University Press, Princeton.
Mittelman, J.H. (2004). *Whither Globalization? The Vortex of Knowledge and Ideology*, Routledge,
Pellerin, H. and Overbeek, H.W. (2001). 'Neoliberal Regionalism and the Management of People's Mobility', in Bieler, A., and Morton, A.D. (eds) *Social Forces in the Making of the 'New Europe'*. Palgrave MacMillan.
Owen, R., (2004), State, Power and Politics in the Making of the modern Middle East, Routledge
Overbeek, H.W. (1995). 'Globalisation and the Restructuring of the European Labor Markets: The Role of Migration', in Simai, M. (ed.) *Global Employment. An International Investigation into the Future of Work*. Zed Books and United Nations University Press, London/Tokyo.
Overbeek, H. (1999). *The Budapest Process: Internationalization of Migration Control*, Paper presented to the 40th Annual Conference of the International Studies Association, 16–20 February 1999, Washington D.C., Mimeo.
Overbeek, H. (2000). 'Globalisation, Sovereignty and Transnational Regulation: Reshaping the Governance of International Migration', in Gosh, B. (ed.) *Managing Migration: Time for a New International Regime*, Oxford University Press, Oxford.
Putnam, R. (2000). Bowling Alone: The Collapse and Revival of American Community. Simon & Schuster, New York.
Richards, A., and Waterbury, J. (1998). A Political Economy of the Middle East, Westview Press.
Roccu, R. (2013). *The Political Economy of the Egyptian Revolution*. Palgrave.
Roccu, R. (2012). 'Of Middle Classes, Economic Reforms and Popular Revolts', in S. Panebianco and R. Rossi (eds) *Winds of Democratic Change in the Mediterranean?* Rubbettino, *Palermo, pp.* 61–82.

Said, M., 2007, 'The Fall and Rise in Wage Inequality in Egypt: New Evidence from the ELMPS, 2006', ERF Working Paper Series, WP 0708, Cairo: Economic Research Forum.Sassen, S. (1988). *The Mobility of Labour and Capital.* Cambridge University Press, Cambridge, UK.

Sassen, S. (1991). *The Global City: New York, London, Tokyo.* Princeton University Press, Princeton, NJ.

Sassen, S. (1996). *Losing Control? Sovereignty in the Age of Globalization.* Columbia University Press, New York.

Van der Pijl, K. (2011). *Arab Revolts and Nation-State Crisis*, NLR 70, July–August 2011.

Vandewalle, D. (1998) *Libya since independence: oil and state-building.* Cornell University Press, Ithaca and London.

Vandewalle, D. (2012). *A History of Modern Libya.* Cambridge University Press, Cambridge

Index

CPI Antony Rowe
Chippenham, UK
2017-07-13 21:43